# EMBRACING
## THE POWER OF TRUTH
Tools for Liberating Your Heart

SHAVASTI

# EMBRACING
## THE POWER OF TRUTH
Tools for Liberating Your Heart

## SHAVASTI

FINDHORN PRESS

© Shavasti, 2015

The right of Shavasti to be identified as
the author of this work has been asserted by him in accordance
with the Copyright, Designs and Patents Act 1998.

Published in 2015 by Findhorn Press, Scotland

ISBN 978-1-84409-661-9

A CIP record for this title is available from the British Library.

Edited by Michael Hawkins
Cover design by Richard Crookes
Interior design by Damian Keenan
Printed & bound in the USA

Published by

Findhorn Press

117-121 High Street,

Forres IV36 1AB,

Scotland, UK

*t* +44 (0)1309 690582

*f* +44 (0)131 777 2711

*e* info@findhornpress.com

www.findhornpress.com

# Contents

# Preface

There are many different ways of reading a book, especially non-fiction. Although you may be drawn to start with a certain chapter, I encourage sequential reading from start to finish.

This book is a journey, in part my own personal journey, and for the most part, a journey into our core and all of the layers that surround it. Some of these layers invite investigation, others illicit fear, even dread. The many layers we have built up over decades are replete with knowledge, experience, regret, joy, sadness, grief, delight, aversion, clarity, truth, lies, avoidances, longing, love, soulfulness, compassion and more.

We are multi-faceted beings – and some of these facets are useful, whilst other facets are absolutely not useful. In my own personal journey I began to see clearly that when we start to meet the simplest of truths, that which can be deemed the absolute truth, devoid of masks and pretences, what shifts is our perception of what is 'good' or 'bad' into that which is useful or simply not useful, life supporting, or life limiting.

As we journey deeper into the power of truth we begin to realize that much of what we thought was true about ourselves, our families, life and goodness may in fact simply be a story – and one that does not serve us.

When we embrace the power of truth, opinions dissolve and the heart is able to speak freely as we are reborn into a renewed freedom that we may not have experienced since early childhood.

As we meet the very worst stories we've told ourselves about our nature we rise, like the phoenix, out of the ashes of disillusionment and illusion to embrace a world in which opinions become obsolete and simple truth becomes paramount.

As you read from paragraph to paragraph I both invite and encourage you to pause, take a breath or two, and allow your *body and breath* to respond to some of the deeper questions rather than your mind.

As part of any path of awakening, the process involves bringing the light into the shadows. At times this can be challenging and uncomfortable. Our mind has an uncanny ability to lead us as far away from the truth in avoidance of that which may be inconvenient or painful. What I've noticed over the years is that we often choose long term suffering in favour over short-term pain.

Whilst this book poses many questions regarding the human condition and the role personal development and spirituality may have in our lives, the questions and statements are designed to invite deeper investigation into the Self and are not asked in order to disparage, denigrate or make a statement regarding the validity of spiritual practices and lifestyles.

The invitation is to investigate and to meet within yourself whether any of what is believed and practiced forms part of a hindrance and is an image rather than that which is authentically you.

As we delve into the heavier topics in the beginning of the book – simply breathe and perhaps take some breaks in the richness that silence can offer, allowing your body and breathing to be the barometer for knowing if something is true for you or not.

The human condition is fraught with generations of undervaluing one another and belittling ourselves. As we delve deep into that which has most often been avoided, we begin to rise up again into the light of the heart and of consciousness itself as the journey through these pages continues towards its conclusion – the Way of the Heart.

Truth brings us onto the way of the heart, and when fully met in its authenticity, is an expression of love.

*Enjoy the journey,*
*Shavasti.*
*2014.*

# Introduction

What is truth? We all, pretty much, know what a lie is. What might a liberated heart allow? How could it feel? We have all had experiences of our heart being closed, either to an individual or to a group of people, or even to ourselves.

We have all, equally, had experiences of our heart being open – perhaps to a child, lover, pet, a landscape, or a dear friend.

If I were to simply present to you some teachings from an awakening heart as a finished product or as something that just simply exists or something that I've cobbled together, it would not be complete. Therefore, as part of this, I want to share with you parts of my own journey and that which may help you to recognize that you are indeed on the same pilgrimage of a lifetime to awaken your heart – a pilgrimage that ultimately longs to arrive at the place in which your heart knows itself as love.

What I'm attempting to do in this book is to block the road to *chasing* the light, and to look at the rawness of what is. The purpose of this book is to appeal to those who have perhaps been on a path for decades and yet peace evades them. Of course, new seekers can enjoy and benefit too. In reality, there is no 'beginner' or 'advanced' – we're either awakening or not.

It is not what we know or believe, it is the quality of our love and sense of peace that defines us.

Although there can be heart awakenings that take place in an instant, and some of mine have been, and undoubtedly some of yours have been too, for they really have taken place in an instant or in a few moments of time; there is in fact, a journey.

It is a journey of unfolding and of releasing our tight grip on the shutters that shield our heart from a seemingly cold and cruel world. It is not a journey of discovering a distant land or a coveted secret, but rather, it is a journey of surrendering to what has always been present but shrouded in illusion and disillusion.

In this sharing I reflect back on the many years my path involved working with Family Constellations, having given some 400 or more workshops, plus the many individuals I worked with, one-on one, using the principles I had integrated not only from Family Constellations, but also Shamanism.

However, there came a stage when I felt that I wasn't learning anything new. There was this constant ceiling that I was bumping up against. I kept on asking, asking, asking – asking inwardly, asking the divine, trying to feel my relationship to something greater than myself, and continued simply asking myself 'what is it that I am missing'?

It is from that point of deeper asking and deeper longing that my journey really starts. Of course, our journey starts from the moment that we are born. Our journey continues through childhood and all of the circumstances of our life, leading up to a moment of something awakening within us. In reality, all of it is part of our journey, whether or not we recognize it at the time. Even jobs that we've done, whether it's working in a bakery or working as a waiter, working as a journalist, working as anything we can possibly imagine.

In retrospect, all of our tasks had ingredients that prepared us for what it is that we want to do later on in life, which is beyond a wanting, it is something that we were born to do, something that feels natural. All of it, no matter how much of a detour it may feel like at the time is designed to fulfil our life's purpose, to fulfil our dharma.

There have been many ingredients, events and seeming detours that have lead up to this moment. When I speak of this moment, I speak of it from the perspective that it is not complete. So when I offer you some teachings from an awakening heart, it doesn't mean that I've arrived somewhere, and now that I'm here there's nothing more to do.

This is just another stage and part of this stage is sharing with you much of what I have experienced, all that I have hitherto realized, in the hope that it may give you something for you to realize about yourself and your own awakening heart.

ᘒᘒᘒᘒᘒ

We now go back to 2007. I was sitting in front of my television, watching Oprah Winfrey, and just as she said the words, "And now for our next guest," three armed men, each of them carrying guns, came into my living room. Or at least one of them was. It is always true with these traumatic events that memory can be a little bit sketchy.

There were definitely three men, and at least one gun. I spent the next hour or so tied up and blindfolded with a gun to my head frequently; it wasn't there constantly throughout the entire ordeal, but the threat that they were going to kill me was very present.

Not only was the threat of imminent execution present emotionally, for it was indisputably felt, but also the words carrying the undeniable threat and intimidation came on a regular basis – "We are going to shoot you now." These words simply kept on coming, along with racial slurs and mockery.

There was a critical and haunting moment during that entire experience in which the gunman held the weapon to my temple and released the safety catch and said, "I will kill you now." That was, to say the least, a major turning point in my life. It was in that moment that I truly understood the expression, "and my entire life flashed before me."

For that's what happened. I experienced every moment, everything that I had done, everything I had felt, every moment of grief, every moment of pain, every moment of joy, every moment of happiness as if on a movie screen; each moment searingly intense.

It was then that I heard a voice, and it was a voice that I'd heard once before. For me, it was a very deep, male, masculine booming voice that called me by name and said, "Do you want to live?"

ᏏᏏᏏᏏᏏ

I have created a deliberate pause in this moment, for that is what happened. There was a momentary pause between hearing the voice that asked a very specific question and me giving an answer. In that moment of pause, that could easily have been millennia, I looked at my life.

I was 45 at the time, single, with no children, and I'd spent many years working, giving workshops and working with many clients. There was a part of me that was tired. I didn't actually have an answer immediately. As I realized within myself, that I was hesitating, I didn't know whether I wanted to say yes or no.

Then suddenly within me there was this deep and profound upwelling of longing. There was something that I longed to do. Ever since I was a young child, ever since I was seven or eight years old, I wanted to speak of the things of God. I had wanted to be a Catholic priest at that age, I was very devoted to that path. However, life circumstances and a little bit of a run-in with the church for asking too many questions sorted out that career decision for me. It wasn't going to be.

There I was, blindfolded, hands tied behind my back, ankles secured with a cable, and I was coming into contact with that deep spiritual longing again. The re-connection with that longing was both powerful and fundamental in terms of creating a road map for the next few years – a roadmap that became more visible with hindsight than in actual moments of pondering my future.

If I stayed with the unanswered longing, no matter how uncomfortable or painful, the next step would manifest naturally as if by an evolutionary impulse that simply must have its own way. I have learnt that it is not we who awaken, but it is that within us which has always been awake that calls us.

It is the ever-present flame of longing that propels us to seek when it is time. For the most part we are either seeking the fulfilment of some religious or spiritual philosophy or way of life, or we are seeking to move beyond suffering to a greater knowledge of the nature of the Universe or God.

However, so much of our longing and thirst is to awaken to ourselves, to the truth of who we are, and for that to happen, we must be willing to *tell the absolute truth*.

In that moment I felt that in addition to my spiritual longing, there were also things that I wanted to do. Although I was an avid traveller, there were places I wanted to see, things I wanted to experience. My longing was to live life as an individual in contact with his own heart. I not only wanted to know what love was, but to live it fully, devoid of masks or pretences that dictated how love behaved and also devoid of any romanticism.

I realized my deep longing to truly, authentically and undeniably be in contact with my heart and to be directly in contact with the knowledge and experience of the divine whilst being grounded in the body. This profound longing welled up powerfully, and along with it, the desire to also speak of the things of God with other people.

My longing to have that union, and also to share that union with others emerged in that moment. Little did I realize at the time that what needed to happen was the destruction of much of my world – the world I had created in defence of my heart, a world that had not yet supported an awakened heart.

ᐁᐁᐁᐁᐁ

Then the next thing happened. To this day it is astounding to me. To this day I greet this crystal clear memory as a miracle that is barely explicable to the logical mind. As I responded "yes" to the voice, I heard the clip of the gun and I felt that the weapon had been withdrawn. He then literally laughed and said, "I'm not in the mood for murder tonight."

He left. He simply left and walked away.

This event took place in South Africa. I consider myself very, very lucky to be alive. I'm guessing I defied all statistics by surviving and in that particular way. In that moment I had been touched by the hand of grace. If you want to call it the hand of God, you may. I often hesitate to use the word God because it has become so loaded; it has been very distorted, misused, abused and misunderstood.

We've been taught so many truths and untruths and we've received so many distortions around the word that it conjures up images that are often unhealthy or lead us to hear something different than what's actually being said.

I heard a voice, I hesitated, I then responded and a miracle took place. It is a miracle as neither I, nor the statistics, expected me to be here. It is a miracle because what was almost certainly going to have one outcome, ended up with a very different outcome. It is a miracle because I was touched by something, I responded to it, and I live to tell the tale. It is a miracle because that which touched me is greater than myself, that which touched me connected to me in a way that was undeniable and there was a dialogue and a response, and not only that, but a change in outcome took place. What was a done deal became undone.

In that moment of realizing what had just happened – beyond being in the very real experience of being held at gunpoint – was the realisation that an intervention had taken place, that something or someone reached me, touched me, appealed to me, asked me – that a voice was heard and that not only was it a voice, but that this voice could actually influence and create a different outcome to the one I was in no doubt would occur.

A bullet was transformed into astonishment and the deep realisation that something else was encouraging a different outcome; I had been given a choice. These events are profound to the extent that they not only create a new life, but they also usher in the destruction of a life once lived. With destruction comes rebirth, with awakening comes the death of so much.

In the days to come I touched levels of rage and anguish I had never known. Every sound was a potential intruder and I was shocked to my core when deep seated feelings of revenge and rage came up to the surface. I wanted to punish them, and not just a little! I was incensed that anyone would dare do this to me, and I felt violated. I was enraged that someone had poisoned my beloved dog, I felt crimson with fury.

But that was just one part of me. In other moments I felt a deep sense of everything being as it is supposed to be and I felt very humbled by the grace that had touched me, and the voice that had spoken to me.

☙ ☙ ☙ ☙ ☙

I wavered like a pendulum from one state to the other – calm to rage, serenity to high levels of anxiety, clarity of thought and mind and moments of total paranoia. It was very much a mixed blessing. My world looked different and I began to see things very differently and to question the meaning and reality of things much more deeply than ever before.

I recall driving my car, just two or three days after the event and stopping on the side of the road, to look up at a single small white cloud floating in a vast expanse of bright blue sky. I gazed upon it for several minutes with absolute curiosity. It was as if I was seeing this sight for the very first time and I felt captivated by its beauty. I even asked myself 'What is a cloud?, 'What is blue, who told me that the sky is blue? Why is it blue? What does 'blue' mean, if it has a meaning? What, I began to realize, was that all of the labels and names we have for things do not describe them.

Somehow calling a cloud a cloud robbed it of the truth of its existence. I became aware of the voice I had heard being everywhere. I wondered if it was in the cloud. If I left the word 'cloud' behind and simply gazed at it without conceiving of it as a cloud, I began to perceive the underlying presence, the underlying life force energy that flashed in and out with, pulses and flashes, across the vast expanse of blue sky and within that which I once called 'cloud'.

On the one hand one could pass this off as the irrational thoughts of the recently traumatised, however, something else was emerging, I was becoming increasingly aware of my place within a much greater reality and questioning so many things that I had taken for granted or simply had never noticed before. Life was different, it took on a different meaning and my place in the world took on a new significance.

Interestingly, John, the little me, seemed far less important and far less significant, but what became much more interesting was my greater self, the part of me who was connected to that voice, who knew deep down what that voice was and from whence it came. What became more important to me was the journey of souls, the journey of my own soul and my contribution to the world and to my own life in a more meaningful and soul driven way.

It is not that these concepts or feelings were new to me, they simply took on a new more profound role in my life. In hindsight I was in a deep process of giving birth to Shavasti, a name that had been given to me in 1994, and there would be many more moments of birth pangs to come, some leading to graceful emergence through realization and yet others that brought me to my knees.

*ᘒᘒᘒᘒᘒ*

Even with those thoughts and insights I was not out of the woods yet. There was still 'just John' who felt traumatised and needed healing in a way that went deeper than any path of self-development I had previously wandered.

I touched depths of loneliness, despair and disconnection I had never before experienced. I simply did not know anyone else with the same experience, at least not in my circle of friends. It was difficult to talk about and I could sense that others had immense difficulty in relating to my story and felt lost for words. In many ways, my story brought mortality too close to home.

The feelings of isolation deepened and I began to live in my own secret world. When meeting friends, I always met them in popular public places that I knew very well and if they were new friends, I would not go to their homes, but invited them to eat in a restaurant with me. This was all because I had the need to know where my quickest exit would be!

In many ways I felt like the alcoholic who kept his drinking secret from others, I didn't want anyone to know exactly how traumatized and fearful I felt. It had become my shameful secret. I was defiled in some way and my anxiety, along with manifesting obsessive compulsive behaviour, became something to be ashamed of.

So why the shame? There are a number of reasons. Firstly, blaming myself for not securing my property more than I had, blaming myself for having my television volume so loud that I could not hear the gunmen enter my home, and assuming that I must, in some way, be exaggerating what had happened, as explaining it to friends and family was invariably met with total silence, and, with some, withdrawal.

Therefore a part of me concluded that it was my fault and on top of that, my story made others uncomfortable, and therefore it was unwelcome. With all of this, the slippery slide into loneliness and despair commenced along with the secret compulsive behaviours, the worst of which was washing my hands every few minutes.

Another event happened that also changed me and shook me. A very close friend – we've known each other for many years – shared with me one day that he had recently had a very similar experience. As he told his story my heart wept for him and part of me was re-living my own experience. However, another feeling came, the feeling of relief. Suddenly I did not feel alone with my experience, there was someone else that understood all that had happened.

I felt guilt for feeling the relief that came with his sharing for I was not happy that it had happened to him, had not wished it, and yet relief was present. How can we feel relief at the suffering of another? When one is in an abyss, company brings some relief.

My love and compassion for my friend deepened, as well as for myself, as I transcended the guilt with an understanding of my response, for I was no longer alone, and my secret fears were no longer a secret, no longer needing to be held in shame.

෨෨෨෨෨

In the seven years following that fateful night there have been many highs and many lows. Lows, as I've never experienced them before, and highs that have been blessings that were in and of themselves life changing.

I met and fell in love with an Indian Guru; flew on a private jet to have dinner with royalty and met Oprah Winfrey; spent many nights crying myself to sleep; made new friends, alienated myself from both new and old friends; made a fool of myself; lived from outrage, and rebelled; felt like a total stranger in company and felt connected to all life when completely alone.

What has emerged is a greater awareness of my own heart, a greater awareness of nature and nature spirits, a greater awareness of the ancestors and ancestral voices, the ability to much more clearly see and feel energies and also the ability to speak to those who have crossed over, working as a medium for some of my clients.

My awareness of the 'other worlds' has become a major part of my life whilst at the same time becoming ever more present in this physical world – balancing life in both worlds to become a more complete human being, little step by little step.

I no longer feel reluctant to show my so called, 'psychic' abilities and feel no need to defend them to the sceptical, cautious or fearful. They are what they are, it is a part of who I am, and it is a part of my service to others and simply a part of my everyday experience, my own personal truth that does not require protecting.

Just like the cloud I witnessed, the term 'psychic' became an unnecessary, even offensive descriptor for something that was natural. Paranormal was normal and 'normal' was strange and foreign.

⌒⌒⌒⌒⌒

As a result of that traumatic life changing event and the time of deep introspection that followed it, I also noticed that the nature of my extra sensory perception changed. Instead of observing from the place of fear and guardedness as I had as a child, my extra sensory perception become much more centred in the heart, thereby increasing my ability to feel into the whole picture, the feelings and motivations behind the story or events.

In other words, my overworked third eye rested and allowed my heart to start doing much more of the work. It has been an opening of the heart, a movement into deeper compassion and increased self-responsibility. My heart had been broken over and over again and eventually it began to break open and I could love the world. Eventually I could breathe more fully and there were many along the way who helped me.

A month after that fateful night I found myself on my way to China to learn Tai Chi; this was the start of my self-healing process. What has followed is an intense path of self-discovery and healing that included working with many gifted healers and teachers around the globe. I am grateful for each and every one of them.

This book is in part not only my own personal story, but the story of many. Although it is a story, offering in part an autobiographical framework for sharing my experiences and the subsequent teachings that have emerged from that, it is not a story in the traditional sense of there being a beginning, middle and an end. As I share experiences and teachings the chronology of certain experiences is not adhered to, but rather shared in tune with my heart's longing of what it wants to share.

Something very profound happened that set me on a path of something very different. As you will discover, there were more events to come that would mould and shape me, sometimes gently, at other times, dramatically. It is that path of something very different that I want to share with you.

You may not have come to this book because you just survived something very traumatic, but you have come to this book, to this sharing with me, because you want to know something about yourself. You want to know something about the nature of life and the nature of the heart, and the nature of human relationships.

With this book I share with you my journey. With this sharing I offer you my teachings and my insights for you to take and do whatever you want with, until you find another piece for yourself that may come to you from another teacher, from within yourself, or from another who shares as I do.

I do not have all of the answers. I have my answers, and it is my wish that my sharing will help you in some small or greater way to find your answers. Answers to the question of who you really are and what your place is in the world, to find some real and authentic freedom, perhaps even the ultimate freedom – the freedom to love and be loved.

*With deep respect,*
*Shavasti, 2014*

# CHAPTER 1

# Tao Time:
# The Dragon's Teeth Mountains

Words merely point towards the truth,
the truth always resides in the silence –

*SHAVASTI*

It has been said that a river never looks back. The Lijiang is no exception as it meanders magnificently through the magical karst landscapes of Guangxi province towards the South China Sea. It is here that I dubbed the karst formations, that garland the Lijiang, 'The Dragon's Teeth Mountains' – for that is what they looked like; large teeth sticking out of the earth as if from nowhere. No gradual slopes, no foothills, just a mountain standing tall and erect with steep inclines that barely a mountain goat could clamber.

Some were majestic, others imposing, and still others beckoning the hearts of poets and artists to entwine their soul with the spirit of the mountains and mark their encounter with either a quill or a brush.

Just a month after my close encounter with death in South Africa, after having been hogtied with a gun to my head, I arrived in China in the dead of night. Earlier that day I had crossed the Hong Kong – China border on foot between a coach that had just dropped me off on one side of the border and one that awaited my appearance, the other side of the formalities.

Having travelled to Hungary and Czechoslovakia during the early 1980s, I had expected much the same as I entered the belly of Communist China. To my surprise the welcome was warm and friendly, a far cry from the Eastern European apparatchiks of yesteryear.

A little while later I found myself sitting in a lounge at Shenzhen airport casually chatting to Chinese businessmen whilst waiting for my delayed flight to Guilin, a city famed not only for its landscape but also for its Osmanthus flowers and the delectable osmanthus wine, a fortified and sweet elixir.

As my taxi left Guilin airport we started the two hour journey to Yangshuo, at first hobbling along an unlit pot holed dirt road, then negotiating sharp bends with oncoming trucks that were bellowing enough black smoke to darken even the night sky. As we joined the main country road to our destination I experienced my first glimpse of the Dragon's Teeth, silhouetted against a crisp and clear obsidian canopy bejewelled with stars.

I was captivated by the mysterious forms, each appearing to be an individual or a presence in its own right, standing tall above paddy fields and orange groves, as if they were ancient guardians whose task was to oversee and protect the land that rests at their feet. As I absorbed the mysterious images I uttered to myself, 'Oh my good God, I'm in the middle of China, how did I get here?'

Two hours passed and in the chill of night my taxi finally arrived at the Snow Lion Inn situated on the banks of the Lijiang. It was very dark, just a light or two casting their beams out into the blackness. Despite my tiredness I was wide eyed for I was indeed in China, a land cloaked in so much mystery for a curious western mind.

The entrance to the inn was a large double wooden door decorated with traditional Chinese characters; it was of course red. I was captivated by the doors themselves and I imagined that they were perhaps just smaller versions of the type of doors protecting the Forbidden City from the invading Mongol hordes.

As I gazed with both curiosity and wonder at the imposing doorway, suddenly a crack appeared along with the unmistakeable groaning sound of such large objects moving. The door opened in a fashion reminiscent of a castle door to reveal the slight figures of two young women. They eagerly rushed towards my vehicle, greeted me in English, and then proceeded to gather my belongings, with the help of the driver, despite the fact that my large suitcase had to be bigger than either of them in both dimension and weight.

Shortly afterwards I was in my room making acquaintance with my first Chinese bed. It was hard. However, I knew that both my tiredness and my jet lag would not keep sleep away, no matter the hardness of the bed. I had been in my room for less than ten minutes attempting some rudimentary unpacking when a knock came on my door.

On opening it I was greeted by Linna, a young woman of twenty two, who presented me with a bowl of hot soup and a bottle of water. I felt welcomed and settled into my room, almost merging with the warm and tasty soup like a young child cuddling up with a teddy bear. The large brown bowl of soup expressed welcome in a way that only soup can. Minutes later I entered a deep sleep only to be greeted by a dawn chorus in what seemed to be just a fleeting moment later.

I could have done with nine hours sleep but the Dragon's Teeth were beckoning to my soul to venture out and explore this hitherto mysterious land that was so richly adorned with thousands of years of history and tradition. I stepped onto my balcony on that early morn to see giant bamboo of the like I had never seen before. Many were taller than a three-storey building, with deep green thick trunks that I was later to learn were fashioned into bamboo rafts.

My images of bamboo had hitherto been of delicate plants being daintily chewed upon by an adorable Panda or as an adornment in a refined royal garden. This bamboo was positively substantial almost to the point of being megalithic. Again, as I looked at my new surroundings the thought and feeling I had had the night before arose within me: 'Oh my good God, I'm in the middle of China'.

Whereas visiting China has become fairly commonplace for many a western tourist in the past decade, in the mind of a child of the sixties, being in China was as exotic and mysterious as travelling down the Nile to Khartoum on a dhow, or traipsing to Lhasa, Mandalay or Timbuktu, the stuff of Indiana Jones. However, a modern aeroplane, not a biplane, dropped me off in the most modern of cities, Hong Kong, bringing me most of the way to my current location.

China had beckoned me and in answer to her call I spent the next few months deepening my experience of her traditions and culture and embarking on my own path of self-healing through Tai Chi and Chi Gong. After a brief stay at the Snow Lion Inn I moved into an apartment in the centre of town. It was busy, full of traders, market people and street vendors offering everything from trinkets to live chickens in a woven basket.

After several weeks of studying at one school, I moved on to another teacher, Mei. She spoke good English and I learnt that it was rather unusual to have a female Tai Chi Master, not only that, but that she personally had to go against the wishes of her family and challenge the culture in which she was raised in order to follow her passion for Tai Chi.

I arrived at her school expecting she would be most impressed with my Tai Chi; after all, I had dedicated six hours a day, six days a week to the task. However, to my dismay she was underwhelmed by my attention to detail and my ability to actually be fully present in my body.

For two solid weeks she had me practise one movement and one movement only – grounding my Tan Tien into the earth, sinking the roots of my feet deeply into its core and allowing the upwelling of pure positive Chi to fill me from the bottom up.

After a couple of days of what seemed like monotonous torture I complained and asked her why she was holding me back when so many other students seemed to be progressing towards ballet-like graceful skills. She looked at me and told me the following story:

> "Long ago a Tai Chi master was travelling across the country on a long journey when he stopped at a village for some rest. The men of the village, on learning that he was a Tai Chi master, begged him to teach them the secrets of Chi and the Tao. He taught them the first movement, grounding into the earth, and did so for more than a month.
>
> One morning the men of the village noticed that that the Master was gathering his belongings as if to leave the village. 'Where are you going' they cried. 'I must be on my way, I have a long way to go,' he replied. The village men were dismayed and said to him, 'How can you leave? You have not yet taught us the other movements? The Master replied 'Did I say that I wouldn't teach you the other movements? For surely I will. I shall be back in a year or two to check on your progress with the first movement".

ᖚᖚᖚᖚᖚ

It was a defining moment. Not only was I humbled by the story but also touched by the care with which it was told. I realized that I had fallen foul of the Westerner's disease: 'I want it now, I want it all'. I continued for another week with the first movement and it was in that movement that magic began to happen. Intense life force energies began coursing through my body, my spine becoming hot and tingly and my pelvis becoming alive with sensations that were akin to sexual orgasm.

Each day I would walk two kilometres to school and two kilometres back. Sometimes with a friend, sometimes alone. As my energies increased, so did my sensitivity. I had been somewhat numb in the aftermath of the armed robbery and the new aliveness was both a blessing, and also a challenge, as a wide variety of feelings began to surface. During my morning, lunchtime and evening walks along the river, to and from school, my relationship to my environment began to change.

I began to experience the river as a being, a being that was as real as you or I. It had pulse, it had moods and it had consciousness. Not only that, my initial experience of the karst formations as beings began to be revealed to me. I would often sit on the banks of the Lijiang simply gazing across her at the mountains that formed the Dragon's Teeth, watching her every movement; fascinated with the array of currents within her.

One bright and sunny day as I sat in the dappled light under the canopy of fresh green leaves that adorned the many trees along the Lijiang's banks, I stared into the crevice between two mountains on the opposite bank. There in front of my eyes stood a vast angelic being, wings spread high and wide, filling the space between the two megaliths. I was captivated by what I was witnessing as I had not seen such things, so vividly, since early childhood. I welcomed the experience as if I was greeting a friend I had not seen in many, many years.

'Who are you?,' I asked

'I am a guardian of this land,' the being replied.

ରୀରୀରୀରୀରୀ

What followed was a dialogue that lasted for several minutes, one in which I came face to face with my own images of what is good and bad and my own feeling that the forces of good were not doing enough to stop all the 'bad' things from happening. What I learnt was that all psychic phenomenon and all manifestations of Gods, goddesses, deities, angelic beings and spiritual sages were but manifestations of the truth of who we are – one that is denied, one that is feared.

I sat in silence contemplating this communication and what my eyes had seen. The Guardian was right. Just as Jesus had once said to his disciples, 'you will deny me three times before the cock crows', I too had denied my true nature for many years. I had had so many glimpses of the truth of who we really are and yet I invariably walked away from it, falling into the trap of believing that it was what I did, had and became that defined me.

ରୀରୀରୀରୀରୀ

As a child I could see dead people, who were very much 'alive': I could also see fairies, devas, gnomes and the spirit of trees. My childhood was alive with the other worlds, unseen by most, felt by many, and yet denied. In the days that followed this fresh encounter with spirit I contemplated not only my own separation from Self but how humanity had managed to separate itself from its true nature.

I truly began to see that when we are separated from ourselves it would be quite easy to toss a plastic bag into a river or to discard waste with no thought to the consequences.

When we are not aware of Self, how can we possibly be aware of our environment? If I am not aware of my own true nature, how can I possibly be witness to another's true nature? If I only look at the world through my mask then I can only expect to see my own projections.

ରୀରୀରୀରୀରୀ

My life story had been one of disappointment; it was the theme of so many aspects of my life – relationships, finances, my work, opportunities. It seemed that so many things simply crumbled just before I could grasp at or take them in. They would be there, all visible in their shining glory and as I would reach out to them, they faded, came to nothing, simply dissolved into nothingness.

The telepathic communication with this Angel went to the very core of my being. I had been reminded of a voice I had once known very well, not only as a child, but also as an adult, about a decade previously. It was so easy to dismiss such voices for everything and everyone around me seemed to be telling me that such things were fanciful to the extent of being some sort of escapism. After all, I had much I wanted to escape from. The tears and trauma of a childhood in which little to no care was demonstrated or given and the recent trauma of having a gun to my head. What was true?

As I sat on the riverbank contemplating my experience my linear logical mind kicked in and called it into question and then I remembered the miracle that had taken place during the armed robbery. The voice. Yes, the voice that had spoken to me so loud and deep. The miracle of the assailant simply walking away. Indeed, the voice. How could I forget so easily? How could I call anything extra sensory into question so quickly after that?

The mind cannot and does not understand that which does not emanate from the mind or that which is behind the mind, the ever-present beingness that is everywhere. I spent years trying to understand, analyze and mentally grasp the many experiences I had had and after years of this exhaustive quest to understand the unknowable, I concluded that the mind cannot fathom the unknowable; only the heart can experience the unknowable within the depths of silence.

It was only in deep silence, the silencing of thought, of worry, of the eternal and incessant questions, that I could hold both the known and unknown in an experience of expanded 'awareness' that required no words and for which no words existed to describe that which is beyond the mind.

In this space there are no questions and no answers and yet everything that is, was and would be was known and yet not known. In the silence was everything and yet it appeared to be nothing; a great spiritual paradox. To the logical linear mind all these descriptions are total gobbledygook for the mind is a mere servant of consciousness, it is not consciousness itself.

❦❦❦❦❦

The longer I remained in China the more I began to question the fundamentals of beliefs and of reality itself. I found myself in a country that had only recently opened its doors to external influences and a country whose history and language stretched back for millennia.

China is a vast and populous land whose people had not been touched by western philosophical thought and belief systems. It was in China that I suddenly and shockingly gained the insight of just how 'Christian' I was in my outlook and in my belief systems. Prior to entering the dragon's belly, had you asked me about my belief systems and way of viewing the world I would never have even seen that indeed much of my thinking was heavily influenced by Christian principles and western philosophy.

My time in China had not only re-awakened within me the magic of being the psychic child with the ability to see into the world of subtle and yet very present energies, but the murmurings of my devotion and longing for the Divine started to be felt once more. The following months and years would see me not only adventure back into the world of spirits, ghosts, fairies and elves, but also back into the world of Gods, Goddesses, Gurus and aspects of religious ritual I had long since walked away from.

China re-awakened my love for nature and it is in China I discovered my love of photography. Through photography, literally looking at life through a different lens, I began to reconnect to humanity again, began to see people for who they are, for the beauty of their being.

The healer's journey has been a grand realization. China had provided not only a safe, peaceful and quiet setting, for that which had been so deeply hurt to start the process of healing, she also challenged the core of my assumptions regarding the nature of reality, values, morality and customs. Somehow all of us assume that our own culture's view of the world is the correct one and I was no exception.

Today, several years later, I more fully own my movement away from the limited and isolated sense of self into a more realized experience of awareness being omnipresent and life being ever present. Today rather than clinging to the hope of there being a greater reality, increasingly I realize that the mundane reality that most of us have been hypnotized by is in fact not the entire picture – an awareness that is not and has not been deduced by logic, reason or rationality, but through direct experience.

Having experienced so much trauma, it gave me a good reason to question everything, to wonder if my broader perceptions were illusions, delusions or mirages created by a distraught mind. In the journey I took to come to peace again, the mere fact of the presence of an awareness both greater than myself and one that also encompasses myself became irrefutable through direct experience and consistent confirmation.

However, in order for this to become more realized within my day to day life I had to become willing to no longer deny that which I knew to be true. It caused me to slowly come out of hiding in many areas of my life, it caused me to become willing not only to know the absolute truth, but also to speak it.

In speaking the absolute truth I am not making reference to being assertive and expressing my opinions, although in part that also happened, but I am talking about speaking the absolute truth about things that may be forbidden, hidden in shame, rejected, disowned or even seen as heresy. It meant being who I am naturally. No justification required, no defences needed, no denials required.

The greatest challenge to living more fully and more truthfully was to cease avoiding myself. I had avoided myself for decades. If I was going to sustain and benefit from the awakening that took place with a gun to my head, I then had to be willing to live in truth, cease avoiding myself and allow a more complete and full awakening to have its own way. What was required was a 'de-cloaking' of myself so that I could completely come out of hiding.

What I discovered was that some things were so deeply hidden that I had forgotten that they were there and still other things were so terrifying to me that it was difficult to face them and believe that I would still be sane afterwards. What encouraged me was the thought, 'If I had survived a gun to my head, then it is clear that I didn't come all the way to China just to die of fear, if it is my time, then it would have happened already.' Reason and logic have their place.

My greatest challenge was coming face to face with an aspect of myself that was still expecting 'redemption' in some way. Somehow, somewhere along the line I had believed that if only I could have a definitive and direct experience of God then all of my pain and suffering would go away – without me ever having to face it.

As I write these words I smile to myself, however, the truth is, it lasted for a long time, it deepened the pain and the illusions, kept God far away and, not only that, I encounter many who are still holding out hope that the realization of our greater awareness with an enduring awakening will wipe away all of our tears without ever crying them.

Coming out of hiding and daring to appear from behind the parapet meant facing what is – grief, fear, hatred, shame, blame, envy, manipulation, control and self-hatred. It meant being willing not only to face the truth of all of that, it also meant giving up all hope that grasping to understand 'why' would ever solve any of this.

It meant giving up the hope that no apology would ever come my way, it meant giving up the hope that there was nothing anyone outside of myself could ever do to magically take it away, and at best what I hoped for is that there may be someone there who would be willing to hold my hand as I face it all, truly facing it all, as it was.

⊘⊘⊘⊘⊘

When I speak of facing the truth I am not speaking of asserting the truth, for asserting the truth is most often the expression of an opinion, which may include truth, but it is invariably not the definitive truth. Facing the truth is coming out of hiding from ourselves. It means overcoming the deep seated fears that many of us have around speaking the truth and facing the truth.

Much of this deep seated pain comes from our early childhood years, a period during which we lived in truth freely. However, this was a freedom that was soon to be experienced as unwelcome, unwanted and unrecognized by the adults around us, which triggered a great and hitherto abiding hurt that we have simply learnt to internalize and hide.

In addition to the memory of this great pain, which in reality is more than a simple memory, it is an energy that we've locked away deep in our core, we are also afraid of losing control of our relationships. Once the truth is expressed we can no longer control other people, or be controlled by other people, through living our relationships from the basis of unspoken rules, unspoken desires and unspoken pain.

The truth places an undeniable spotlight on everything and once it is out, we have a greater chance of getting toothpaste back into the tube. Once truth has been expressed and spoken, especially to ourselves, it is visible and undeniable, even though it may be accompanied with the fear that all of that which used to be internal and hidden, is now hanging freely on the outside – something that can cause us to feel exceptionally vulnerable and open to rejection and attack.

It is for these two reasons – the memory of truth being unwelcome and surrendering our ability to control others once the truth has been fully expressed, that causes most of us to shy away from the truth.

Only our deep longing to be free from the prisons we create can sustain us through beginning to tell the truth and facing what is. Our deep longing can summon forth a great yielding to grace as we dare to be bare and allow the truth to unfold in its own way. Awakening has its own way. It is not we who awakens, for we cannot awaken that which is already awake – it is that which is already awake within us, the undeniable truth of who we are, that summons us.

Once we heed its call, truth starts to become the only acceptable currency with which to navigate and experience the world. The happiness that we all long for comes from living honest, sincere and truthful lives. It means living without pretences and masks, it means choosing our relationships instead of allowing them to be our only or best option, it means consciously choosing every expression of our lives whether that be work, career, play, self-expression, creativity or even parenting.

When we don't live in truth we are either being controlled or we are attempting to control others. In reality, nothing is under our control and we only have the illusion of control and, for the most part, we remain empty handed.

## Enlivening Truth

You may be wondering why truth is so important. When we seek healing we are in reality seeking to return to wholeness once more, we are seeking to remember the truth of who we are. Healing takes place on many levels, not only healing of the body, but also healing of the psyche, the mind and the spirit.

Truth is such a fundamental part of that, facing it forms the foundation for any journey into spiritual awakening and is the building block upon which you can launch yourself into transcendental experiences of the greater Self.

Whilst the fundamental truths of human relationships and the relationship to ourselves does not define what may be called pure consciousness, it does form the foundation upon which pure consciousness can take form and manifest in our lives. In other words, the first and fundamental steps of awakening involve being willing to not only know, but also to tell the absolute truth. For many, the first glimpse of awakening comes either with or very fast on the heels of facing truth, no matter the discomfort.

The truth is enlivening as it always frees us. The truth is always of a higher expression for it must be understood that there is a vast difference between offering an opinion and expressing truth. Coming to truth is not about liberally offering opinions, for opinions are more often than not a distortion based on our projections and belief systems. We often express an opinion in order to *hide* from the truth.

When we express the truth it is truly intimate. It is more often than not followed by a deep silence in which the depth of the truth resides. When truth is spoken we become naked, we become visible, and we cease being shrouded in our fear, projections and demands. As speaking the truth requires such nakedness on our part, it explains why so many of us often avoid it with half-truths, opinions or even outright lies.

We may even feel reluctant to bare ourselves with a particular individual, feeling perhaps that it is not safe – this feeling arises from the deep memory of early childhood when our deepest truths were met with dismissal in one form or another. As we become more accustomed to speaking the deeper truth of who we are, and how we feel, the easier it becomes. Each and every quest for healing, spiritual enlightenment, the attainment of happiness, requires us to meet truth.

Without it, no amount of intellectual information and understanding on an intellectual level will ever deliver what we want without dedication to knowing and telling the absolute truth. However, in order for us to speak from that undefended place of truth, then we need to have met all of the places within us that are afraid of coming out of hiding. We need to meet shame, blame, self-hatred and the fear of being totally alone.

As we encounter all of the hidden places we hold inside, somehow deceiving ourselves that they are also out of sight and have no impact on our lives, we also begin to encounter that which is behind the smoke and mirrors we've created – pure essence. It is this place, beyond the inner veils of illusion and self-deception that we begin to encounter that which forms the foundation for a very transpersonal experience of Universal truths, Universal realities, of that which can be called God.

In order for us to have any sort of sustainable experience of the transpersonal, we must first encounter our foundation. If we don't face that which is, then our new found 'truth' can simply be a new set of projections, wishful thinking and differing forms of idealism that ignore what is present right in front of us in the here and now.

# CHAPTER 2

# A Broken Heart

## Facing it all. Facing the Truth

I have already shared with you a dramatic account of a very real life-threatening event. I've also shared how I had seemed to have reached a ceiling in my work, a ceiling in my understanding, a ceiling in terms of my perceptions of the world and of reality – it was as if I constantly had a word on the tip of my tongue that I simply could not grasp or remember. There was something that wasn't quite right. So there I was, face to face with a gun.

These life-threatening events have a very profound effect on most people, if not on everyone. It certainly did have a profound effect on me. In presenting my work as it is now, I want to share what transpired from all of that. What materialized was an awful lot of learning, much of it through tears of profound and debilitating grief accompanied with bouts of depression I tried to keep hidden from view.

I had it in my mind that a deep spiritual awakening was going to be a big "aha" moment, one that would be blissful, joyful and happy. In previous years I had experienced many spontaneous moments of expansion, which could last for days. Well, that's not what happened. That isn't at all what happened.

After the trauma I spent about a year being quite numb. When I wasn't numb, there were two primary feelings: fear and hatred. Earlier that year, someone with whom I had had a relationship with was killed, and died in circumstances that deeply unsettled and shocked me. There had also been other events in my life and the gun to my head was the culmination.

Close friends had died, two dogs had been poisoned by would-be burglars – one of them had died in a very unpleasant way – and the constant stream of stories regarding violence, murder and rape took their toll.

Less than twenty four hours after the armed robbery I found myself in my bedroom at home with the door firmly shut and locked. I was consumed with hatred, utter detestation. I simply wanted to go out and punish those people, and not just a little. I wanted to hurt them and to hurt them badly. In fact I could have punished anyone who reminded me of them; anyone who was like them; anyone who had the impudence to even look at me; anyone who had the audacity to ask me for anything. That was the state that I was in.

I was white with fury, absolutely consumed, almost frenzied with an outrage and grief that I could barely contain. My own inner sense of safety, propriety and wisdom – whatever you want to call it, taught me enough not to go out too much, not to leave the home, and not to expose myself to people who might remind me of those individuals.

That entire journey, that whole experience shocked me to the core of my being. I had never experienced hatred on that scale. Not ever. I didn't even know that I was capable of it. I simply did not know that I was capable of that kind of hatred. It was monstrous and destructive and it longed to be cruel.

I knew enough to know that I was in danger, in danger of submitting to these darker feelings. It is not that I suppressed them, but I knew enough to control my movements and to stay out of other people's way, in order to keep myself, and them, safe. My state of mind was such that anyone and everyone was a potential threat.

One of the things that I realized – but not overnight, it wasn't an instant thing, it took time for glimpses of it to appear on the horizon on my awareness – was that hatred is born out of a love that has been betrayed. I began to investigate within myself the betrayal of love, not as a mental concept, but as something within myself.

I had touched a hatred so deep and profound that to approach it with my intellect was not only foolhardy, but would rob me of both resolution and opportunities for rich experience.

Where does hatred really start? There's an awful lot of hatred in the world – that is clear and obvious to see. Furthermore, it is not just 'bad' people who hate, a lot of 'good' people are unaware of the depths of their own hatred and some even justify their hatred of 'bad' people as if it is taking the moral high ground. Hatred abounds.

My own hatred could be explained because a gun had been put to my head, and earlier in the year my dogs had been killed, and there were lots of people around me who had been affected by the violence in South Africa – friends, clients and staff alike. I had witnessed and experienced this violence first hand, and because of the nature of my work offering Family Constellation workshops, virtually every weekend I was privy to and heard and shared in such horrendous stories.

It all becomes rather taxing after a while and one of my coping mechanisms was to numb myself. I became acutely aware that hatred existed in all the world.

It existed even outside such clear events that we can point to, underline, and see. If you have a gun to your head or if you are raped or your country is at war, if you have experienced great trauma, if you've just been betrayed by your husband or your wife, or someone very close to you, then of course you can have hatred.

However, what became apparent to me is that even outside of the context of such clearly identifiable events – hatred exists.

In realizing this and in experiencing this from a much deeper place, I realized that my own personal hatred had its origins and roots that were beyond the armed robbery. What the armed robbery did was to bring it up to the surface. It was deeply hidden.

I began to see, and I began to realize that it was also deeply hidden within humanity, even though we see evidence of it everywhere. Almost every day we hear people say, "I hate this" or "I hate those people," "I hate the people from that country," "I hate the people from that religion," "I hate people who like that music," "I hate skinny people," "I hate fat people," "I hate people with red hair," "I hate people with dark skin." We have a lot of liberal use of the word "hatred" and many of us find reasons to hate others.

With this investigation an awareness emerged that informed me that hatred was pandemic, for it was everywhere, and not as hidden as I thought. It was present in the media, in politics, in religion, comedy, entertainment and in fashion. However, most of us when we look at the topic of hatred, believe that we are not affected by it and that we don't actually have it, and that it belongs to those 'other' people. As the veils began to lift and I could see it with such clarity in the world around me, I proceeded to investigate it within myself.

What was the source of my own hatred? I was certain it wasn't the armed robbery. So what was the real source?

What I came across, over and over again, was that hatred is born out of an innocent love and a devoted love that has been betrayed. As this realization unfolded it also became abundantly evident to me with many of my clients.

During the past 18 years of my healing practice I've noticed that when I learn something new about myself, new clients come my way to show me different aspects of the topic at hand which then gives me an opportunity to work with the subject in many different ways and to get to know it more intimately. Sometimes they arrive just before I've learnt the lesson, which is again, the hand of grace.

I began to see hatred and hear about hatred from my clients and began to realize from whence it was born. As we come into this world, we are unchained, unfettered and we are open, living in truth. Quite literally, we have not yet developed filters and screens within and around our chakra system. The entire system is designed so that the father holds the mother and the mother holds the child, and the child is imbued with love, devotion and exquisite adoration.

It is from this experience of paradise we get our deepest sense of self. We feel welcomed into the world. As infants and as young children we are very much like puppy dogs. We love unconditionally. We are happy to see our parents. You might have experienced at times or many times, as I have, how the smile and the little chuckle of a baby, or an infant, can literally light up an entire room.

In this way we are full of divine innocence and we are full of love and we love everyone we see, and we particularly love our parents. This is paradise.

However, for most, if not all of us, almost from the instant we are born, our parents and society begin to project images onto us of how it is that we are to be. So if we are male, there are certain images that are projected onto us, and if we are female there are other images that are projected onto us.

In some cultures perhaps our whole life and our destiny has been mapped out for us. If we're a girl we're going to get a good husband one day and have children. If we're a boy we're going to have a certain type of career.

Each moment of receiving that as a projection is absorbed as the message that who we are and what we are is not quite what is wanted. What is wanted is something else. What is wanted is not who we are, what is wanted is who we are to become. At a very young age we're exposed to not having received life for *our* reasons, but having life given to us is to fulfil the reasons of others. It is in these fundamental moments that our innocence and our essence are betrayed.

For many of the adults around us, the light and the truth of who we are is intolerable. It is not that they hate us, for many loving parents can unconsciously dim the light of their children, unconscious of their own fear of the truth of a child born in innocence. This experience is the birth of hatred and it starts with self-hatred that is later to be projected out onto the world.

It is not my purpose here to paint a picture that states that parents are evil or bad, because the same thing has happened to them. The same thing has been happening for many generations. Even within spiritual communities this takes place. In fact, I would even dare to say especially within spiritual and religious communities that this takes place.

It happens so overwhelmingly because there are many images about what it is to be good, what it is to be spiritual, what it is to be devoted, what it is to be good in the eyes of God. Those images can be extremely powerful.

In fact, they can even serve to strip us of any sense of our divine selves, of any sense of our souls, of any sense of our source. There is great irony in all of that.

ⓐⓐⓐⓐⓐ

My onward and inward journey led me to investigate the truth of hatred. Again I say to you that hatred is born out of a love betrayed. In relating that back to the armed robbery one could say that I didn't love those robbers and therefore if hatred is born out of love betrayed, then how did that happen? However, I did love, I was in love with Africa. I went to Africa because I fell in love with it, fully and completely and totally.

There were many experiences that challenged the existence of that love. I had a strong longing to embrace South Africa and also to be embraced by it. When the longing to embrace something is met by violence, violation and harm, then the longing can easily transform into hatred.

The only way that I knew at the time, that I was capable of at the time, in order to really cope with the deep and profound grief was, to transpose that energy into hatred. Hatred actually serves a purpose. It serves the purpose of stopping us feeling the deep disappointment and the deep, profound and unbearable grief of having lost something that we loved so greatly.

As we come into the world we have great love for our mother and father. Hatred is born when the innocence of that exquisite love is unrecognized and lost.

## Self-Hatred

Hatred, especially self-hatred, exists to a certain extent in every single one of us. It behoves us to not rid ourselves of hatred, not to supress our hatred, not to punish and banish our hatred, but it behoves us to realize and meet the hatred.

It is required that we realize that in fact our deepest nature is to love fully and completely and without condition. To realize that when that is not met, instead of facing the deep and devastating abyss of disappointment, grief and hurt around that, it is easier for us to sit in hatred than to sit in something that gives us the feeling that maybe we even want to die.

If we meet the loss of love, then we might be faced with the realization that we live in a loveless universe, and that there is nothing and no point: no love and no God. And so this is the birth of hatred. Hatred has the purpose and the function of keeping us well away from the ocean of grief that we are unable to face, self-hatred serves the function of stopping us from facing the possibility that we are not wanted, that we are not enough and that somehow there must be something wrong with us.

In reality we can spend decades trying to fix ourselves. Most of what we come across is in our personality. We see the neurosis, we see the dysfunction, we see all sorts of personality traits that we either try to hide or spend most of our time despising. We have learnt to hate our body and spend so much time, lost in comparison. We compare what we see as perfection, happiness and goodness in others, to our own lack.

However, none of this addresses the real heart of the matter – Self-Hatred. What we generally attempt is to fix everything in the futile hope that one day we'll be ok, that one day we'll be acceptable. However, when self-hatred is not faced, we never enter the realm of our core wounds – betrayal, abandonment, rejection.

When this is not met, then our ability to even recognize the underlying sense of emptiness can never be met and when that is not met, we cannot experience what IS there, which turns out to be the better, greater and more magnificent part of ourselves – the very essence we learnt to lock away all those many years ago.

When I refer to an ocean of grief, it is not because the grief itself is so large that it can never be resolved. I call it an ocean of grief because that's what it feels like. It feels like if we actually touch that place, if we touch the reality of what life is like on earth, with all of the cruelty, all of the hatred, all of the wars, all of the injustice, all of the unfairness, all of the abandoning, all of the betrayals – if we touch that, it might become unbearable for us.

However, my personal experience has begun to inform me that when we truly face it, when we truly touch it, this big bad wolf of hatred and profound grief is not as big as we imagine it to be. What we begin to discover is that its bigness, its largeness exists because we are so afraid of it.

We've given it so much energy. When we touch it authentically, when we meet it, when we're willing to die to it, to actually be willing to die to the truth, we begin to earnestly venture into the realm of the heart.

At first we don't really touch this place of loss and deep separation, because there is an intense fear that it will somehow destroy us. Then there's the other fear that this grief is so large and profound, a veritable ocean of tears, that we might discover that there is nothing else: only the grief, only the sadness. We fear that we may journey into this vast ocean of desolation and separation only to discover that there's no "there" when we get there.

That is actually what stops most people from investigating this to any great depth. It is certainly what stopped me from investigating it until the hand of grace pushed my fate in one particular direction and I really had the choice of dying or diving. That was the choice, to die or to dive. That is the fear.

That is the fear that I had, that when I get there, there will be no "there" there.

Years later I laughed and laughed and laughed and I laughed, when I realized that of course, there is no "there" there when we get there. *Because it's here, it never was there. It has always been here.*

⊘⊘⊘⊘⊘

The uncovering of the awakening heart, the uncovering of what is beneath the hatred, comes when we are willing to die for the truth and willing to give up everything for the truth. There is a phrase from the Vedas that says *"Vedeshu durlabam adurlabam atma bhaktau"*.

That particular text, which is part of the Brahma Samhita, says that the Vedas, or ultimate truth, are sealed. The truths of the Vedas are closed. They are inaccessible. *"Adurlabam atma bhaktau"* – but they are accessible and open to the devoted heart (soul).

When we are willing to face anything, to discover any truth, willing to even risk the revelation that there is nothing, no point to life, no God, no meaning, that we're just a bunch of chemicals; when we are willing to risk it all, then revelation comes.

I so wanted to know the truth, I really didn't care if it killed me. After all, I'd just had a gun to my head. That is when I began to uncover, realize and discover for myself that when we're willing to sacrifice everything for the truth, then the truth itself will be revealed and that the truth that is revealed is far more profound and even simpler than we ever imagined. *Than we ever imagined.*

So for me it was an enormous experiential discovery that the source of hatred was in fact an innocent love that had been betrayed.

## Original Sin – The Curse of Generations

In investigating hatred and self-hatred we must become aware that we are not islands. Collectively we carry the hatred of many generations. Our families have been cursed many times and our ancestors have in turn cursed others.

In our ancestry we have both victims and perpetrators, each of them with their own shade, texture and volume of hatred. Hatred is not just a feeling, a belief or an idea, it is an actual energy that has slithered its way down through many generations to us. It is thick and viscous and like all other negative and heavy energies, it tends to stick to us.

Some of us are born into hatred as if it is a family tradition and when we're born into it, either through our culture, family, ethnicity or national tradition, we become so accustomed to wearing the mantle of self-hatred that we hardly even know it is there.

Our inner light becomes dimmed by it until we start to hear the whispers of awakening that beckon us night and day. When born into a world that hates itself we can very easily learn how to hate others without question, even without knowing them.

We are not born with original sin, it is passed to us like a baton in a relay race – except in this race, no one is a winner and we end up losing ourselves in the constant struggle to reach the finish line of personal, planetary and ancestral redemption.

What we don't realize is that every moment of hatred towards another is equalled or surpassed by hatred towards the self. Hateful communities that may be tied up in either a radical political ideology that breeds hatred, or a religious, racial or cultural dogma that likewise propagates hatred are full of families that project hatred not only to their perceived enemies – but also onto their children.

What is generally communicated are very strong and fixed ideas of what is required to be considered good, what is required to belong. Together with all of that there is usually an insistence upon unquestioned loyalty.

In reading the title of this section, Original Sin, your first reaction may be, 'I was not raised in a religious family', 'I was never taught this', 'I'm not a Christian' – which is understandable. However, for the past 1,500 years, every generation, and that is between 45 and 60 generations, has been raised with the teaching that they were born in sin, are sinners and also in need of deliverance from sin.

The ugliest face of this distorted teaching has been the various inquisitions, the witch burnings and other heinous acts of torture and war done in the name of Christ. All of that lives in our cellular memory. Every witch that was burned, every ancestor who was spurned, every pregnant teenager sent away in disgrace, every un-christened child that was sent to hell, every orphan who was told he was worthless – every one of them who was stripped of their humanity by the dogma of original sin that has taught us for generations to hate ourselves and to hate others.

I speak here from the perspective of being raised a Christian. However, distortions exist in all religions and in all cultures. Very often in the East suffering is seen as a result of bad deeds in a past life. In other words 'you are suffering because you are bad'. It may not be called 'original sin' in either Buddhism or Hinduism, but the distortions and the abuse certainly do exist.

Misogyny thrives across all cultures and generations of women have been taught to hate, loathe and distrust their own bodies and in more recent years, misandry is also finding expression in spiritual and healing communities in which the Divine Feminine is seen as superior and one in which the problem is seen to be the masculine and the solution is seen as the feminine.

This collective avoidance of self-hatred is causing many men within spiritual circles to be de-masculinised to the point of losing their identity in a world in which it appears as if they are paying a penance for the sins of their fathers.

I had not considered myself a Christian at all when I was in my 40s; I had long moved on from my Catholic upbringing and had rid myself of the teachings of the Jehovah's Witness sect that I was briefly a member of in my teenage years. However, on entering China, a country that had never been colonized and had in effect been a closed society and culture for thousands of years, I then, to my shock, realised just how Christian my thinking was – and in almost every way.

I began to see that even with my open and liberal view of morality, some of my philosophies, my view of the Universe and my place in it, had all been shaped by Christian thinking. We may not be church going or practising Christians, but after 50 or more generations, this thinking is very much part of who we are and is embedded in our cultural values and norms, even when we are not conscious that our moral and philosophical view has its roots in distorted Christian thinking.

## The Original Sin Teaching, Parenting and Society

The basic teaching is that humanity fell from grace, committed the deadly sin of disobedience, was cast out of paradise and was in need of a saviour to become the ransom sacrifice to absolve us of our sins. There is indisputable richness and deep meaning in the story of Adam and Eve, when it is received as a metaphor for the birth of sentience and our journey through the pitfalls of self-awareness and self-evaluation.

However, taught as a literal truth, as it was for generations, it instilled within large sections of the population, for fifty generations or more, a deep fear of God and a deep fear of falling from grace. What is apparent is that when religion is dominant, God is far, far away.

This deep and abiding religious wound is still very evident in western culture, not only through all of the expressions of self-hatred, but also present in the way in which those who are centred in reason and logic approach both spiritual and psychic phenomenon.

Any suggestion that anything exists beyond what we can measure with the five senses rears the ugly spectre of 'God' and all of the associated wounding that took place over tens of generations. What I believe that this demonstrates is the deep seated belief in the 'person' of God as bestowed upon us through theology and that the mere existence of extra sensory phenomenon brings along with it the unwanted prospect that this personal 'God' may in fact exist.

The existence of 'God' remains unwanted in some circles as we are yet to fully release our notions of a deity with personality and will – a tribal God like Yahweh.

There are still large sections of western culture that are still unable to leave the ancestral image of God behind and move towards the experience of a benevolent consciousness that pervades all things.

At its most horrendous, Christian teachings told parents that if their young baby died before the ceremony of Christening, then their child would either end up in a place called 'Purgatory' or even in the fires of 'Hell' for an eternity. Apart from being heinously devoid of any love and compassion, it was a teaching that ensured the obedience of the masses, controlling the population with fear, terror, shame and blame.

This is one of the grim legacies of Christianity, a punitive view of individuals, families and nations. It is ironic that the individual in whose name all of this came to pass is an embodiment of love.

As these belief systems have directly impacted parenting for generations, at the core of western culture and most western individuals is self-hatred. There is the notion that we must achieve something, become something or do something in order to be 'good'. Our belief in our inherent badness runs very deep.

We grasp at objects, status, ideals, spirituality, images, ideas about body, diets, food and fashion, all in the vein hope that somehow, somewhere, if we're 'good enough,' then the inherent, generationally taught, culturally and religiously imposed self-hatred will dissolve.

It won't. It doesn't. It remains and becomes a millstone around our necks that causes us to chase after the next saviour – in the form of career, a special diet, yoga, sports, fashion, money, sex, a lover, spirituality, or we become addicted to a narrow set of emotions such as anger, bitterness, cynicism or we grasp onto positive thinking in a way that borders on creating another abusive dogma to be adhered to. None of these new 'saviours' will satisfy until we face self-hatred.

# The Individual God

One of the legacies of the Abrahamic religions and Christianity is the creation of an individual, singular God who has a personality, a will, a rule and a desire. In the creation of this concept of an individual God as a singular entity, this God then became external to us and our relationship to Him was either to be in or out of favour, according to the prevailing dogmas at the time.

This also very much mimicked our relationships to parents. Daddy was either happy or unhappy with us, and as with all dominant fathers who could turn on us in a bad temper, much of our time could be spent trying to anticipate and figure out his largely unexpressed wishes and will.

Just as we may run around trying to get the benevolence, love and attention of an aloof father or mother, our concept of an individual God that sits up on high is also an aloof one, whose grace we may also chase through being 'good'.

Much of Christianity in its current and historical form cannot, in reality claim to be Christian, but rather, it is very Paulist in nature. Much of Christian thinking finds its roots in the writing of Paul who is mistakenly called an Apostle, even though he was not one of the original 12, and converted to Christianity some 70 years after the reported death of Christ.

Paul, for one reason or another, clearly could not embrace the simple teachings of Jesus, which are identical in places to the teachings of the Buddha and Krishna. In effect, what Paul did was to re-establish a more Levitical view of the world – God is to be obeyed and feared and these are the rules you must follow.

The establishment of Paulism as the official 'Christian' religion was of course political – placing God outside of the individual, assigning clergy as the only way to 'God', introducing the teachings of Hellfire, Purgatory and being Born in Sin that all amounted to controlling a vast uneducated population for the purposes of garnering power and wealth.

However, as educated as we may be, 50 generations of this religious atrocity have left an almost indelible mark on the western soul – a footprint of self-loathing has been left on our relationship to self.

The Curse of Christianity, as a doctrine based religion, with its strongly Monotheistic 'personal God' thinking is that it places all that is divine outside of the individual and then does two things very clearly: it says that 'sin' is the nature of the individual, thereby we are inherently bad, and then places access to God through one or more individuals.

This very recipe keeps us in the loop of seeking external validation for our goodness, none of which can ever satisfy – when the centre of our being is never touched, nothing ever touches it.

When we've been culturally trained for well over a thousand years to believe that what lies within us is bad, sinful and separate from God, then it is little wonder that self-hatred is a virulent disease in western culture.

# Within

So what if we were now to challenge this premise and to start allowing ourselves to discover the truth of what is within us? This is often a challenge as we have built many rings of defence around our central core.

In an ideal world, parents are in touch with and live from their own true essence and freely bring their children into a process of merging love* in which our own essence is reflected back to us. As each generation of separation from our true nature has advanced through time, we have become increasingly isolated from the truth of who we are.

This isolation from our very own nature has led to a great deal of loneliness in western culture especially, and one in which objectifying individuals has become the norm instead of the exception. When generations of a culture have been told that they are inherently bad, then they will simply begin believing it.

You may even be reading these words and exclaiming, 'none of this applies to me', however, when we truly examine our beliefs around achieving, doing and becoming, in order simply to have value – the picture becomes crystal clear.

There is a great difference between engaging in careers, activities and spiritual practices for the sheer joy, love and creative expression of it than to grasp at self-esteem and self-worth through the medium of our choice.

With our inner work we stumble across the rings of defence that we've built to hide our innocent essence away from harm. As our essence and innate goodness was not reflected back to us and as we continued to be subjected to the punitive nature of Abrahamic cultures and religion, we then began to hide the most precious and beautiful parts of ourselves away.

Around this delicate innocence that also brims with exuberant life forces are rings, like the rings of Saturn, that cloak our light with grief, profound sadness, resentment, bitterness, hatred, anger, rage, despair, hopelessness, worthlessness, self-hatred and self-loathing.

With all of these rings in place, going within to find inherent goodness can be a challenge as we bump into everything we've stored up, denied, was too afraid to feel or acknowledge, or simply numbed ourselves to.

As we venture into this world we begin to glimpse glimmers of what was once lost, forgotten, told it wasn't welcome or shamed out of us in the name of obedience, compliance and agreement to a collective belief system that has had us hating ourselves.

As we embrace the courage to face the big bad wolf of self-hatred that has stalked us for generations, hope begins finally to emerge, the light of truth and consciousness is shone upon our true nature and we can start to truly experience what Jesus, Buddha and Krishna all have said:

'*The Kingdom of God is within*' – J E S U S
'*You will find the Lord dwelling in your own heart*' – K R I S H N A
*The way is not in the sky. The way is in the heart.*' – B U D D H A

In facing the big bad wolf we begin to discover that all the love we've ever wanted has always been right here, right now. Each of us was born to be magnificent and as we have the courage to step out of the hypnotic state that most of the world is living in we begin to discover that the pilgrimage to our heart through the medium of truth is rich and rewarding.

As each layer becomes revealed we begin to experience the voice of the heart as wisdom, its expression as love and its manifestation as beauty.

## Steps to Freedom

It would simply not be true to say that all, or even most of our inner conflicts can be attributed to Western Christian thinking. One only has to look at other non-Christian cultures to know that they too have their own set of problems, some unique to them, and many others in common with westerners.

Many of our personal issues arise out of personal traumas and from direct experiences within the drama that is childhood. However, it behoves us to realize that we are not islands and that we are also barely a generation away from the direct influence of daily religious dogma and strict social norms based on the same.

You, me, we may not be church going Christians, and we may even be affiliated with a liberal spiritual or religious tradition – however, as I wrote above, 1,500 years and 50 generations or more of Original Sin have left their mark and have separated us from the knowledge and experience that within us is a wellspring of goodness, grace, creativity, aliveness and love that could be called 'God' by any other name.

Goodness is both our birth right, natural inheritance and the very nature of our being. The time is 'now' for authentically and diligently reclaiming all that was lost in the dogma of Original Sin. Once this is done we will fully realize that the one and only Original Sin is how we have denied who we truly are.

As I've already stated, I don't have all of the answers. I have some ideas about why we're all here, but I'm more concerned with 'who am I?' Not how I got here. I'm here, I arrived, I don't particularly remember arriving, but I am here.

And so for me, the more important question is, who are you? Who are you really? In order to uncover who you are, it is important to uncover what you have taught yourself that you are, as that's probably not true. It's time to look at all of the images that you have concerning goodness, what it is to be good, what it is to be successful, what it is to be spiritual, what it is to be kind, enlightened, loving, knowledgeable, smart, a worthy, worthwhile human being.

There are so many big fat lies that we have bought into, that we've believed. And there's no one there, really, to blame. Not even ourselves.

Most of the covering of our inner self happens so young that we don't even remember doing that. In fact, in defence of our wound, we constructed a whole personality, forgotten that we've actually done that, and then we believe that the constructed personality is the real us. And all of this has been in defence of innocence, because we've come into a rather challenging and rather brutal world.

෨෨෨෨෨

In looking at all of this, there is very little mileage and very little value in looking for the culprit, even if you think the culprit is yourself. The culprits aren't mom and dad, the culprits aren't grandparents, the culprits aren't the people who adopted you or put you up for adoption. All of these contributed, but the same things were done to them and to everybody else.

Depending on your age, perhaps your parents lived through a war, were part of a war, were children during a war, and perhaps their own parents did things to them, quote-unquote, that are far worse than what they did to you. We're not looking for anyone to blame here. We're looking at the truth of what is.

Acknowledging simple facts is a simplistic way of asking questions where the truth of what is an illusion becomes clear, and the truth of who you are can be met when there is the courage to die to it.

What is your longing to have an awakened heart? What are you willing to risk? What are you really willing to risk? Not so long ago, one of my own teachers asked me a question, and she said to me, "Shavasti, why do you long for self-realization or enlightenment?" I answered truthfully, and I said to her, "Because then everybody will love me and I will be safe."

I told her the truth. And so it's important to look at the truth of motivation. Why are you looking for spiritual growth? Why are you looking for spiritual insights? Why are you looking for healing? Many of us are looking for spiritual truth because we want to improve our experience of this reality, and there is absolutely nothing wrong with that.

We want to have more pleasure. But there's another part of it, which is simply to know the truth, the absolute truth of who you are. *That is part of what I want to share: All of my experiences that have led me to many journeys into the absolute truth of who I am. And when I use the phrase, the absolute truth, it is not a dogma, it is not a teaching to be adhered to, but a realization of something that exists.*

Not a rule, not a regulation, but something that exists. When we travel into and beyond the ocean of grief and fear that dominates human experience, we begin to discover another truth, that there is no "there" there when we get there.

## Breaking the Heart Open

Most of us enter the world of healing, meditation, yoga, new thinking and spirituality because we want to either feel better about ourselves or to improve our experience of reality – some of us enter because we have a burning desire to know the truth of who we are, or even the truth of humanity, our origins, our purpose, the reason for our existence.

However, very few of us, consciously, want to know the absolute truth. What truth always brings is transformation, what truth always demands is that we relinquish our attempts to control our relationships and other people, and that we relinquish control in the full knowledge that we had none in the first place and all of our attempts to control simply led to increased suffering.

The quest for truth is inconvenient – most of us at one point in our lives, or almost always in some areas of our lives, limit the truth we speak with the notion that somehow we can control others or control relationships. We don't speak our needs clearly, sometimes dropping hints, sometimes through never fully completing a sentence –while leaving it up to the other person to fill in the gaps and anticipate our needs.

What is destructive about this fear based behaviour is that we then become angry, resentful or feel hard done by when the other does not respond to our unspoken need!

When we seek the truth, the unequivocal, undeniable truth of not only acknowledging what is and what was, what becomes apparent is that there is a world of difference between our opinions and what is really true, and a world of difference between what 'IS' and the story we've told about it.

We often get caught in needing to be right and our need to be right often overrides any other consideration – especially the truth.

When we seek the truth, then much of what we've held in place either through lying to ourselves, or to others, comes into focus and this is simply too uncomfortable for many of us. We fear being alone, we fear being an outcast, we fear that our own sense of worthlessness may actually be true or undeniably confirmed.

On the one hand we want to be happier, we want to be 'more spiritual', we want more 'union with God' and yet a good measure of all of that is revealing the most precious parts of ourselves that we've locked away and denied.

In encountering that which has been locked away and denied, we begin to see the self-betrayal very clearly and with that revelation, our stories of blame also begin to crumble. The truth does not bring comfort to us at first; it comes to destroy our world with the Sword of Michael, the fire of Shiva and the ferocity of Kali.

However, when we value truth over and above our fearful attachments, truth then becomes our refuge, comforter and the doorway into that which we have long been in search of – freedom and peace.

When we have freedom, true freedom, not the freedom that is dictated to us by politicians, not the freedom to behave as we wish, but the truest freedom of all – the freedom to love – with that comes peace: an unending peace.

However, the only doorway to get there is through truth. Here we have our dilemma. We want to be healed, we want more harmony in our lives, we want to be happy, healthier, and wealthier and have a more pleasurable experience of our work life, day-to-day activities and income. There are so many things that we want. However, none of them can change unless the truth about them and the stories we've both told ourselves and have agreed to, are faced.

Truth is such a charged and difficult word. It is very similar to the words 'God' and 'Love'. So much has been said, written, dictated and done in the name of God, Love and Truth – most of which does not contain the undistorted essence of either. So how can we know what truth is?

Truth is always simple, the statements are always simple. If we need to use a lot of words to explain our truth then we can know that we're stuck in our own story about it, or bound by an opinion or a belief.

❦ ❦ ❦ ❦ ❦

I spoke earlier about hatred and in the process of opening the heart, every nook and cranny of the heart needs to be met: All of the secret hatreds, resentments, self-criticism and judgements that form a barrier around what we're really afraid of – deep grief.

Hatred is such rich territory for self-exploration. Not a territory to wallow in or search for reasons and evidence with which we can reject the self even more, but, it is the territory that has the most doorways leading to love. When we re-alize the deeper function of hatred and start to acknowledge the depth of the wound behind it, hatred begins to lose its meaning as anything beyond a defence mechanism – even as destructive as it is.

As a general rule of thumb, the more intense the hatred, the deeper the wound, the more devastating and threatening it feels to even encounter such a wound. However, with courage, you will soon be able to experience the pain of childhood walking beside you as a friend, teaching you how to invite the stillness of compassion.

## Meeting the Grief & Loss

You may be wondering if grief and loss even apply to you as you read this – after all, perhaps you've never had the experience of losing anything or anyone. However, the loss I speak of here is much more fundamental, it is deep down inside our consciousness and it is where we have separated from the truth of who we are. This is the greatest loss of all – the loss of the truth of who we really are.

Much of what we identify as our 'self' is in fact a construction of layers of defence around our original wound. That is not to say that our personality or ego is all bad, or that logic and reason have no place in the world. However, as we look at the constructed self, the defended self, it is designed to circumnavigate our core wound and it is also most often obsessed with being good.

This entire process of creating a personality that conforms, shape-shifts and navigates what it believes others want from us, and also what is defined as a 'good' person, has eroded away our contact with our authentic self. Here in the space between our true self and that which we've created in separation from the true self is a terrifying schism; it has often been described as the 'abyss'.

It is terrifying for as we enter the schism itself, before touching the whole and complete self, it can feel as if everything we are and thought we were is about to crumble and fall into annihilation. The truth is, the defences we have constructed do start to crumble. The fear that we feel is that we separated from our true and authentic self so long ago that we now believe that the false self, the one trying to be good, the one searching for meaning, is the real self.

Terror ensues, hopelessness ensues. In the schism there appears to be nothing, a lack of self. However, in truth, contained within and around the schism is all of the life force energy that we have used to hide away that we have experienced to be unwelcome.

We learn from a very early age that truth is not welcome and that we live in a world of direct contradiction. We are told that to lie is wrong or a sin, and yet we observe the adults around us being habitually untruthful whilst at the same time having our own truth censored and suppressed.

As children we are naturally curious about everyone and everything and just like our favourite pet dogs, as children we have an innate ability to love anyone. We're neither sexist nor racist, we don't notice anyone's social standing, disability or inabilities – we simply love. Through the process of being subjected to the repeated rejection of our innocent love, we begin to hide it away.

For those of us who have experienced violence, abandonment, trauma, sexual, religious and other forms of abuse on top of the feeling of not being welcome as we are, the burying can be much deeper – out of pure survival. In the process of all of this hiding we begin to adopt the sexist, racist, cultural and religious basis of discrimination.

As all of this develops and we adopt belief systems that are specific to our culture and country – we begin not only to lose contact with our true and authentic self, we often don't even remember having one and don't realize that there is a true and authentic self to be experienced – so deep the schism can be.

As we begin to awaken to this and learn to surrender our stories of who did what to whom and whose fault it was, the heart begins to stir. This can be the first murmuring of the Profound Grief – the Wound of Separation.

As we explore our grief we may indeed come across layers of loss regarding life circumstances; the death of a parent, sibling, grandparent, childhood friend or pet. However, the Profound Grief is that which we are generally terrified to feel. This Profound Grief represents the loss of innocence, the loss of personal truth, the loss of love and the hopelessness that encases the disillusionment that the world is no longer the world of wonderment it was when we were new arrivals.

The heart of a child simply cannot fathom why the adults behave as they do, cannot comprehend the insanity with which most adults seem to live with – espousing high ideals but acting from their opposites. The heart of the child must bury itself in order not to flounder and drown in the cold and murky wells of devastating disappointment.

This is the Profound Grief that awaits those who have the courage to want more than to simply improve some of their experience of life. This Profound Grief awaits those who long to know the truth of who they really are. This truth, rather than being a million miles away, sits quietly, not lost, already found, always and forever present the other side of the schism.

It dwells in the land of the forgotten and yet, when we meet it, we realize that it was never forgotten, when we find it, we discover it was never lost, when we feel it, we discover it was never not felt, when we surrender to it, we discover that it always had its arms gently wrapped around us. The power of that which lies shrouded behind and under the Profound Grief is so great that its presence has always been felt.

In reality, it has never been us who has gone in search of our true Self, it is this very Self that has been calling us, and although its voice is silent, its call is indeed heard night and day.

ⓞⓞⓞⓞⓞ

As we begin to approach the Profound Grief we start moving through layers of all of those things that cause us to wall off our true Self in the first place. As we go to this depth, more often than not, there is no story. There can be some flashes of memory here and there, but mostly it is simply emotional energy that has been stored in both the physical and auric bodies.

One of the greatest hindrances to this process of awakening to the greater fullness of who we truly are, is facing the conflict we may hold around those who have hurt us. Whilst in any kind of self-investigation we may stumble across anger and a whole host of emotions, as we approach Profound Grief, something different often emerges which can cause sufficient conflict to cause us to stop the process of opening to the Grace of the Heart once Profound Grief has had its way.

As we enter the depths of our wound our adult reasoned mind can feel very challenged when in our depths we feel not only love, but also the deep loss we have experienced in losing the father who beat us, the mother who abused us, the uncle who raped us, the sister who betrayed us, the teacher who humiliated us and the grandmother who always said 'No' to us.

What we touch as we enter Profound Grief is the innocent love with which we met everyone as a child – we begin to touch our innocence again and experience directly what was lost. Our adult mind wants to cling on to the idea that the people who did this to us are bad. However, in encountering our lost innocence, we begin to remember the quality of our love and that, which was lost.

*As our heart awakens to itself, we discover that everything is already forgiven.*

Our cultural belief systems can also scupper all attempts to traverse the territory of Profound Grief. Cultural beliefs and attitudes may make it impossible to feel anything else other than disdain or hatred for our abusers – believing in some way that feeling love for them lets them off the hook. It doesn't, it lets us off the hook.

Karma will have her way no matter what, and it is none of our business. As we move through this ring of woundedness we start to hit a profound loss of love. We long to remember those who hurt us through the eyes and heart of innocence, we miss what was lost, we long for the once innocent love and what we ultimately discover, is that the innocence was not lost, has never been lost, it was present all the time – buried under the fear that somehow we are bad and that there is something wrong with us.

What a triumph this is when we uncover this treasure trove of wishes yet to be fulfilled, loves to be finally shared and nurtured and munificent, bountiful and exuberant life force energy that so wants to live and thrive – more than all of that, it longs to embrace the world! How blessed we are when we have the courage to face the truth of who we love and how much we love them.

In this process of traversing the schism between our separated self and authentic Self there may be several layers, some more challenging than others, and often quite unexpected.

We can find ourselves grieving a loss we never considered important. This happens because we have a tendency to place more importance in the stories rather than the feelings that were felt and the deeper separation that came about as a result.

## Meeting the Place of Separation

As we surrender to our deeper grief; the grief that the world is not as kind and loving as we want it to be, the intolerable suffering we see all around us, our own personal loss and betrayal of self, we start to feel the place of separation within us. This is not just a psychological barrier, it is an energetic one and it is, for the most part, housed within the body, often deep in the gut and lower belly.

It is an energy, it can feel and look like a wall, it can feel and look like a sack of dark nothingness – no matter its form, it is an energy and it can be experienced as something that has inertia until we begin to step inside of it. Some have called this the abyss. It certainly feels bottomless, it certainly feels like a place of utter destruction and a place of no return.

At first it can be terrifying to enter the schism, the place of separation until we begin to realize that it is an energy – it is not dead at all – it is compacted life force energy that only appears to be an abyss.

One of the greatest fears that arises as we meet this place is that most, if not all, of our identity has been built on top of this place. Starting in our formative years we began to construct an identity that we thought would be pleasing to those around us, sometimes this identity was created for pure survival. Women create identities to fit in with societal expectations of what a 'real woman' is and boys create identities in similar fashion, often ones' that dictate that 'big boys don't cry'.

However, here we are, facing the place of separation from ourselves. However, on first approach we have no proof that anything other than destruction and annihilation awaits us.

All we can feel is the separation – it's a lonely place – no God, no light, no sense of anything having any meaning, no rescuers, no saints, no angels, no gurus, no prophets, no nothing – it is a place of total separation and it can feel like death on a grand scale: a death from which nothing will ever, or could ever, survive. We may shake, we may sweat, our hearts may pound – we may even call out 'Father, father, why hath thou forsaken me?'

We may have spent many years either approaching or avoiding this deep place of separation for the separation itself is sustained by self-loathing, self-hatred and the feeling that no matter what we do to improve ourselves, we simply don't like what we see and it is never enough.

In our quest to 'fix' ourselves we may have moved from teacher to teacher, healing modality to healing modality, book to book, workshop to workshop, all in an attempt to fix what is wrong and yet somehow we still end up feeling dissatisfied.

All of our quests for new teachings, new teachers and new processes, although they may have given us many invaluable experiences and enriched our lives with better relationships, improved health and a more successful career, really only ever satisfy temporarily.

This abyss of separation contains and has wrapped around it all of our unwanted, denied and unconscious feelings; it is the embodiment of hell and is our very own personal hell. It is my firm belief that all of the mystics and holy men of old who wrote of hell and a place of separation from God wrote about this domain that lay within us until it was/is met consciously.

 round round round round round

This personal hell has gravity – each and every time we reach for the stars, it has a way of pulling us back and we can become like a hamster on a wheel, forever reaching for spiritual bliss, insights and enlightenment, only to be pulled back by the gravity of our hitherto avoided hell.

When we contemplate stories of the great enlightened teachers such as Christ or the Buddha, we begin to see that they also met their own personal hell before realizing God for themselves. They faced their fears, their weaknesses, their temptations.

What is generally not understood, by many spiritual seekers is that the temptations were not in a literal sense money, food, fear, sex or power – but they were representative of what can only fulfil the constructed self, a realisation that when we grasp onto them they can only bring temporary relief and are otherwise dissatisfying.

The irony of all this is that the separated self has capitalized upon these stories and has made a spiritual dogma out of them, which only seeks to keep the status quo between the separated self and the dissolution of separation, as we approach essence.

So strong is our identification with the separated self that we will even weave distorted spiritual teachings into its existence in order to once again fully and totally avoid the abyss.

New dogmas and 'truly spiritual' teachings emerge – it is better not to have desires, money is evil, power is evil, following a certain diet is *more* spiritual – the list goes on and on. Truly, such teachings are the devil himself dressed up to look like an angel of light.

The separated self seeks to keep itself in separation because we have become so identified with it that its deconstruction equals annihilation – who are we if we're not identified with being something or someone? Thus we have the construction of the spiritualized ego that seeks to convince you that if you do all the right things, eat all the right foods, believe in all the right beliefs, do the right exercises, mediate correctly, that all of this will 'fix' you.

It even has within it the belief that perhaps it may become enlightened – this is the proverbial carrot on a stick. The spiritualized ego is the most deceptive of them all and it has captured millions across the planet with the belief that if we are simply 'good enough' or 'obedient enough', then the grand prize of Union with God, Self-Realization or Enlightenment will be ours.

෧෧෧෧෧

It is only reunion with our core essential self that can satisfy. However, as we separated so very long ago, and for the most part we've even forgotten that we did, the separated self now believes that 'IT' is the real you, that 'IT' is the one who is in charge and is the most important part of your existence.

As we approach the abyss and the ring of torment that binds it like a metal band on a barrel, our constructed self, or ego, will do anything to stop us risking annihilation. After all, our constructed self emerged as a survival strategy in a world that did not welcome truth and could not tolerate the light of innocent love.

As we fall into the abyss and risk the feared annihilation the terror of separation can be felt intensely. However, as it is met more fully and surrendered to, the energy that is held in place within our body begins to move up and out of the body, often either through the top of the head or out through the mouth.

As we use our gentle breath to allow this movement to have its own way we begin to get glimpses of what may lie beyond the abyss, on the other side of separation, and our system begins to calm down.

Moving through our places of separation as a means of reclaiming our whole and complete self is an experience that transforms lives. Not only do we begin to remember who we once were, we also experience that indeed it is not lost, but simply buried within us. It didn't go anywhere, it never left, it was never lost.

We, the seeker were lost, our essence self, our whole self, was never lost – it sat silently waiting. As we continue to surrender our stories, what dies is everything we are not. What comes to life is who we truly are.

When we surrender to the Profound Grief and take courage in facing the abyss and our deepest existential fears, what awaits us is the experience of ourselves at the level of essence – not as an escape, not as a fanciful idea, not as a part in the drama of a spiritual by-pass, but the real authentic you who is brimming with life force energy and is at peace with itself and with the world.

For the lucky few, some hit this place and everything else falls away permanently, no longer identified with the constructed self, with images and beliefs as to who they are supposed to be, finally free or Self Realized.

For most of us, this experience can either be a single experience, or one of many experiences that slowly allows more and more of our true nature to emerge and transform our vision of ourselves and our place in the world. This release into freedom seems to come in two forms – either the balloon is popped, or the knot is undone, and the air is let out slowly.

Most of us fall into the latter category with perhaps there being a separation of months or years between each experience of deeper awakening, between each experience of releasing the heart. The awakening, or living from essence, can last for minutes, hours or days.

However, no matter how long it lasts it will leave permanent footprints on our path, transforming aspects of life with the new light of consciousness that has now become conscious. It is not possible to touch the truth and then fully retreat back into the lie that we are small, insignificant and loathsome.

*MERGING LOVE: *A term used by HH Almaas to describe the symbiotic nurturing stage between mother and infant. At this stage we are not aware of our separate ego identity from our mother.*

# CHAPTER THREE

# Acts of Separation

## Images, Beliefs and Denials

Who are you? With this question it is then important to explore who we are not. It is important to start identifying all of the images and notions of who we believe ourselves to be, as they have been not only influenced by cultural and ancestral imprinting, our identities have also been deeply influenced by spiritual imagery – giving way to many ideas of who we 'ought' to be, in total contrast to who we truly are.

In reality, the truth of who we are is much more exquisite than anything the ego could conjure up. Part of our work is to challenge what we've been taught – not in order to create a new image of who we believe ourselves to be, but to allow all images, thoughts, ideas and beliefs about who we think we are and who we think we should be to dissolve, so that what lies within us can be free from defence and allow itself to become manifest in all of its exquisite glory.

This is not done through positive thinking, through use of will, through recreating a new personality, adjusting the old one – it is done through surrendering to the wound of separation. However, before that takes place, we must first ask the deeper questions regarding what is true – deeply enquire into the truth of belief systems.

Most of us, without even realizing it, are acting from an image of who we're not, rather than living from the deeper truth of who we really are. Given that we've been bombarded with images of loyalty, cultural values, images of gender, sexual orientation, race, ethnicity and what is defined as a 'good' person by our religion, nation or culture – it is not surprising that so few of us are truly in touch with who we are.

At a very young age our feelings were discouraged, especially in boys, and we were told to 'think things through' and that certain feelings were neither welcome nor acceptable.

One of the great challenges for each of us, as we begin to awaken, is that because we have constructed so much of our life around images and beliefs of what it is to be good, much of that construction has been in avoidance of the curse of self-loathing and self-hatred that has been passed down from the many preceding generations.

What is time, and again, evident is that even in our attempt to become more of who we truly are, it is more often than not simply grabbing hold of new images that perhaps represent a better version of who we think we are, in avoidance of what we fear we may be. As we try to live from those new images there is simply a prolongation of the suffering caused by living in separation from our authentic centre.

There are many great misunderstandings in terms of what is required for personal development, spiritual development, and healing. Many individuals seek solace through a spiritual practice, through seeking out a guru, and through many aspects of spirituality that are very transpersonal in nature. It is not that any of these things are wrong or bad, but it must be understood that spirituality is not therapy and although it can be very healing, we must be aware of what it is we are bringing into the circle.

We must be aware that spiritual practice seeks to take us beyond the day-to-day personality and ego that we usually identify with and is therefore 'transpersonal'. Therapy helps us to bring awareness and resolution to our personal issues.

When our underlying wounding has not been addressed, when it has not been felt, when it has not been looked at or acknowledged, we have very little understanding and experience of how we have constructed a defence around our essential Self. When that is not understood or experienced we can have a strong tendency to live from our upper chakras through constructing another false image of self – this time a spiritual one.

It is very easy to recognize other aspects of the false self for they can perhaps be identified as negative, for example, arrogance as a defensive posture. It is important that we recognize that there is a big difference between transpersonal work and our own individual needs to heal what was not given, what was taken away, shunned and abandoned when we were in our formative years.

In other words, there has to be sufficient foundation for a healthy person to thrive upon before transpersonal work can have any deep, lasting or truly positive effect on our lives. The very substance of transpersonal work is to move beyond identification with the constructed self, in others words, the ego.

However, of what benefit is that when the individual in question is fragmented and shattered in unhealthy ways? What I'm saying here is that their needs to be a healthy ego in place before it can be de-constructed for trans-personal experience. To quote Jack Engler, 'you have to be somebody before you become nobody'.

When we ignore our foundational healing needs we run the risk of becoming an individual who lives from idealism, or living from what has been termed as a spiritualized ego, becoming blind to humanity and blind to the individuals standing right in front of us, perhaps even projecting an image of what we want to see onto them, or some notion of their potential.

At its worst, we can fall into spiritual narcissism and simply be out of touch with the reality that most people around us are experiencing. One could argue that it is not such a bad thing to not see the reality of others, given the mass belief systems. However, given that all of the great teachers to have walked this planet of ours have spoken in depth about compassion – how can we encounter anyone from a centred place of compassion if we are not present?

When we avoid the healing that is necessary for our very foundation as a relational human being we grasp the idea that a spiritual teaching or a spiritual practice can give us something to make us good. However, what generally happens is that the schism between who we think we are and the truth of who we truly are, at our core being, merely widens.

This is one of the main reasons why appalling, anti-social, highly dysfunctional and deeply narcissistic behaviours can sometimes be observed without difficulty in ashrams, spiritual communities and spiritual centres. When we grasp at that which will make us 'good' we deepen the rift with our essential self, and the self-hatred with all of its distorted behaviours simply becomes amplified with all of the energy we are bringing into our system through various spiritual practices and from living in our upper energy centres or chakras.

In saying this, I'm not speaking against spiritual practices or gurus. I have a guru and I have a spiritual practice. However, when we look at ourselves as individuals, there are three very distinct avenues of healing, all three of which are very important. There is foundational work (pre-personal), personal work, and then there is transpersonal work. All three areas of work are limited without the inclusion of the other.

☙☙☙☙☙

Foundational work is literally an experiential exploration and healing of the wounding that led to the formation of all of the barriers and defences we've built around us and how this has become the foundation of a defended self that is locked in prolonged suffering. Foundational work is not about looking at what is wrong with the personality, but it is about witnessing how we have constructed defences around wounds that we may not even be conscious of.

One of the challenges of healing our foundation, the pre-personal aspects of our self, is that there is rarely a story attached. Most of us can tell a story about what was said and done to us and around us – and these stories can also easily become a repetitive narrative for our lives. However, since our foundational wounding took place at such a young age what we are generally left with are pure feelings – no story, no specific memories, no explanation.

What is surprising for so many of us is simply how intense it can be when we start to unravel the tightly wound knots of suffering that started to form before we could even speak or walk. A mother or father shouting is much more terrifying to a three month old baby than it is to a six year old, and that same shouting is far more frightening to a six year old than it is to a 15 year old.

Therefore as we enter into the realm of our foundational self, the energy of separation that is generally held in the lower belly, we can feel feelings of sheer terror. What can add to that fear is the mind's inability to construct a memory around what is, essentially, raw feelings.

For the vast majority of us, we seldom experienced our divine essence being reflected back to us in the course of our formative years. We were subjected to the images of the family that we were born into, including the culture, ethnicity, race, country and nation.

We were also formed further, by the schools that we went to, by the rituals and the habits of the culture in which we exist. All of these images that we either rebel against, imitate or live up to serve the purpose of giving us a deeper sense of belonging.

However, as we identify with that belonging, and identify with the images as 'absolutes' about what is true, false, good or bad, we begin to lose contact with who we truly are and become willing to betray as many parts of ourselves as possible in order to fit in, in order to be part of a group, clan, culture or a society.

It is not that all values that we have been taught are bad, the issue remains with our identification with these values and beliefs as if something 'other' will make us good, valuable and worthy instead of our innate true self.

ᘒᘒᘒᘒᘒ

Some of us have done the complete opposite to that. We've rebelled against everything that we were ever taught. However, the rebellion in itself also becomes part of a constructed aspect of our defended personality that is also not the truth of who we are.

In reality, whether we are compliant or rebellious, neither of those opposite ends of the scale express the truth of who we are. As we come into this world we arrive as little beams of light, an embodiment of the exuberance, the grace, the abundance, the exquisite love of the divine.

However, even before we are born, the circumstances of our conception, the environment of the womb itself, the nature of the relationship between our mother and father, the environment of the country and land our gestation takes place in, and the experiences of our ancestors, are already beginning to influence how we will see ourselves and perceive our place in the world.

It is not a simple case of being born untouched from a womb; as this life begins we are immersed in a far greater field of energy and consciousness than existed prior to our conception. This field of energy and consciousness contains the collective experience, mental patterns and emotional responses of our entire biological family and of our ancestors, stretching back several generations.

Imprints of domestic violence, war, famine, grief, death, trauma, political and ethnic allegiances, tragedies and religious ideologies have left their footprint on the energy field we have just entered the world through. Some will also argue that in addition to this we also arrive with imprints from pervious lives. What I do know is that we seem to be born into families that are working with similar themes to the personal themes of our own soul.

What is clear, and in recent years this is being verified by some areas of science, is that even before we are born into the world, there are indeed strong influences already in place that contribute to the image of who we believe ourselves to be.

As we grow inside our mother's body we are merged with her at the very deepest level and with this merging we feel all that she feels, all of which has a direct influence on our body chemistry and emotional well-being. If there is alcohol, nicotine or recreational drugs in her system, this too will be felt and experienced; also if it is present with the father.

The energy of our father influences us directly too. For example, during conception it is not just the sperm that reaches the egg. With ejaculation the father's auric field expands and projects outward along with his ejaculate to meet the egg in the uterus. The egg that then develops to become us, is bathed in many layers of the father's energy field and consciousness.

In essence this consciousness is saying, 'Hello, you belong to me and are a part of me'. Therefore, as your physical body is forming, even before it even becomes two cells, it receives an injection of your father's emotional state, his belief systems, his experiences, his trauma, his upbringing and the traditions of his ancestors.

It is a very complete 'calling card' that leaves a footprint, or rather, a template for the life we are about to emerge into. In part this also explains why even adopted children, on meeting their biological families, can identify habits, opinions, feelings and beliefs that are identical to their biological father, mother, brother, sister, and yet they have never met them.

We are energy beings, not just physical beings. In fact, we are primarily energy beings.

&#8279;&#8279;&#8279;&#8279;&#8279;

Here we are. We are first an individual cell, and then we are multiple cells, and then we're a foetus and then we're a baby. And then we're born. And already at this stage we have been exposed to the feelings and the belief systems of the family into which we have been born. What this tells us is that even on the level of our external personality and on the level of our physical being, we are certainly not islands.

Here I return to the deeper question again: *are you willing to risk everything to know the truth?*

As we venture into this world of self-discovery, we're seeking personal fulfilment and perhaps our notion of what spiritual growth is. There are many images along the way that we can grab onto. They can be the stories that we tell, the stories that we can hold onto, they can be descriptions of where we came from, the kind of family that we came from, all in order to explain our lack of fulfilment and unhappiness.

On top of that, there can be many images that we have inherited, taken on, that have been imposed upon us, thrust upon us, about what it is to be good or to be happy. Or to be considered successful or spiritual, what it is to be a man, or a 'real' man, what is expected from us as a woman, or what a 'real' woman is.

Here is the poisonous combination. We have a story of who we think we are and then the images of who we believe we should become, both of which are the devil in disguise.

They're simply not true. As we look honestly at all of our images we begin to see the 'not enoughness' contained in all of them: we're not successful enough, we're not intelligent enough, we're not pretty enough, we're not talented enough, we're not masculine enough, we're not maternal enough, brave enough, good enough – we're simply not *enough*.

Here's the absolute truth with all of that: we're not enough. That is the truth. You, me, anyone can never be enough. We are limited by our human frailties and it is our concern that we're not enough that leads to the suffering in its avoidance. Once we meet the actual fact that we're not enough, what follows is peace and a chance for the heart to express love, manifest beauty and be present with our own inherent magnificence.

Once we make peace with not being enough and we've built up a tolerance towards truly and deeply encountering the belief that not being enough makes us bad, it is from here that the images and the 'shoulds' can start to crumble.

What we notice is that as we encountered one of our greatest fears, or perhaps the deepest shame of feeling that we're never enough, is that we get glimpses of the truth of who we are as it becomes evident through the encountering of our 'not enoughness,'; that we were not annihilated in the process. This brings great relief.

As a part of my own personal journey with the deconstruction of my defended self, I studied spiritual paths and truths because I believed that is was going to help me to discover something, and that surely it would be good? However, those spiritual truths often became images that I hung onto which had the effect of keeping me away from a deeper discovery of Self and the innate freedom that comes from knowing absolutely that all is well and has always been well.

Here is a paradox. Our pursuit of spiritual truth can be the very thing that holds us back from ever discovering, experiencing and living the truth, peace and freedom we long for. It is rarely about the content of what it is that we are studying, but it IS about how we habitually create objects, images and dogmas out of things.

*None of these things are wrong for I am not speaking a word against them as personal preferences.* The cautionary tale here, is attaching some notion of a spiritual value to them – attaching to them the idea that they will make us good which translates into a 'better person'.

As soon as we grasp onto a form and make it part of what we believe may make us a 'good' person, then we can know absolutely for sure that we are in avoidance of Self-Hatred and our deep fear of not being enough, or not being welcome, or simply not belonging.

Western culture in particular is already notorious for projecting impossible images around acceptable body types for women and all of this becomes distorted in both similar and different ways within the realm of spirituality and spiritual practice.

Similarly western culture has over masculinized men to the extent that many have an inability to identify feelings and have many conflicting images of what it is to be a man. In addition to cultural indoctrination regarding what constitutes a 'man', there has also been the many generations of wars that have taken a terrible toll on male lines and their inherited coping mechanism that seeks to nullify feelings.

In generations gone by many men have witnessed their friends, brothers, fathers, uncles and sons die on the battle field – this adds up to a lot of inherited numbness. What we often see in spiritual communities is how men are often moved to de-masculinize themselves in order to fit in with a more female dominated modern spiritual era.

# Core Beliefs

We each have a set of beliefs that we hold about ourselves, sometimes conscious, sometimes frequently stated, sometimes just outside our field of vision until we get quiet long enough to hear their tormenting whisper. They are often hidden but somehow almost always visible as they leave footprints on the chapters and paragraphs of our life, as we meander from hope to promise in search of happiness and spiritual fulfilment.

When we begin to examine our relationship to ourselves we see that there are a host of satellite beliefs that appear to orbit one central core belief. We may not at first be aware of this belief, however, on closer inspection it is revealed that each of our satellite beliefs has a common theme and they are in effect pointing inwards towards that which sits around our true core.

The true core is our divine light, it is the essence of who we are, it is that which we truly are, that which is and always has been free and that which is neither bound by fear nor dogma, that which is aware of being an expression and extension of something much greater than itself.

This core is the silent witness that dwells in the stillness of well-being, no matter what our current experience is. As this exuberant core became shrouded by what we thought others wanted of us we created a barrier between our Divine Core and the outer world. On the far outside is our personality and, between the face we show the world and the Divine Core, is a ring or ball of thick viscous energy that is weighed down by our satellite and core beliefs.

Working with our core belief *cannot be done in the mind.* It simply cannot. At most we can place a sort of Band-Aid over the core wound. There is a great temptation to believe that we can resolve the core belief through new thoughts alone – after all, the core belief sits right at the threshold of separation from our core self.

Separation form the core Self, from our Essence Self IS separation from God, it IS the ultimate experience of loneliness and isolation, it IS fear of annihilation, it *does* feel like a fate worse than death.

Once we're aware of the hidden beliefs and feelings, it takes much more energy to hide them from others, when in reality they are not hidden at all.

Our beliefs are so often VERY visible to others for they are the observers of our actions, the recipients of our defences and judgements and therefore, in reality, there is no hidden truth – not if we're completely still for a few moments and can tolerate telling, seeing, feeling and knowing the absolute truth of how we feel.

As we become acquainted with our satellite beliefs we can move towards the core through noticing the common theme. It is important to know that the core belief is created in response to an event or a series of events. As these events most probably took place in very early childhood, there are often no memories, simply a raw feeling.

Here are some of the most common core beliefs:

I am bad
I am not welcome
I am not loved
I am unlovable
I don't deserve to be here
I am ugly
I am wrong
I am not enough
I am all alone
God doesn't love me
I am stupid
I am evil
I am not good enough

What is very important to remember is that the core belief is an energy and it can be seen in the auric field. It can often be seen as a Dense Spherical Object that floats in and around the aura, but most often, it is lodged inside the body, usually in the lower belly around the area that is also called the Hara or Tan Tien below the navel, or slightly above the navel region.

Another form the Core Belief and Satellite Beliefs can take is that of Energy Sphincters along the body's vertical energy channels. They seek to restrict the flow of energy so that the heavier emotions associated with beliefs such as, 'I am unwanted' and, 'I am ugly,' are not felt.

The Core Belief ends up becoming this dense object because it has been a re-curring theme in our lives and with every incident we seek to suppress the terrible feelings associated with it. Here we have an object in the human energy body that is a manifestation of raw emotion coupled with a belief – a belief being either a thought that has been thought many times, or a thought that really penetrated us during a traumatic experience.

The experience of being an infant and left to cry between feeds can be one of many such ways in which a belief coupled with terror can become lodged in our system. Witnessing violence as a child, being called stupid, being over disciplined, being asked to take too much adult responsibility, and birth traumas, can all contribute to a deep sense of separation and despair as an infant, young child and teenager.

ৎৎৎৎৎ

Our Core Belief gets wrapped around our Core Wound which in turn is wrapped around our Core Essence. Our Core Essence is the abode of all our goodness. Once we begin to unlock our Core Essence we no longer need to go in search of that which may make us good or valuable or more lovable as it is all here already; it is who we are, it is present, and therefore everything we've ever wanted is in fact here already.

What is required is an absolute commitment to tell the absolute truth, to know the absolute truth and to have the courage to face it all no matter how ugly, hopeless or utterly terrifying it may appear to be at first. In our search for happiness we often ask for things like 'enlightenment,' or 'spiritual realization,' or even 'self-realization' in the hope that it will be one superbly delicious spiritual experience of bliss that will make all the pain go away.

There is not one authentic piece of writing, modern or ancient, that emanates from someone recognized as 'enlightened' who speaks of such doorways into oneness with God. What they all invariably speak of is the dire separation they have felt, the torments of their inner demons and a deep sense of abandonment as they enter their own personal hell before finally allowing the light, their light, to be unveiled and the illusion that we are somehow separate, bad and unworthy is lifted like a silk veil.

You may be thinking, 'How can I do this? How can I get to my core?' My answer to that is you probably need help with it. There are very few people capable of going into a cave and facing it all on their own with no assistance from the outside.

However, there is so much we can do to prepare the garden for greater liberation from the greatest lies we've been telling ourselves. The most important step is to start telling the truth and to welcome whatever is present. With our commitment to telling the truth we also need to be willing to stop telling our story, to stop regurgitating the same story we've been telling ourselves for years.

The story is something like, 'I feel like this because my father...' Or, 'I cannot achieve this because my mother did....', 'I am not free because my partner...'

When we're willing to stop telling the story then a more beneficial truth can emerge. In identifying your story as a 'story' it is not that it never happened, or was never said but is what we decided to believe about ourselves as a result of those words, actions or events.

Giving up the story often requires giving up the need to be right and at times letting go of our refusal to forgive or seeing our attempt at forgiveness as simply another story that serves the status quo. However, there is another aspect of telling the story that remains invisible until we stop telling it – sorrow, heartache, grief.

When we get stuck in telling the story it also serves the purpose of keeping us from ever surrendering to the underlying wound. Story telling is another avoidance strategy, even when it looks like it may not be. For example, in telling our story we can cry, we can get angry, we can express hatred, disdain, resentment, righteous indignation, self-pity, fear and horror, and yet still not relinquish our control on our deeper feelings.

We can be outraged at our treatment at the hands of another, we can feel abandoned and hurt by them, but however, at the core there is often a totally different dialogue. This dialogue is about the 'ugly truth' – meaning, the ugliest thing we've told ourselves. Often as we've been abandoned, neglected, not protected or abused, our conclusion can be, 'I am unlovable', 'there is something wrong with me'.

The story, therefore, becomes the buffer that orbits the core wound keeping us at a safe distance, never having to feel the devastating feelings of separation.

 round ornament divider

Why has it been so easy for us to take on this idea that there is something wrong with us? It starts in very early childhood, starting with the construction of a false self, a false personality, and a defence mechanism that serves to protect the innocent centre of our being.

As we come into this world, we are beaming sources of light. We've all experienced young babies that can light up an entire room with their smile, with their gurgles, with their little giggle. We all enjoy bathing in the light of that. We're so drawn to that because their innocence, their exuberance, their exquisiteness and their divinity remains intact.

As young children, we have undeveloped energy systems, not yet matured and chakras are emergent. Owing to this, we are exposed to all of the energies around us. And the energies around us are made up of mental energies and emotional energies, astral energies. And so there are energies from physical and non-physical beings.

If your parents are not happy with one another, we feel that. If your mother is depressed, you feel that. If your father is angry, you feel that. If your father is away at war, you feel your mother's feelings about that. As infants we are psychic sponges.

We are literally bombarded with emotional and mental pollution. One could ask the question: 'why do we have this energy system that's so open?' Why would one choose to come into this world when it's quite clear that we will become overwhelmed in one way or another? I have to say I don't actually have an answer to that question. I really don't. Not a complete one.

As I set out to create this book of insights, teachings and experiences of developing and witnessing an awakening heart I knew in advance that I did not have all of the answers. Through my own explorations, both on my own and in the presence of my own beloved teachers, my clients and students, I have discovered how the heart closes and what is required of us to let go and to allow the fullness of our being to thrive again.

However, I do not know for certain why it is that we choose to come here, not for certain. When I share teachings, it is always my preference to share what I know to be true based on experience rather than what I believe to be true. Beliefs can be as unpredictable as a leaf floating and tumbling on a breeze, eventually they fall to the ground and submit to decay.

In an ideal world, when neither our parents, grand-parents and ancestors have been affected by the traumas of war, sickness, early deaths, famine and political strife, there is a free flow of love that cascades unhindered down through the generations – each generation holding the next in undefended love and able to welcome the essence of a new child.

In such circumstances neither the mother nor the father are hindered by their own childhood or other collective traumas. In this unhindered state, love flows freely and we as infants are brought into our mother's heart centre, or heart chakra through the act of breast feeding and other forms of nurturing and holding.

Ideally, the father embraces the mother in his protective energy, allowing her to sit in his heart unhindered. He embraces both the mother and baby in this way. He surrenders his own importance to the importance of the child and holds each of them in his own heart.

This supports the mother in merging with her baby so that this infant, so that YOU, get the experience of being filled with love. As we are filled with this love our essence begins to shine. We feel welcomed, wanted and valued.

This is the original 'Holy Trinity', the sacred triad of Mother, Father, Child and when love's flow is unhindered and unfettered by the demands of culture, inherited trauma and challenging life circumstances this Holy Trinity of the Heart is truly Paradise.

This is the paradise we all seek to experience in our physical existence and we often go out and seek that in partners and lovers – not realizing that they too had paradise ripped from them, or perhaps did not experience it in the first place. Therefore our quest for this perfect symbiosis and union with another human being will become disheartened, as it is apparent that few, if any, have an ability to give this.

The solution then is to heal the wound of the Lost Paradise and find every nook and cranny of our heart that has either recoiled from the deep and devastating disappointment of never having received it, or the trauma of having it ripped away from us. In reality, very few of us received enough.

We got just enough to survive and those fortunate enough to get more than 'just enough' often fare better in life or can struggle with allowing themselves to be happier than others around them.

As we come into this world we are immediately subjected to the images of both our parents and of the culture around us. For many girls born into the world their welcome into the world is their father's disappointment that they are not a boy.

Many cultures place a premium on male children, to the great cost of girls. The cultural demands can be influenced by religion, economy and tradition. However it is also true to say that boys equally have a lot of expectations projected onto them.

Either way, rather than merging with both parents to form the Paradise of the original Holy Trinity, this merging is hampered by the energy of expectation.

## Recovery from the Lost Paradise

How do we recover from this Lost Paradise? How do we recover from never having experienced this Paradise in the first place? And how can we know that our lives are being affected by the wound of having lost or never had Paradise? What are the symptoms?

The symptoms of the Lost Paradise can be seen clearly across the globe and is rampant in modern western culture. When we didn't GET enough, IT is never enough and WE are never enough. When Paradise is lost it can leave us in a place of being in the eternal pursuit of happiness.

In this process we can chase lot of objects and life conditions in the hope that they will deliver lasting fulfilment and fill the empty space left by the paradise lost. However, as years turn into decades and we are faced with saying, 'maybe this time' yet again, we begin to realize that no object or life circumstance can fill the empty space left by the experience of losing paradise.

This can be very frightening, for we do not yet know that, in reality, paradise has not been lost, it is simply shrouded and has been with us always and everywhere as the silent witness to our lives. Even with this realization we can resist it and negotiate, create and pursue another strategy for getting the fullness we are looking for.

We can capitulate and surrender to 'maybe this time', and tell ourselves, 'just this one more time' – this yo-yo of suffering can be entangled with trying to get acknowledgement from a parent, trying to find the 'ideal partner' who will fulfil and provide everything we did not get when we were children, or be tied up in the belief that a certain social position, a certain sum of money, status or spiritual practice or teaching will finally give us something.

The hope that one day, some day, we will get what we need merely seeks to avoid the pain of separation – for hope is better than despair. The last thing we want to hear is that the solution lies deep inside us. This resistance or stubbornness is born with experience of not having received enough from our parents and so we go in hunt of 'other' who will give it to us – at times we don't even seek, we simply demand that the world gives us what we missed out on. This of course simply adds to our suffering.

As we enter this territory we are horrified by the answer that the only place we can find resolution to all of this is inside us – after all, our deepest fear and often our hidden belief, is that the only thing that can be found inside us is disgusting, unlovable, unwanted, bad, ugly and totally unworthy.

This is what happens when paradise is lost or simply not present enough. We cannot comprehend as infants or young children why paradise was not given fully, and in our non-comprehension of that we concluded that there must be something wrong with us, something wrong with me.

So when we hear that the only solution is to find it within we can be angry, want to protest, even call the other, who tells us such a terrible thing, that they are a liar. When I first encountered this in myself, I was convinced that my teacher was in cahoots with everyone else who had told me I was not worthy. I intensely believed that my teacher was saying, 'You will never get what you want, so you must learn to go without, and it is not truly spiritual to pursue what you want in life'.

This is what I heard over and over again, until I really began to see, sense, feel and experience the deeper truth. What I had not wanted to do was to face the ocean of tears and what seemed like a bottomless pit of unbearable grief.

What I had not seen was that it was not the pursuit of career, success, financial comfort and love that was the issue, the issue was hoping and believing in the lie that they or anyone else could heal the lost paradise.

My own paradise had been so deeply damaged and wounded that I did not even know how to start unpacking the layers of defence, or how to manage the intense fear of 'going there'. It is important to say here too, when your personal paradise has been ripped away with the traumas of violence, sexual abuse, divorce and rejection it is a big challenge to let even a healer or a teacher in to those spaces. It simply feels too threatening.

The process can be gradual and with each layer, the truth of 'only within' becomes increasingly apparent. As we surrender to that truth our focus starts to shift away from going outside of ourselves to find fulfilment, to an emergent curiosity and anticipation at discovering greater depths to our own heart and untainted essence. This is the beginning of freedom.

Even as we mature in our journey of personal discovery and development we may still be tempted to believe that a lasting peace with ourselves and the experience of living with an awakened heart can be found in some object, circumstance, belief or other person. One of the greatest temptations in some spiritual communities is to pursue bliss.

There is a belief that if only we could have enough blissful experiences and sufficient spiritual experiences – which can be very intense and have value, that 'that which is hidden', around which we live a lie about ourselves and our lives, will never need to be faced.

The relentless pursuit of bliss, be that via chanting, yoga, ayahuasca, meditation, ecstatic dance and any other form you care to name, is no different to the pursuit of sports cars, money and sex. There is in fact, nothing wrong with any of the things mentioned here. There is nothing wrong with money, chanting, sex, sports cars, ecstatic dance – nothing wrong with any of it.

However, induced spiritual experience simply allows us to visit the abode of the gods, it is only when we face that which we seek to hide from view can we ever have an opportunity to live in paradise with an awakened heart. An awakened heart allows us to live as more complete human beings, in communion with the paradise that is all around us.

The sad truth is that the more we pursue bliss, the deeper and more challenging the split may become. As the split widens between what we present to the world and how we truly feel about ourselves, we have to tell even bigger lies in order to sustain the lies already lived.

When our spiritual path or practice becomes a source of our worth, or status, or that which makes us special, then we can know that somewhere and somehow we are telling a lie about something or still desperately trying to conceal an 'ugly truth'. The deeper the denial, the more dysfunctional our behaviour can become, even falling prey to spiritual narcissism that seeks to see itself as special and feed off the adoration of others, all the while hiding a terrible truth.

The more apparent this 'terrible truth' becomes, the harder we have to work at hiding it. However, here is the absolute truth: it is not invisible, it is indeed very visible. It is not even invisible to those joining us in playing the same game of pursuing bliss and spiritual narcissism for they have agreed to the unspoken rules of denial as have we.

This has been a tough pattern for me to break. The easiest way for me to identify it would be whenever I felt tinges of guilt around not doing my daily chanting or praying. I've even caught myself apologising to God for having missed my worship for a couple of days!

What helped me with all of this is to realize and experience what spiritual practice was all about and what it really meant. What unfolded from this was the deep realisation that the pursuit of god is indeed the pursuit of the heart and that Devotion to God is in fact Devotion to our very own Heart.

What became equally clear to me is that those who love god but do not love human beings have totally missed the point, and those who love human beings and do not love God never get to see the potential and the deeper truth of the person standing right in front of them.

Recovering from the lost paradise involves realizing that your very own heart wishes to know itself as love. Once that is pursued, then all else will follow.

# CHAPTER 4

# Surrendering Strategies
## Intellectual strategies,
## Aversion and Avoidance

I n the previous chapter I began to speak more in depth about being separated from our authentic self. These concepts are not new. However, like all teachings, if they are only understood in the mind and are not experienced directly and if they are not experienced kinaesthetically, then the teachings remain in the realm of the mind.

What must be stated repeatedly is that that which stands in the way of resolving our suffering is an energy – it is not a single thought or belief, but it is an accumulation of thoughts, beliefs, grief, terror, self-hatred and despair that have clumped together to create an energy form that has gravity, texture and density. For those with extra sensory awareness, it can be clearly seen and felt in the human energy field – the aura.

We can get caught up in continually trying to ask the mind to do a job that it simply cannot do. This comes from the belief that the mind is our source, it comes from the lack of realization that the intellectual mind is merely a servant of consciousness and is not consciousness itself.

Our culture also rewards memory as if memory is an indication of intelligence; it is not. Intelligence is not indicative of consciousness either. A rose has consciousness, but it does not have intellect in the way that we would measure intellect – it will not debate either Plato or Shakespeare with us, it is content to be at peace with its own innate magnificence and does not question its existence.

ღღღღ

The reliance on the mind leads us to believe that if only we can understand our problem or challenge sufficiently, then we will be able to resolve it or perhaps even modify our behaviour to avoid the problem. The belief that the mind is the host of our consciousness and therefore the centre of our being, leads many to believe that through simply changing a thought about something then we can be healed.

Whilst it is true that some habitual negative thinking can be transformed, curtailed or eradicated through employing some of the useful mind tools available, they do not address the underlying issue of core belief.

If the mind was capable of resolving all of our issues, if positive thinking alone could resolve our basic defence mechanism, and all of our dysfunction, then the world would have healed itself a long time ago.

We believe that we make political and other decisions based on logic and reason – this could not be further from the truth. We are emotional beings and most, if not all of our decisions, are made from our emotional centre and not from our intellectual centre. One of the proofs of this is how once we've decided that we like a particular person or politician, even when faced with evidence of contradictory statements we will find a way to either justify or ignore the contradiction.

Therefore, if we are to make any progress at all in terms of healing life's disappointments, difficult relationships and issues of health, wealth and purpose, we need to encounter the world of our feelings, and to do that, we must also understand the difference between emotions and feelings.

Emotions are an outward expression, the energy almost always projects outwards, and feelings take us inward. Let me give you an example: an emotional response may show anger or irritation at a friend who is consistently late to social engagements, a feeling response may have us express feelings of being undervalued, disrespected, and forgotten, ignored, for example. Notice how much more personal the feelings are? Being aware of our feelings not only helps us in getting to the truth of a matter, it also assists in allowing relationships to be based on honesty.

Once we start to engage with our feelings, what then happens, is the realization that it is frequently the same feelings, or the same two or three feelings that are being activated with almost every incident that we have an emotional response to.

As we embrace that, we begin to see that our core wound is indeed active. Far from slumbering in the abyss it sends out pulses into our life and commands and controls almost all of our responses and indeed our relationships. What most of us are good at is identifying the behaviours that are either destructive or limiting and then we hope to modify our behaviour.

However, no matter how much we modify our behaviour, if the core wound is not resolved it will find expression and we can find ourselves back on the hamster wheel re-experiencing the same situations and emotional response over and over again.

Our strong tendency to want to search in the mind for our problems and solutions is because we are afraid to feel. We are perhaps not afraid to express emotion, however, that at times can simply become a regurgitation of the same emotion over and over again, and certain emotional responses can become a part of our story and our own personal drama, similarly played over and over again.

We are often afraid to feel because as we move beyond an emotional response to the depth of feeling that is compacted under all of the layers, we start to run into a territory over which we feel we have no control. Most human beings are very uncomfortable with the idea of having no control.

No matter how much evidence we have that reveals unequivocally that we don't have control, and never did have control, we still hang on to the idea that we have control and need to be in control.

This need for control finds it roots in our early history as a species, needing to control our environment for survival purposes, and more importantly, in the fact that as infants and young children we had zero control over what was given to us, what was done to us and what was said to us – we were helpless, totally dependent and completely vulnerable.

Many of us carry within ourselves a deep feeling of 'never again' – never again will I have no control over who or what enters my personal space, what is done to me and what I shall feel. Feelings of terror go hand in hand with fear of destruction, a fear of total annihilation and therefore any territory that requires complete surrender to enter can cause feelings of terror to arise in us.

The challenge with the deeper feelings around our wound is that their origin has its deep roots in exactly the same phase of our lives in which we have zero control. As we approach the feelings of worthlessness, being ugly, unwanted, stupid, unwelcome, et al, we enter into the deep memory and trauma of not having had any control, and so the fear can overtake us.

We often then believe that if we surrender control to the deeper feelings, we will either become lost in those feelings, or become those feelings forever. Fear of death can also often arise at this point. When we were infants our nervous system was still developing and we were fragile, nowhere near as robust as we are as adults.

With this in mind it is important to know that whenever the shaming words were said – the shouting, the aggression, the violence, the abandonment or sexual abuse took place – it overwhelmed our system.

As we approach such feelings it is important to truly realize that things have changed. We are now adults and largely in charge of all aspects of our experience. These raw feelings that we have hidden away for so long can cause intense anxiety, and if that happens, it is important to know that you have touched into your early experiences of these feelings.

Allow them to wash through you and if you are like most other people, you may need to get support for your process. Given that our core wound can evoke so many primal feelings, it is not a surprise that many of us choose to live in our heads so to speak.

What is really important to say here is that as we approach our own healing and personal development we must be willing to make a choice between long term suffering and short term pain. There is no pain free way of healing the core wound. If you want your lover or partner to heal it for you, they will eventually leave or withdraw, in some way, from you.

We cannot resolve that which has been held in the depths of darkness by running towards the light – we can only heal this by taking the light of consciousness into the abyss. A single candle is sufficient to light up the abyss and to start revealing the lies we've been telling ourselves and to begin the process of allowing the deeper feelings to be metabolized.

These deeply held feelings, because they were so overwhelming when we were but young children, have gone un-metabolized, undigested and unrecognized for many years and they sit in the dense *energy* that is the manifestation of our original wounds.

No matter how often we reach for bliss, expanded consciousness, enlightenment or Self-Realisation, unless our core wound has been met consciously and diligently, it will act as a gravitational pull that will keep you from becoming more fully awake, keep you from stepping more completely into your essence.

This is literally the same process of facing our demons as expressed in the stories of both the Buddha and Christ and in the many personal memoirs of other enlightened individuals.

## Addiction to Thinking

One of the reasons why we attempt to resolve our dysfunction with the mind is that we've become addicted to thought, action and use of will – surrender is not a word most people are comfortable with.

So what happens when we suspend rational thought, thinking things through, and all the mind chatter? What is the cause of our incessant mind chatter? Consider silence for a moment. Complete silence. What does it evoke in you? When we begin to delve into silence, at times what can emerge is terror. Silence is the equivalent of nothingness, and nothingness can evoke existential terror – the fear of non-existence.

☙☙☙☙☙

For many years I meditated with purpose. I was either busy running a specific type of energy through my system, working with a particular chakra or visualizing a goal I had in mind. There was no real silence.

However, over the years that changed and at first my response was 'of what use is this silence? I'm not doing anything!' Understanding my need to be pro-active and the opposing need for me to surrender offered me a great leap forward in my work with individuals and groups.

What I learnt was that a totally silent mind has access to anything we need in the moment. What I learnt was that when I ceased searching for answers, they would appear, when I stopped looking, I could see, when I stopped trying to figure it out, the answers would simply come.

It is out of the silence that healing emerges. However, there are some other things that can appear in the silence and it goes some way to explaining our inability and reluctance to be in silence. What we learn is that once the mind chatter is suspended, our unspoken content becomes more present and palpable.

In other words, the way is clear to access our core wounds and to witness more openly our habitual defences around it. Not only that, within the silence we can also access the healing solutions with little to no effort.

If you are disturbed by a lot of mind chatter, simply ask the question: what is the function of my mind chatter? What does it seek to keep away? As we silence the mind our inner world opens up, thereby giving us wonderful opportunities to face and resolve that which has been long hidden from view and yet has controlled our lives.

Stillness can be brought into our experience through following a few easy guidelines: Focus on your breath and not on the thoughts that may come, don't attach to your thoughts or judge them, let them be. When we see 'failure' because we're thinking and not in 'silence', then we're giving the thoughts more energy. Chanting a mantra also helps the mind to become still. Repetition allows the active thinking mind to take a rest and it takes us into an altered relaxed state.

Addiction to thinking is again related to having been overwhelmed as young children by our sheer helplessness in being unable to stop what was hurting us from taking place. With this strong fear of losing control, mind chatter then becomes the tool we use to control everything.

We think it through, we weigh it up, we scrutinize it, debate it, reject it, bring it back again, look on the flip side, the bright side, the dark side, discuss it, measure it, deny it, dismiss it, blame it, categorize it and finally tell ourselves that now we understand the issue from every possible angle, it is resolved.

Or at least that is what our mind wants us to believe.

As we came to believe that the mind is the centre of our consciousness, or indeed, consciousness itself, we've become not only convinced that all is possible through the intellect but we've become afraid of 'no mind'.

In this modern era, the servant has been lauded as the master and the master, consciousness itself, has been dismissed or denied. As the mind believes itself to be the centre it is then not keen to enter either the place of separation or the wound, as both risk annihilation and both exist in a dimension that is outside of the mind's scope. Raw feelings equals no story.

Both are very threatening and trigger fear within us. Our rational mind is designed for navigating a physical Universe. It is designed to calculate, assess, measure, compare and compartmentalize physical world challenges and issues – such as building houses, counting sheep, writing rules and regulations and other practical applications.

All of the world's greatest creative geniuses will tell you that none of what they have done emanated from their mind through reason. The creative and intuitive aspect of consciousness actually emerges from silence, and so does healing.

Works of great art, music, poetry and even philosophy are not cobbled together by the intellectual mind trying to figure out what may make a good piece of music or art. Highly creative people will tell you that 'the song wrote itself', 'the painting painted itself' or the 'book wrote itself'.

Out of the silence, which is the abode of infinite un-manifest possibilities, arise the solutions to our problems, our greatest achievements in creative expression, and a deeper knowing that is beyond words. My work with groups and individuals has shown me time and again that the truth of anything resides in the silence after the words have been spoken.

When we say, 'I'm sorry' to someone, it is not the words that have the real impact, it is the moment of silence when you look at the other just after having said the words. This is when the love, the regret and the desire to make amends is received, not before. It is from within this very same silence that all love, creativity and knowledge emerges.

As we quieten the mind and enter the silence, that which sits between the perceptions of who we think we are, the vast un-manifest force of the Universe becomes apparent. I have said repeatedly that the basis of our core wound is that our essence was either not welcomed, wanted or recognized in its fullness. In our attempt to protect the most precious part of ourselves from the brutal world we found ourselves in, we built up layers of defence around the terrible wound of not having been embraced as pure love, which is the true nature of ALL human beings.

Our deepest longing is for the heart to know itself as love and for the heart to know itself as peace, and to realize the natural state of acceptance that the heart embodies. Love is our very nature and in our wounding we are struggling to come to terms with our very nature not being embraced, nor welcomed, not kept safe from harm and not celebrated.

As children we recoiled from this rude awakening and in many ways we are still in a constant state of recoiling, triggered by anyone or anything that resembles the personalities and circumstances involved in our original wounding.

෧෧෧෧෧

All of the mind chatter simply seeks to keep us as far away as possible from this primal wound. There are many levels to the wound as you have already in all probability discovered – abandonment, betrayal, negligence and suppression. As the deep wounds of abandonment and betrayal become unbearable we separate. Behind the separation is our original essence, the core of love of who we are.

In this process of separation we begin to mimic the attitudes, characteristics of what we observe around us and begin to interpret what is wanted or needed, in order to be deemed welcome, as belonging and as good. At this point we open ourselves to absolute conditioning.

As the process continues we lose more and more contact with our core until we reach the stage of perhaps forgetting that we ever had a core and believing that the constructed self is in fact our true and authentic self.

This is at the core of all human suffering, it is at the core of all human cruelty, it is at the core of all human hatred, injustice, war, crime and our challenges in loving one another. Our lives have become defended and it takes a very courageous soul to absolutely choose to step out of the cycle of suffering into a far deeper realization of who we are.

In our quest to do this we will chase many new images and construct perhaps new aspects of the false self in an attempt to get away from what wounded us so deeply. We may become anti-establishment, live and proclaim alternative life styles and may even start to develop a spiritualized ego, all of which is simply a 'better version' of the original false self we have sought to escape.

With the creation of new versions of a false self we're still not out of the woods yet for as time goes by we begin to discover that we are still not satisfied and still do not feel whole and complete. The realization of this can bring about a spiritual crisis as we come to realize that the separation is still intact and that we are still running from, and avoiding, Self-hatred.

As we start to surrender our addiction to thinking we allow something new to emerge. At first it may fill us with fear, then with grief, however, the rewards are immeasurable as we will soon begin to taste that which we thought we had long forgotten, that which we thought had forsaken us, that which we thought was so far away that it could no longer be found.

Astonishingly, we will discover that that which we seek, the truth of who we are, has always been as close to us as our next three breaths.

# Beliefs in Good

We can become caught up in the idea that somehow our personality can become enlightened. As so many aspects of our personality are dictated by culture, gender, ethnicity, national identity and what we've inherited from our ancestors, it is very clear that not only is that which has been identified as the ego is impermanent, it is not who we really are.

What we have learnt from our environment is a set of values that determine who is good and who is bad and what constitutes goodness. Challenging everything we believe is part of the process of awakening to truth and the inherent power it contains. As previously mentioned, we do have natural inner impulses, an inner compass if you like, one that tell us that it is wrong to murder, steal and violate another person's sovereignty.

As we are well aware, these natural impulses can be overridden by those in deep separation from themselves. What I want to make clear at this point is that challenging our beliefs in what makes us 'Good' is not about becoming a rebel and throwing out all societal rules concerning manners and appropriate behaviour: it is about the images we have around doing, achieving and having something that will make us somehow good.

A little earlier I used the word ego, a word I generally like to avoid if possible, along with words like God and Love. These three words have probably had more written about them any three words in human history. They are totally subject to belief, distortion and projection – they can even be the source of wars, murder and ostracization.

Among western spiritual groups a belief has arisen that we must be without ego and, along with that, piggybacks the belief that the ego is bad and is equivalent to desire. What has happened is that the new 'thing' that will make us 'good' is not having any desires and not having any ego.

When we cling onto such beliefs we are truly placing the cart before the horse. It is not the 'not having desires' that leads to awakening, it is the awakening itself that changes our desires and eventually leads us to be content with all life circumstances. This is another example of the said ego's distortion of spiritual teachings in order for it to ensure its survival – it is truly the ego having the last laugh.

The moment we hook into a belief that is supposed to deliver on the promise of making us 'good', we've fallen into deeper separation – even if, or especially if, the new belief is attached to a spiritual teaching or practice. I say 'especially if' because the deceptions of the spiritualized ego are the most conniving and convincing – the Devil dressed up as an Angel of Light.

In addition to any beliefs and images we may have around spirituality, it is important to look at how we see ourselves as a man, a woman, as a friend, a lover, and member of our culture, community, race, religion and nationality.

What constitutes a good woman? What constitutes a good man? What constitutes a good citizen? Parent? Grand-parent? Spouse? Partner? The mind is *always* comparing itself to others and it is invariably never enough and not as good as. At times we can feign superiority in order to hide our deeper feelings of inferiority, however, when it comes to images of what makes us 'good' the emphasis is almost always on 'not good enough'.

All of this can lead to perfectionism, piety and arrogance. Perfectionism is largely looking for what is wrong and constantly correcting it and when perfectionism has a grip on us, magnificence rarely gets a chance to shine.

One of the greatest freedoms we can experience comes from having a healthy relationship to being wrong. This involves firstly allowing ourselves to be wrong, to be in the state of wrongness instead of avoiding it. What this state allows for is coming to the realization that our wrongness about something, an action or idea, does not equate to our 'badness'.

Hand in hand with the freedom to be wrong is also the great freedom of not knowing. When we truly surrender to not knowing, through accepting fully that we do not know, and then relinquishing the control that we believe that knowing will give us, what ensues is not only greater peace but it also has the effect of giving us access to that which is beyond knowing and that which simply emerges from the silence.

We are so programmed to be uncomfortable with not knowing. This comes from our upbringing and from an education system that equates memory and knowledge with intelligence. Buried within us is the fear of humiliation, failure and possibly the memory of punishments that were meted out because we did not know or did not have an immediate answer. If we are to challenge our ideas of what makes us 'good' then we have to court being wrong, make peace with being wrong and also surrender any Self-importance tied up with it.

# Romancing the Unknowable

How can we romance the unknowable? If something is unknowable, then surely it is simply unknowable?

No. It doesn't work that way. The unknowable becomes knowable once we surrender our search for it and once we realize that our mind is a servant and *not* the centre of our consciousness. Our consciousness is vast and has access to limitless knowing.

However, none of that knowing comes from the mind. The intelligence and the greater knowing are non-local and access to that is through silence; it is through becoming an empty vessel that we can receive a broader spectrum of simplified truths.

The broader, more profound and greater truth that assists us with healing and with the awakening of our awareness and consciousness is always simple, for it is absolutely known. As our dear friend Albert Einstein said *'if you can't explain it simply, you don't understand it well enough'*.

Everything that emerges from the silence is simply and powerfully stated. Simplicity itself is in fact the healing. Once we encounter simplicity and the mind ceases its chatter, pure, unadulterated, untarnished and undistorted truth emerges which speaks directly to the heart and in reality, emanates from the heart. *The heart truly does not have any opinions; opinions are a function of the mind.*

Many of us habitually confuse 'speaking our truth' with expressing a passionately held opinion. The truth is always undeniable when it is heard and our body recognizes it.

࿔࿔࿔࿔࿔

In the few years I used to teach others how to facilitate Family Constellations, I was constantly asked about how I knew what to say and what to do. It was a challenge for many of my students to hear my reply: 'I didn't know'.

The more I facilitated this profound work of engaging with the ancestral field the more I began to trust in a knowledge, wisdom and power that was far greater than myself. As the years went by and I amassed the experience of having given well over 400 workshops I eventually only worked from complete inner silence.

This doesn't mean that I didn't talk on my workshop, what this means is that all of my work with individuals stemmed from silence, and what that in turn means is that there was not a reasoning thought process that said, 'she needs this, therefore I must do that'.

Each movement and each sentence expressed came from not knowing. My trust in this took me to a place of total surrender when working to the extent that on beginning a sentence I did not know how it would end; I simply allowed the words to be spoken as they wanted to be spoken.

It very much took a healthy relationship to being wrong as often I communicated facts and circumstances that I could not have known about. One could call this psychic ability or channelling if you wish, so my question is, from whence do psychic impressions and channelling emanate? They emanate from the silence, not from the mind.

I know this to be absolutely true because my mind still does not understand how I am able to do many of the things I do on a daily basis!

Once we become comfortable with not knowing, with being wrong, and release any notion of self-importance around being right, the unknowable becomes accessible.

I am smiling to myself as I write this as I remember, all too well, those days just after I truly got the secret to not knowing and how to be in deep silence, for I would sit in silence hoping to pull or magnetize the 'unknowable' to me. What I was yet to fully learn was that we truly and absolutely need to surrender any hope or wish of knowing and accept fully and completely the possibility of being wrong, in other words, surrender the neurosis that our ego is apt to live with.

In my early days there was the pressure to perform in many ways and at times it was like pulling a healing out of a hat like a white rabbit. Such were the days of more youthful uncertainty.

Unless you are one of the few who have experienced an instant almost overnight awakening that has remained, then this process of surrendering the mind to that which is the nothingness and 'everythingness' of silence is gradual.

## 'I just don't know how!'

'I just don't know how,' is an expression I have both used and heard more times than can be counted. In surrendering our thoughts and ideas about something, in surrendering our story, we're being asked to approach an issue or a problem in a new way, not in the old way.

Previously we have come from the place of wanting to fix, get rid of and change something. When we surrender to the greater intelligence that is around us, within us and indeed is us, we have to be willing to approach it in new ways. 'I just don't know how,' is the mind struggling to understand something that is not in its realm; at least that is one part of the story.

'I just don't know how' is often indicative of our need to be in control. Surrender is a very dirty word for many, a very threatening word. It sounds really nice when we're told of the benefits, hear the stories, and receive the promises of the great healing that can take place when we do surrender. However, what if your entire life has been based on your capability? What then?

So many of us were asked to do too much too soon. We may have taken on an emotional responsibility, a financial responsibility or a physical responsibility far too young – thereby leaving the innocence of childhood early.

Taking on an emotional responsibility takes place frequently in households in which divorce has taken place, when one of the parents is unhappily married and seeks comfort and friendship from one or more children, when long term illness causes a child to be supportive and take responsibility, when an early death takes place, and when one or both parents confide in their children and treat them as friends. This is especially true when we're asked to hold secrets.

When we're asked to do too much too soon there is a truth that first must be met. This truth can be a challenge as it can bring to the surface any distorted and misplaced loyalties we have. The truth here is that if you were asked to do too much too soon then you did not get enough.

It can be a great challenge to acknowledge that for some of us. If you have been the special child with the special relationship with either mum or dad, or the child that your siblings looked to as a parent then you may have a certain amount of 'specialness' in your view of yourself.

Being the 'special' or 'important' child can become a destructive part of our identity, not only because of the effect it can have on our adult relationships, but because it is part of the defence that can seek to deny that insufficient was given, that in fact, our childhood was sacrificed in order to meet the needs of one of our parents.

When tragedy strikes, although not healthy, it is almost certainly unavoidable. However, the betrayal goes deep when a child is placed as the friend of the parent who is either lonely or finds themselves in an unhappy marriage. When parents place the bonds of adult friendship on a child a major betrayal has taken place and the child, if that is you, can suffer feelings of guilt and never being happy with their skills, talents and abilities as a result – it is a case of never being good enough.

Not being 'good enough' manifests as a life trend because if we are brought into an adult relationship when still a child we can only ever fail. In fact we fail daily. We just do not have the power to make the parent happy. It simply cannot be done.

Additionally, at such a young age we do not have either the emotional or mental capacity of an adult and therefore will always fall short of the friendship requirement – to come in as an equal or even as one to receive guidance from.

Over the years I have had many a parent, usually mothers, who want themselves and their fifteen your old son or daughter to come on a workshop. On explaining that it is a workshop for adults only, I have frequently been told, 'my child is very mature for her age, we're best friends and she will be ok on your workshop'.

෨෨෨෨෨

Perhaps you were not brought into friendship with a parent and neither treated as the 'special' child. However, many boys and young men are bombarded with images of what it is to be a 'man'. They are told not to cry, and are even punished, bullied and teased for showing emotion, feelings and vulnerability.

Vulnerability is seen as a weakness and I have experienced many male clients who have stopped their inner work immediately after surrendering to deep grief and expressing a deep need to be held in safety. So deep is the cultural imperative for men to be 'strong' that any sign of vulnerability is deemed either shameful or experienced as terrifying.

This fear of vulnerability can overtake anyone who has prided themselves with their capability, and what it triggers is the deep fear that everything will fall apart and that they will become incapable as soon as they surrender. What is often apparent is that those who rely mainly or solely on their capability as an identity, are 'too capable' for love and often cannot commit to or sustain intimate relationships.

Most often, when we just don't know how, it is because we're being asked to surrender our capable self that knows how to fix things and be present with what is. We, at times, can exclaim, 'but I don't feel anything'. With experience you will begin to know that there is no such thing as 'feeling nothing' – there is experiencing numbness, but there is no such thing as feeling nothing.

When we get caught up in the story of 'feeling nothing' it is because we're actually afraid of and in resistance to what may happen. What if I lose control? What if some intense feelings come up? What if I'm wrong?

As we may have built up an entire identity around being capable or 'polite and reasonable,' to the extent of never expressing a need, never having any sort of outburst, overcoming 'I just don't know how,' will take patience.

We need to show courage and actually risk humiliation by doing it anyway. When a child is chastised frequently for crying, the fear of disapproval or doing something wrong, wasting the other person's time, can become very present as we start our inner work.

With patience, and perhaps with guidance, together with a longing to resolve the diversion that is our mind chatter and the deeper longing to allow our heart to be free, we can use the energy of all of our frustration to take us into the world of feelings.

In this way, frustration is our friend. Frustration itself can take you on a valuable journey that can reveal doorways into your inner world. Surrender, surrender to it all, even to being frustrated. Surrender even to the numbness, become aware of how it has been shadowing you for a very long time, curtailing what could otherwise be a very rich and pleasurable emotional life.

As we surrender to numbness and fully accept that we 'just don't know how,' we can become aware of just how much of our life force energy is locked away, simply not lived, not expressed, not seen.

You may be very successful in business and yet have little to no pleasure in your life, you may be applauded for your skills and yet see little value in what you do and in who you are, you may have everything you've ever dreamt of and feel empty, bewildered and wondering why is it that you are not happy when you have it all.

You may be very much loved as a mother or a father and yet feel that your life has little meaning. All of these feelings point to something deeper and what I want you to really hear right now in this moment: there is nothing wrong with you. *Nothing at all.*

No matter how pointless you may think your life to be, no matter how worthless, or selfish, how ugly or uncomfortably special you may think you are, there is nothing wrong with you. This is said with confidence, for everything you can point at that is supposedly 'wrong' with you, is not truly real. It may feel real, it may interact with others and the world in a very real way, it may cause some very real problems, it may cause a lot of pain to both yourself and others and yet *in reality* it is not real.

When we feel unworthy we can either wear it on our shoulder as constant self-deprecation, which has an impact in our life, or we can do everything possible to keep that sense of unworthiness hidden from sight.

All of our 'bad,' 'wrong' and dysfunctional behaviour, everything we consider to be 'wrong' about us, either comes from a false image of how we think we 'should' be or it is an expression of a defence mechanism around our wound.

Self-Deprecation can have many purposes: it can serve the purpose of deflecting any criticism before it comes our way from others or it can be a mechanism for soliciting the attention and affirmation we never received as a child.

The feeling and the belief that there is something wrong with us is deeply rooted in us as individuals and also as a culture. As we step onto the path of healing our life we can get lost in all of the details that seemingly point to the evidence that indeed there is something wrong, terrible, ugly or bad about us.

However, once we truly start to see that, all of that evidence sifting is merely a diversion. As we approach our wound, we approach the place of separation we hold within ourselves. We are not ever going to allow that to be felt. It is the place of absolute annihilation, it is worse than death, it is separation from life, from God, from love, from ourselves.

As we approach this place of separation, our defence mechanism has one more trick up its sleeve. The shadow. Meeting and surrendering to, "I don't know how!" is exceptionally powerful – accepting fully that we don't know, allowing ourselves to fully 'not know'.

It may be counter intuitive for you to do this, however, in surrendering to not knowing how, relief and peace result, and deep silence follows quickly.

## The Final Frontier (Well almost)

As our place of separation from essence represents almost certain annihilation, our strong impulse to survive places one final firewall in our way before we reach the core of our wound and our inner experience of separation form self, from God and from life. The final firewall is our shadow self.

Our shadow self contains all of the feelings we have stuffed away and have labelled as bad. As the final defence, the shadow or Lower Self, marches in with the evidence that we are 'bad', that the other is bad, the healer or therapist is bad, the guru is bad, good people are bad and that the Self is bad.

The Lower Self knows that the time of meeting the place of separation is near, it knows that the event of experiencing the place of separation is close at hand and it seeks to prevent this from happening at all costs – it does so for it fears total destruction.

What if after all of our healing, after all of our therapy, after many years of meditation and contemplating our place in the world we discover that there is absolutely nothing? No God, no meaning, no life, no intelligence, just nothing. A solitary existence, that seems to have no meaning.

This is indeed terrifying for we come face to face with the fear of non-existence. As we approach this our false self, the self we believe ourselves to be, puts up one final fight before falling upon the sword of absolute truth.

I return here to one of the original questions laid out in this book. Are you willing to know the absolute truth? Are you willing to die? In saying that, I am not asking, 'do you want to die,' or if you are suicidal, for those are totally different matters to where we are right in this moment on this page.

How hungry are you to know the truth of your existence? How willing are you to experience what is still yet to be discovered beyond your inner world of separation? Many have convinced themselves that they have found this place through not living in their bodies, but by almost always reaching upward towards some higher dimension or a projection of what that dimension may be like.

This journey is into the core of our being, it is not a journey into other worlds through the prowess of our third eyes, or ajna centre, and it is the ultimate journey of discovery. It is not only experiencing that which we were before separation, but it is discovering who we have always been, it is a discovery of the whisper and call to awakenings that has always been present.

This is a grand death, when it takes place, for many of the structures we've put in place – many of our strategies, our defences, personality traits, beliefs and fears can simply crumble and return to ashes within an instant. We may have many encounters with our separation from the true self and each time we will rise from the ashes of what we thought was true, like a phoenix.

How willing are you to know the truth? Many, including myself, have imagined that the process of awakening is a series of wonderful 'aha' moments coupled with some inner work to resolve some 'issues'.

However, what awaits us is the fire of Shiva, the destruction of beliefs that served to keep us safe but in reality kept us far away from the love we've always known was there but could not feel.

Once the schism, the place of separation has been traversed is another realm altogether. It is a place of 'nothing, yet everything,' or 'deep darkness and yet vibrant with a light', it is a place in which there are no questions and no answers, it is a place of peace and revelation.

However, something needs to be surrendered over and over again in order to enter – our story, our strategies, our need to be right. We must be willing to face the unknown, to risk it all in order to know the truth of our existence.

This lower aspect of all of us can either express itself unconsciously or be investigated consciously. It holds onto all of the hatred, nastiness, bitterness, rage, resentment, jealousy, avarice and it defends self-importance. Many of these qualities are clearly deemed as 'bad' by many. However, now that we understand that hatred has a function, so too do all of these other 'negative' qualities.

When we are willing to meet them fully, with honesty, with clarity, to know what they are through direct experience, we can then get to experience what is behind these feelings.

Once we've encountered these destructive forces they cease having the hold on us they once did. Once we face the 'ugly monster' we see that all along it was like a frightened child who has cast a frightening shadow on a cave wall. We begin to truly see it for what it is and our heart fills with compassion.

So we nurture this compassion for ourselves: no longer can hatred, jealousy and rage stalk us and keep us on the run. Each and every time we need to we can simply turn, face it, and look it straight in the eyes and each and every time another aspect of its hold on us will diminish.

## Relationship to our Wound

As we first start out on our journey of discovery, for the most part we want to improve our life experience and definitely get rid of our pain. At this stage we many not even call it a wound.

All we know is that our life is either not working for us or that we're in some sort of pain; the pain of rejection, the pain of loneliness, the pain of loss, grief, low self-esteem, disappointment or the pain of dissatisfaction or emptiness. We don't yet recognise the wound behind all of these feelings but no matter what it is, we want rid of it.

Our desire to simply get rid of our wound is one reason why many spend years, even decades wandering from teacher to teacher, modality to modality, guru to guru and technique to technique – continuing on in the hope of finding the magic wand that will make it all go away.

This is the main reason why personal development or healing techniques that both promise to give you instant results or train you to be a 'practitioner' in a weekend or two are very popular. They promise quick and painless relief from pain and human suffering. However, what happens for the most part is a heart by-pass and in place of deeper opportunities for healing, what is on offer are vehicles for avoiding what is abundantly visible – human suffering.

Furthermore, what the quick fix approach supports is the Mind Myth, which is the idea that if we understand it, we can resolve it in our mind, and if we simply think differently, then all will be well. As has been previously stated in this book, the mind is but a mere servant of consciousness, it is not consciousness itself.

Consciousness is the entirety of our being, not just our mental capacity. It is our emotional being, our mental being, our relational being, our spiritual being and our eternal being. Just as our consciousness is layered, our energy centres are stacked in a vertical structure.

The main energy centres are our chakras, each with its own manifestation and expression of consciousness. What is not realized is that the system is identical to that of a skyscraper. Each floor or level supports the one above it. So many of our attempts to improve our lives focus on, and attempt to fix, everything through one or two levels of consciousness with the result being that relief is for the most part very short lived and not permanent and we run the risk of creating an even deeper split between our authentic self and our false self.

Both positive and negative thinking patterns can be an addiction. In the same way that there are those addicted to chasing and being in bliss, and those who are addicted to expressing their rage and anger, there are those who are addicted to their victimhood.

Consciousness is the entirety of our being; we then end up lacking in one or many areas of our lives if we believe that the mind is consciousness itself. The limits we experience in our lives are in direct ratio to our Self-awareness, the awareness of our consciousness on many levels, not just the mind.

Most of this energy is held in our lower body. With extra sensory vision it can often be seen as either a very dense ball of black energy of varying size or as a viscous sack-like form of energy that is often denser than its viscosity indicates. It is not necessary to even have the gift of clairvoyance to experience this particular manifestation of our wound. With just a little surrender and Self-awareness, it can be felt.

I mention this here because one of our natural longings is to open our heart and to experience the heart knowing itself as love – one of our deepest longings is to be free again to love and be loved as children do.

When we chase the light, when we use our will and discipline to pursue a strategy of positive thinking to deny what is or use techniques to by-pass habitual behaviours, what we are in fact doing is denying our heart its support system – without the support system the heart cannot sustain an opening.

I am not saying don't use techniques, what is being encouraged is the awareness of when we may be tempted to use them as a by-pass.

❀❀❀❀❀

As our wounding took place in our formative years, this is then expressed in our energy system through how and where this foundational wounding is held. For the most part, our foundational wounds are held in, around and associated with our first two chakras.

Our second chakra, just below the navel is the main chakra through which we relate to others emotionally and get our human needs met. Emanating from this chakra we have cords that connect us to our mother, our father and other meaningful relationships in our life. As we are totally dependent upon our caregivers and literally cannot survive our infancy without them, we then take on whatever flows to us.

If we were neglected, abused verbally, physically, emotionally or sexually then all of that experience will have gathered in and around our second chakra. When we have a healthy first chakra we feel physically vibrant and deeply connected to the Great Mother – the Earth. We have a deep sense of belonging.

However, if our formative years involved physical trauma, birth trauma, physical abuse and violence, being born in a country at war or some other palpable physical threat then we will likely have a disconnection from both our body and the earth.

If you are a sports person and take your physicality as an indication of your first chakra health you simply need to ask yourself: where is my centre? Do I live from my mind and from will?

These two charkas alone can hold a lot of unprocessed fear, self-hatred, deep grief, pain, sorrow and a host of other emotions connected to not having received enough. As we approach and start healing our foundational wounding, more energy can flow through these two chakras more freely and move its way up to the heart where they will find their fulfilment.

When the first two chakras are open and balanced the heart has a support on which to rest. The other thing that happens is as our emotional richness deepens in quality through healing the wounds of our second chakra, our world of thinking in the third chakra becomes more refined.

As this happens we perceive the world less and less according to past experience, and our use of structured viewpoints of the world and reality become more fluid – freeing us from some of the thought patterns inherited from our ancestors, culture and the world at large.

What technique driven mind tools seek to do is to refurbish the third floor of the building without taking care of the foundation. When the foundation is not solid, then the floors above live a very precarious existence. Using this analogy further, the heart can only shine in all of its glory when its support structure is in place, is felt and is operational.

A third chakra working on its own in the belief that it is the centre of all existence, is a lonely state of consciousness. As meaningful relationships are nurtured in the second chakra, a third chakra (mental) will need to move from one idea to the next, one project to the next, one concept to the next in the hope of feeding itself until it is satiated.

Without the input from our first two chakras, it will never know peace – and neither will we. It really is as simple as that.

# Heart Bypass

The truth of another and the truth of who we are can only be seen through the heart. This is not sentimental, for the heart, when awakened, is the bridge between the lower and upper chakras and when we view others, the world and ourselves through the heart, we are using all of our consciousness, not just our thinking mind.

We create a Heart Bypass when the trauma and drama of early childhood has been overwhelming for us – if it has left us scarred and shamed, full of unacknowledged worthlessness and self-hatred we are then reluctant to face the Profound Grief all over again.

The Heart Bypass in this case is created in avoidance of the 'ugly truth' we've told ourselves in an attempt to grasp at the wonderful images, ideals and feelings of how we want the world to be.

As humans we are at our best when we are in alignment – when our spiritual body is firmly grounded in the physical body, living fully in the physical world, and when words, actions, deeds and words of encouragement are expressed through an awakened heart.

# Use of Will

Along with an addiction to positive thinking comes living a will centred life. When we live our life from will we value our capability more than our ability to surrender, we value effort and determination more than openness and we favour strategy more than we value allowing.

None of these qualities are bad things in and of themselves, however, an addiction to positive thinking, which is really a defence around vulnerability and the truth of how we actually feel about ourselves, is often polarized into viewing outcomes as either successes or failures that determine the self as either good or bad, enough or not enough.

As we get older, the more we have to use will to keep our positive thinking ship afloat, the more control we will need to exert on ourselves, our feelings, our emotions, our environment, circumstances and on other people.

This is where the cracks really begin to appear in the fabric of the reality we have created. Strong use of will coupled with a disallowance of negative thinking, along with a heart bypass add up to personal relationships that simply do not work, or which turn out be disappointing.

When we've set up these circumstances in our life, relationships are a challenge as we invariably relate to everyone through our image of how we want things to be and not how they are.

We can also perhaps become callous and intolerant towards those we see as either needy, negative or as failures, for in truth, underneath all of our capability, strong use of will and our relentless positive thinking is a very deep need indeed.

Addiction to positive thinking and achievement is the desperate search to fill ourselves up in the places that feel so very empty, secluded, separate and alone.

## Facing What is Real

There is absolutely nothing wrong with re-framing circumstances into the positive and looking for what can be gained. However, an impulse to re-frame everything in every moment, to disallow yourself and others to feel less than positive is not only bordering on abusive behaviour – it is in fact abusive behaviour, especially towards the self.

Life teaches us that we get what we feel, not what we think, therefore the disallowance of any 'negativity' is counter to the opportunities that exist for healing.

When we are motivated to invest so much energy into berating ourselves into a positive view of the world, we are running at high speed away from something that we are not wanting to face.

When we cease denying our own vulnerability, we will then be able to tolerate the vulnerability of others, no longer abusing them directly or indirectly with our intolerance for authentic doubt and difficulty. No one wants to be around those who wallow in suffering; likewise, no one wants to be around someone who is blind to the truth of who they are.

When positive thinking becomes our main form of medicine, there is a strong tendency to want to fix that which is not working and to 'get rid of' unwanted feelings.

When we become trapped in the grip of an addictive and abusive cycle of positive thinking it then becomes increasingly difficult for us to face the reality that we are perhaps not at all happy with our life's circumstances and that, in reality, we experience little to no peace, little to no contentment and little to no authentic self-worth and very few truly meaningful relationships.

Dwelling on doom and gloom and addictive positive thinking are but opposite sides of the same coin. Given time and a willingness to tell the absolute truth, we will then find both inner and outer resources that can gently hold our hand as we delve into our worthlessness and self-hatred and then come out the other side as a renewed compassionate human being.

# Healing the Heart

Stepping off the positive thinking, will driven and the 'I want to fix it, get rid of it now' treadmill, takes as much courage as it does to put down a cigarette for the last time or to refuse that alcoholic beverage.

It can, in its extremes, be as damaging to your self-esteem and your relationships as any other addictive behaviour that seeks to numb and deny what is really present. When we have the courage to face what is, name what is, and above all, feel what is; then the shackles that have bound the heart can be unleashed.

As the heart is unleashed the goodness of who you are will be realized and once that happens, blessings and opportunities begin to flow more effortlessly through your life.

What is really and truly required for opening the heart and to sustain ourselves as the renewed compassionate human being, is to reposition our relationship to our wound.

Once we begin to find the gold buried under our wound, at the base of the abyss, we will begin to appreciate how the wound has made a valuable contribution to who we are as a human being.

What the world needs now is increasing armies of compassionate people, individuals who can face what is rather than avoid it, point a finger at it, blame it or ignore it. Humanity is caught in the illusion that if we can only stop those other people over there from doing what they're doing then we can be happy.

We are caught in the illusion that if we can identify all of the 'bad' people and rid ourselves of them, or publicly shame them into better behaviour that is in more agreement with either our personal or cultural standards, then we and the world can be at peace.

There has to be a time when we collectively realize that this is exactly what we have been doing and all it does is contribute to more suffering as the 'good' triumphs over the 'bad'. It is all rather subjective. Our job then is to realize that we can *only heal that which happened, we cannot heal that which should not have happened.*

Let me repeat that. We can only heal what happened. We cannot heal what should not have happened. Acceptance of what is and what was is a significant key to personal, tribal, ethnic, national and global freedom from the past.

Most of us spend most of our time resisting what is, bemoaning what should not have happened to us and are trying to find peace with something we say should not even exist.

My invitation to you here is to fully allow your wound to exist, if only for a few breaths. The invitation is to allow for the possibility that your core wound and also the thing you've spent your life running from can be of great benefit. If you can allow that possibility for a few moments, then read on to discover what your relationship with your wound can be.

## Your Wound as a Burden

We can know when our wound is an unconscious burden; when we are still stuck in blame and self-pity; when we regularly allow ourselves to be triggered by others. We invariably view the world through the veil that the wound has placed on our vision of other people and the world at large.

When our wound is a burden we take less responsibility for ourselves, our reactions and we frequently go either into conflict or withdrawal. We interpret the actions of others through the lens of our wound and we frequently re-create the same circumstances over and over again, often with different people.

When we are in burden, we use much of our energy to push against the world, giving much of our focus to that which is not wanted and very often slip into a narcissistic view of ourselves as being better than those 'others'.

With our burden, we can tend to take a 'higher' moral ground and judge others, tell ourselves, and even others, what should be done, how life should be led and what is the right thing to do, all of which is designed to keep us away from the dread of our deepest wound – separation from true self.

However, when we step back and look through the eyes of greater clarity, the occurrences often have more to do with our reactions than actually what happened. Neutral bystanders will invariably see things differently to our own wounded self.

We become stuck in burden when we need others to change; to give us what we didn't get. We remain stuck in burden until the moment we decide to simply give up the need to get what we didn't get from others and start to focus on self-care and fulfilling our own needs. We remain stuck in burden when we stubbornly refuse to accept that we simply didn't get what we needed – when the fear of facing that painful truth seems far too much for us to bear or to integrate.

We remain stuck in burden when we allow our suffering to continue as a way of demonstrating to others 'Look what you did to me!'

ᕤᕤᕤᕤᕤ

It is good to examine why we often choose to live out and express our wounds as a burden, thereby creating much dysfunction and increased suffering in our lives.

At the core of every wound is the belief that somehow it may possibly be true that the reason why we didn't get the love we needed is that there is indeed something deeply wrong with us and that somehow it is our own fault, and that we are indeed simply unlovable.

So, in feeling the wound, do we then simply enter and re-enter catharsis and express our pain, to no end? It is my belief that whilst at times catharsis can be useful and can be a gateway to something greater, it can frequently become the proverbial hamster wheel, keeping us in a place of going over and over the same territory.

What keeps us on the hamster wheel is the deep, profound and often hidden fear that it may just be possibly true that it is indeed all our fault and that there was a good reason why our mother, father and others did not love us enough to keep us safe: that there is something fundamentally wrong with us, that we are in some way bad.

We go through life seeking approval from authorities, from friends, from partners, parents, spouses, clients and anyone who may respond to our need. However, no matter how much approval and love is poured upon us, we never really let it in, for at the core this belief simmers and smoulders in the cauldron of our distorted, and often imposed self-view.

I have discovered that at the core of all self-healing we must have the courage not only to uncover and reveal that hidden and distorted belief, but we must also have the courage to truly face the possibility that it may indeed be true, for that is what lies at the gatepost to our magnificent essence.

We have to have the courage to face the possibility that it may indeed be true.

◎◎◎◎◎

This belief stands there like a bloodthirsty hound ready to pounce upon us as soon as we approach. It is not that the hound or the monster is out to get us, it too believes that it is there to protect us from ever getting to this horrible truth.

It seeks to protect us from the hidden belief that we truly are all alone in the Universe, that love, God, and our magnificence are all but illusions. The hound believes itself to be our friend. However, we are called upon to challenge this belief and to face our deepest fear.

The possibility that this belief is indeed true keeps us away from ever uncovering the truth of who we truly are, it keeps us away from our Divine Magnificence for we cannot possibly entertain the idea that our deepest fear may indeed be true – for if it is true, it is our eternal death knell, it is the ultimate annihilation of the self, the pit of destruction and also the void of eternal aloneness.

However, when we look at the symbolism of Christ on the Cross, there is a death that occurs – all of the investment we have made in the defence of our ego or false self.

It is said in the scriptures that Jesus' last words before death were, 'My God, My God, why hast thou forsaken me'. This is the point in which he faced the dreaded truth of the possibility that there was no God, no love, and the aloneness of our existence.

However, if we look much closer at the symbolism of the Crucifixion, he was nailed upon a cross, arms wide open, heart fully exposed, with a wound in his side about which he could do nothing.

As an archetypal story, much like the mythology of Greece and the ancient world, it can be seen as a means in which we can see and understand the deeper workings of the human psyche and we can use the story of Christ upon the cross as a means of translating our human experience.

As we cross the threshold of our wound into the feared void of there being 'no there when we get there', we do indeed cry out with the same anguish – *My God, My God why hast thou forsaken me?*

This is the magical moment in which grace can enter and fill us, as we face the 'dreaded truth', surrender our defences, surrender to not knowing, surrender all of our investment in our suffering and like the Christ, simply give up and surrender the distorted mechanisms that our wounded ego has used to keep us away from the feared possible truth.

It is at this point we enter the void of nothingness. Take a deep breath.

ﾍﾍﾍﾍﾍ

When we have the courage to venture deeper than simply dipping our toe into the nothingness, the nothingness becomes something more profound than any words that can be used to describe it.

In this place we have no questions and there are no answers. Just silence, simply a void, which is a world away from numbness, for numbness in itself is a feeling and a means through which we avoid feeling the distortions our wounds have created.

As we surrender to the void of total nothingness something new emerges, something that is beyond words, time and space, something magnificent that our day to day lives cannot really explain.

On total surrender to the void, on total surrender to the possibility of absolute nothingness being all that there is – a silent, dead world in which there is no God, no love, no meaning, and no purpose – only solitude in its deepest meaning, a new awareness emerges and our experience of the void transforms and changes us forever.

Instead of experiencing it as being a place of 'no questions and no answers,' it becomes a place in which everything is known and accepted, a place where the past, present and future exist as one, and a place from which all life and consciousness emerges.

As we surrender to the total crucifixion of the investments we have made in our wounding and face the possibility of our annihilation – we enter into a world of pure and unadulterated love.

If love was a material, it feels like being wrapped in a blanket of pure love, a blanket of total acceptance of what is – it is indeed falling into the heart of God and experiencing our own true nature, and that indeed, our deepest and most dreaded fear has been an illusion all along.

Take a breath.

❧❧❧❧❧

In this place, love is beyond a concept, it is palpable, it has substance and we have the experience and absolute knowingness that everything in existence, whether or not we see it as good or bad, emerges from this vast tangible field of unending and eternal love that is both the heart and mind of what we think of as God.

It is indeed the All That Is, and will ever be – it is the realm of the eternal. In this place we touch and meet God, in this place we exist in harmony with our beloved God, in this place, we experience ourselves as, 'All That Is', not alone, but connected with every particle of our being with all All That Is.

We are the saint and the sinner, we are the victim and the perpetrator, we are human and we are God, we are the flower, the dog, the cat, the vast mountains, the stars in the heavens – we are all of it, both great and small, being of vast importance and of little significance – we are all of the opposites simultaneously and, above all, – we are simply the presence of love, the presence of the Divine, both within and without, and there is acceptance of it all and we begin to see the truth that if we have a question, the answer is *always* love.

It is the fear of annihilation and the crossing of the threshold of nothingness before we pass into the threshold of 'All That Is,' that keeps us eternally on the hamster wheel.

We dread the hidden belief, we dread the possibility that it may be true, so we are stuck in perpetual repetition of painful circumstances and often kid ourselves that many of our therapies are indeed working – we enter catharsis and feel some relief from that, we try to 'understand' our issues and create stories as to why this or that person did this or that and our reaction to it – and try to make at least a structured mental peace with all of that.

We develop our minds and place everything in order – however, all of those structures keep us well away from the very thing we are seeking – the unveiling of our true nature, of our Divine Essence. All of that also seeks to keep us away from the dread of our deepest distorted belief, the lie from which most of us have lived our lives and continue to do so.

So what happens once we've surrendered to that place of magnificence? Well, in short, we return to our normal lives, forever changed, and for the most part we go back to our defended ways and cling onto the remaining pain that we have.

Take a breath.

⊘⊘⊘⊘⊘

We live in a very structured world that has powerful belief systems and we return to our day-to-day relationships. However, and this is very important for us to understand, we now have a road map and whilst we will continue to be strongly influenced by the prevailing belief systems, we have within our experience that something else, something wonderful is also true and within our grasp.

We may indeed spend the rest of our lives repeating this journey of the Crucifixion, each time coming back transformed and changed as the hand of grace enters into our awareness again and again. We've been told many times that it is not the destination, it is the journey that counts, and this is no different.

We allow the Crucifixion of one aspect of our distorted self, then we go back, again and again and again, each time we become forever changed, each time bringing back with us more of our true self, more of our Divine Magnificence, each time allowing more of who we really are to express itself through the illusory fears of human existence.

The journey becomes our focus, not the outcome. When we fixate on the outcome, it can easily became a way of avoiding human life and human relationships, and we can create an imagined 'Nirvana' from fixation on the outcome, slipping very easily into adopting a mask of peace and serenity, and living from a place of idealism rather than authenticity.

The place beyond the void can become a distraction if we lose sight of its true location and its true purpose – its location being deep within us, and its purpose is to be seen and felt in everything and in every relationship.

We don't escape to the place beyond the void, but we bring these evolved parts of ourselves back time and time again in order to become heaven on earth, rather than trying to leave earth in search of heaven.

⊘⊘⊘⊘⊘

In Biblical scriptures we are warned that Satan may appear to us as an Angel of Light. Again, if we read scripture in similar fashion to how we approach the ancient Greek and other mythological tales, as descriptions of the working of the human psyche, we can see clearly that Satan is a representation of the illusions and distortions of the wounded human and that the Angel of Light can at times be the projection of our own narcissism.

The biggest temptation on returning from our first experience of the eternal All That Is, is to see it as the goal, and forget the journey. When we forget the journey that each of us is on, we leave compassion to one side and can be tempted by an inflated view of ourselves and begin to see others who have not partaken in this journey, as all 'less than'.

The Angel of Light is deceptive and offers such sweet temptation that it is often difficult to identify and a challenge to resist.

ൟൟൟൟ

Surely after being in the All That Is we are forever changed and therefore none of this is important? Not so, we return to our normal world, indeed changed, indeed altered, but still into a world dominated by fear and illusion.

We begin to forget very clearly that in that place of absolute oneness, we were also in total and complete acceptance of what is – including our own suffering.

When we return, although having the map in our hands and a changed perception of how things are – we are still challenged by the suffering we see around us and quickly return to our own suffering, not as before, but we return to suffering nonetheless, for we have returned to the world that sits behind the veils of illusion.

We see the deceptive Angel of Light everywhere. We see it in Gurus and Spiritual Teachers who begin to suppose that the messenger is more important that the message, we see it in ourselves when we begin to see ourselves as 'more special' than others, rather than embracing the effortlessness of simple acts of love, and we become the Angel of Light (Deception) when we take a paternalistic view of others who do not belong to our 'special club' of enlightened individuals.

The key to our return from the All That Is, is to surrender even more to the acceptance of human suffering, and of our own. The more we resist it, the more the Angel of Light will seek to pull us away from the world and human relationships, simple acts of love, and therefore keep us in our suffering.

In this way we are in danger of becoming Lucifer, the light carrier who fell from grace. It behoves us to face once again the pain of separation, pick up our mantle of suffering, and enter the void once again, facing the same fear over and over again, and to continually surrender to deeper levels of grace and compassion in the face of human suffering.

# Your Wound as a Teacher

This is the next stage of living and working with our wounds. During this phase we are still reacting, projecting, blaming and falling into self-pity, but we have simply become more aware of what we are doing.

At this stage we are able to retrospectively view what happened, our masks, defences and reactions, with a little more neutrality and honesty. We have become much more self-aware and with this awareness we are able to take much more self-responsibility and begin to truly address the wound and its workings in our lives.

One of the challenges at this juncture is to be gentle with ourselves. If we have come from a family in which children were guided and disciplined through a lot of criticism, then we are likely to beat ourselves up a lot at this stage – which simply piles even more negative energy onto our wound, making it more difficult to reach a solution.

Gentle self-awareness is what is required here and a reminder that if you have a question concerning your self-healing, the answer is *always* love. When the wound is our teacher, we can more easily identify with the Angel of Light (Deception) that will even have us at times resent that it is us who seems to be doing all the work.

We will at times fall into the deception that we are the 'good' and 'enlightened' one and feel very pleased that we've done our self-examination work whilst the others are still screaming and shouting. If we are not vigilant, then we may even adopt a false sense of pride that will tell us that although the other person was 'wrong', we did the 'right' thing by working on our 'stuff'.

Take a breath.

෧෧෧෧෧

Whilst the teacher stage is far more comfortable than the burden stage of our journey with our wounds, it can be fraught with pitfalls, deceptions and self-punishment. We can easily at times drop back into the burden, but it rarely lasts for long as once we have the increased awareness, we cannot pretend not to have it, and if we do, it will be short lived for we now know that we have a choice.

We can momentarily forget our new awareness, but it won't be lost. The key is to take a deep breath and be kind to ourselves.

One of the greatest pitfalls of the 'Teacher' stage of our relationship with our wound is that we can easily fall back into the 'Burden', when we lament that everyone else is not taking the same responsibility as we are. When this happens, we've momentarily gone back to what we've known for a long time – The Burden.

We may indeed have spent many years, if not decades, in the 'Teacher' stage of our relationship to our wound.

The key is, and will always be, acceptance; it is the allowing of the Crucifixion to take place and to be at peace with it. Not one single hair upon another person's head needs to change in order for us to change or to be happier with who we are. Take a breath.

At the 'Teacher' stage we can still cling onto the need for the others to change, we can still resist what is, but our new awareness gently and always magnetically draws us in the direction of our longing – connection to all life. We may indeed spend much of our time with a foot in each camp – one in burden, one in greater awareness. It is a process.

It is also useful to be aware that surrounding the core wound of separation are a host of what I call satellite wounds, orbiting the core wound, sometimes as a distraction, sometimes deceiving us that the satellite wound is 'the big one', when all along it too was simply a diversion away from solving our deepest core issue – separation.

So many of us can spend much time, even years gnawing away at what is simply a satellite wound. We venture forth to work on our 'Mother Stuff', 'Father Stuff' and other 'Stuff', while never really addressing the heart of the matter, the central core.

Like the hamster wheel, the satellite wounds in orbit around the core can keep us in the same place, however, I encourage them not to be dismissed out of hand. Our satellite wounds can be a fruitful and fertile territory for preparing ourselves for 'the big journey' to our core.

Whilst this is not entirely true as an analogy, we can see working on the satellite wounds as the dress rehearsal for the real thing. I say that this analogy is not entirely true, for we can ride a satellite directly into the core, using it as a catalyst for our deeper work, and this is what most of us do. We need to know that it is safe, we need to know that the wound won't kill us, annihilate us, or send us off into a permanent state of mental anguish.

We can play with the satellites for quite some time before we are more confident that it is safe 'to go there'. In similar fashion, as we begin to dissolve and dispel the outer layers of illusion that the satellite wounds have kept us in, the core wound becomes less defended and we have greater access to it.

With all of our satellite wounds, it can seem a little like walking a maze that continually takes us down a dead end, however, it is not always so; sometimes we can think it is a dead end, but on closer inspection, the dead end conceals a secret passageway, hidden and perhaps obscure, that will lead us into the heart of the maze.

I have learnt that at this stage, when feeling that we are lost in the maze and also perhaps, feeling that we are only succumbing to the deceptions of the satellite wounds on not really 'getting there' or anywhere, we can use frustration as an ally.

Frustration is our friend.

Take a breath.

ൟൟൟ

Frustration is our friend? Yes, frustration is our friend. When we are frustrated we are not in stagnation and we are not numb. This means that energy is moving and that some of the parts of ourselves that are frozen deeply inside the wound are on the move.

I encourage all of my clients, including myself, to ride the wave of frustration, for it can bring great rewards. What we mostly do is respond to frustration by retreating into despair and then when the despair gets too much, fall into numbness.

All this does is keep us on the hamster wheel. It keeps us away from the goal of addressing and resolving the wound and our deepest fear. In this way frustration is simply resistance in another form, but when we are conscious of its operation and our general response to it – despair and numbing ourselves – we can use this energy to our advantage.

Frustration tries to convince us that we simply cannot get to our wound, whilst in fact, *it is a sign that we are indeed at the threshold of release, realization and freedom*, and that the fear of our most dreaded belief is about to be approached and felt.

But didn't we discuss all of this in the previous section? Didn't we move beyond this when in the 'Burden' stage of our wound? Yes, we did, if we want this process to be linear, which is what the mind wants it to be – linear, structured, safe. However, it is not like that, it is not linear.

ൟൟൟ

Frustration represents all of our life force energy that we have employed to keep the 'dreaded truth' away from us, but it's an illusion. We can experience it as an illusion, but it is a massive wall of energy that seeks to take us in the opposite direction in the unconscious hope that we will again habitually use numbness to take us back to the starting point.

As frustration is one of the false signposts, one of the deceivers along our path, we can take advantage of it and simply allow it to be present. As we ride the wave of frustration it will quickly reveal itself to be the deception that it is – for as we allow the energy to flow, we will soon surf into our intended conscious goal, instead of allowing our subconscious resistance to be in charge of our journey.

101

Frustration is a clear sign that we are approaching the feared, dreaded and distorted truth of our aloneness and unworthiness. It is one of our psyche's 'fail-safes'.

We decided long ago that we never ever wanted to experience our separation directly again, we never again wanted to experience the abandonment again and we never ever wanted to discover that the real (illusory) reason why we were not loved in the way that we needed is that because there is something wrong with us.

So we have built up a storehouse of energy that fights tooth and nail to keep us from ever feeling or approaching that 'dreaded truth'. Frustration is yet another deception, however, instead of dismissing it, we need to take it by the proverbial jugular and ride it like a bucking bronco in the rodeo of our personal salvation.

Instead of trying to tame the bronco – that simply requires more energy – we allow ourselves to be thrown and we surrender to the fall. We surrender to the wound, to what is, and we allow our soul to purify us with the ensuing tears.

Once we've been through this process once, or perhaps more than once, we allow the frustration to become another teacher. We recognize it for what it is, a wall of defence, and instead of pushing back against it, we start to surrender to it increasingly, allowing the wave to well up within us, for it is simply all of our life force energy that we have stored in the wall of frustration.

When we push against it, all we are doing is shoring up the wall and making it stronger, thereby increasing our resistance and making it even more challenging to overcome.

Frustration is life force energy.

Take a breath.

It is all the energy we have invested in believing that we are less than, in the belief that we are not loved, in the fear that we can be annihilated, it contains, in essence, the very thing we seek – the authentic self, authentic power and connectedness to all life.

Frustration is indeed our friend, it is a signpost that we are close to our intended unveiling. It is also deceptive, appearing to be in the exact opposite direction of where we intended to go, but in fact, it is our 'last ditch' attempt of keeping us from the wound.

I have learnt to celebrate frustration and to see it as my friend, it always lets me know that I am simply a hair's breadth away from resolution and that my old friend 'fear' is trying to get the upper hand.

Indeed, many, many times the Angel of Light can appear on our path and try to deceive us – Frustration is simply one of the allies of this deception, when the Angel of Light leads us off onto yet another illusory path, the Angel of Frustration steps in to try and save the day. The trick is to make friends with it.

# Your Wound as a Companion

At this stage our wounds become our friends. In every situation in which we can find ourselves triggered into defence, we become gently aware of our own wounding in the background and we gently make the choice not to go into defence.

If we do go into defence or have a reaction, we start to take immediate responsibility for it and gently take ourselves off into more self-healing work that feeds and nourishes our soul.

Whilst it is true that others can hurt us in the present and that our reaction is not always from a place of being triggered by an event in the present that stimulates an old wound, when our wounds are our companions, we react with much less voracity.

When our wound is our friend, our compassion increases and we are much more easily able to see others beyond the veils of their own wounds and defences. We recognize them for who they truly are and how they are feeling in the moment.

When our wound is our friend we no longer blame or push back, but stand with both feet firmly on the ground with an open heart – feeling no need to be forgiven or to forgive, but simply to be in the present moment with what is presenting itself.

When our wound is our friend, we don't make the other wrong and we can choose to withdraw peacefully until a better opportunity presents itself to deal with the matter at hand more constructively.

As we embrace our wounds, firstly as teachers, then as companions through life, it is at this stage we begin to submit to our destiny – our childhood and other circumstances are what they are and are unchangeable – with the exception of our feelings and reactions.

In submitting to our fate we begin to see the opportunities for growth inherent within the wound and we start seeing the many opportunities that have been presented to us.

For many of us, it is the very seeking for solutions to our pain that leads us onto a path of encountering our own soul and the much greater part of ourselves – yes, even to the Divine.

Our wound serves as a motivator that will not allow us to be comfortable until we begin to acknowledge it and start giving it the attention that is required. Our long-term suffering is caused by our long search, and oft times desperation to get our pain to go away.

Eventually we may turn to spirituality in the hope that a Guru, teacher, spiritual practice or spiritual community will make the pain vanish – if we follow the teaching or the teacher, we will be delivered from suffering.

However, with compassion, sincerity and with kindness it is both my wish and invitation that you throw yourself into the heart of your wound. When we do this all of the planning and strategies of the mind come to a halt; we are silenced. When we fall into the centre of it, the fire of Shiva, the light of our own soul begins to burn through our stories, projections and illusions.

When we have the courage to stop all strategies and surrender to what is present, liberation is at hand.

# CHAPTER 5

# Fate and Forgiveness

Let us now look at healing relationships as an important part of liberating the heart. We are by our very nature relational beings. The primary relationship that we are in is the human trinity: mother, father, and child.

That is the most important foundational relationship for that trinity is the primary influence in the formation of how we manifest through our body in this lifetime.

It is the foundation of who we are as a human being. When we come into existence in this form through the trinity of father, mother, child, it becomes the foundation of who we are, because we inherit not only our physical characteristics, physical strengths and susceptibilities, but also emotional disposition, belief systems and mental structure.

We simply do not arrive into this life out of thin air onto a totally clean slate. We are born into something and that 'something' is an energy that has consciousness. Within that consciousness is the expression of a collective family 'soul' that spans many generations.

The inner ring is made up of your biological parents and siblings, the second ring is aunts, uncles and grandparents, the third ring being great grandparents and so on and so forth. These rings are like the rings on a tree – *they are the record holders of each generation's experiences.*

Those experiences can include great triumphs and deep trauma, crime and compassion, success and failure, kind-heartedness and cruelty, seasons of plenty and seasons of scarcity, each etched out on the family soul leaving a footprint that besmears, celebrates or simply keeps a record.

Everything that has happened, all of the curses placed upon a family, and all of the cursing a family has participated in, and every proclamation or excommunication by the church or state, every disinherited, denied and unclaimed child – the so called 'illegitimate'; these are all imprinted.

These rings contain the experiences of enslavement and of being the enslaver, of being the conquered and the conqueror. The rings of a family tree hold a record of the great social and political movements that have divided nations, brought nations to war, have separated many in the name of religion or ethnic purity and all of the unbearable crimes humanity has exacted upon members of its own and other species.

Part of the Profound Grief I wrote of earlier is associated with our deep need for both personal and collective redemption – the inner voice that says 'what have we done?' There is much to be faced with this but not in the way of piling guilt upon ourselves, for this we have already done and it simply serves to continue the cycle of victims and perpetrators and keeps humanity under the thick veil of self-hatred.

When we face our personal or collective need for redemption what we are in fact facing is both the individual and collective moments of separation from the heart.

As a species we are capable of such grace, such beauty, such creativity – music and poetry to lift hearts and minds, smiles and caresses that can reach the very soul of anyone who receives them.

And yet, we are capable of the deepest, gravest and most horrific nightmares and it is for all of that personal and collective regret that we seek redemption from, as we seek to regain the flicker of innocence that seems to so dimly shine under layers of self-doubt and shame.

Epigenetics, a relatively new branch of science, is beginning to confirm that DNA can and is changed through traumas which are passed down to the subsequent generations and manifests as susceptibility to certain diseases.

This confirms what Shamans and energy healers have been telling us for centuries and what Family Constellation work has been pointing to for the past three or more decades, within the context of a more western approach to the human psyche.

## Fate & Destiny – Forgiving our Past, Embracing Roots and Accepting what IS

What we are born into is our fate. We are born into a certain family, we are born into a certain physical body. We have a gender. We come in either male or female, straight, gay, bi-sexual or we have some other fate in terms of our gender identification, or perhaps even physical identification as to what our gender is, if we have hermaphrodite or androgynous tendencies or appearance.

The physical package that we're born into becomes a big part of our fate, especially if we are born into a culture that has rigid rules around the roles of men and women or distorted moral codes that it applies to those who love the same gender. That's the package that we get, and we're supposed to do something with it.

We not only get mum and dad, but we get siblings if they're there, we get a gender, we get a nation that we're born into.

Our country is part of our fate and the circumstances in our country are part of that. We get a religion or a philosophical teaching, a way of life and a way of looking at the world through our culture's lens and filter.

We get a culture. We get a set of rules. We get a set of manners. Those sets of manners are also important, because what's considered polite in one country is deemed very impolite in another country: that alone should inform us that much of what we believe is simply inherited and not the definitive truth. All of that we are born into is part of our fate. Fate is a given, destiny is what we do with it.

When it comes to healing on any level, the most important quality or virtue is courage. In order not to relive our personal, family, national or ethnic history we must have the courage to face our past, or indeed to examine what we are creating in the present. *What is absolutely necessary is our willingness to tell and know the absolute truth.*

Without this courage to face the absolute truth, all other qualities we consider to be good and virtuous, such as love, forgiveness, acceptance, tolerance, kindness, charity and understanding, are only temporary states of being for none of them can exist in our world unless they are supported by courage.

Likewise, courage does not exist unless fear is present. Fear of judgment, fear of exposure, the fear of being shamed and the fear of being undefended, the very real fear that if we do reveal our light it in some way could be extinguished and we would fade into non-existence.

Without courage we can simply succumb to our fate and allow it to be the cornerstone of our lives, dictating the outcome of every relationship and life experience: in essence, more like a millstone than a solid cornerstone from which to build something that expresses who we truly are, as opposed to the distorted self-view born from our wounding.

However, all of the limiting life patterns that we experience really emerge from resisting that which was given, our fate. Yes, this sounds like a contradiction. In order for us to evolve our fate into a destiny of our choosing, *we must first submit to whatever happened, to the fate that was given. We cannot heal what should not have happened, we can only heal what DID happen.*

This means having the courage to cease resisting what is and what was. It means having the courage to accept everything that befell us in childhood even when it seems so terribly unfair or wrong. Feeling that something is either unfair or wrong does not have the power to change the fact of what actually happened – we simply do not have that power.

However, on the one hand we can long for healing whilst at the same time preaching or complaining that it should never have happened to us, it should never have happened to me. A challenging question can be: *why not?* Why shouldn't it have happened to you?

With that I am not suggesting that you deserved it, asked for it, or in some way are only worthy of such treatment, but when we carry ourselves in the world with an attitude that bad things *should not* happen to us, when clearly we have little to no control of so many of the world's events, this feeling simply serves to set us apart.

Somehow we make ourselves 'special' and look for reasons as to why it should not have happened to us. When we bow with humility to what actually happened, to what DID happen, to what IS, much of our suffering is relieved.

When we cannot accept our fate, we cannot accept ourselves. Our fate forms the building block of who we are, it has set the stage for our development and our direction in life. When we condemn and resist our fate, seeing ourselves as above it, we fall into the trap of never being able to accept ourselves as we are. Something can always be better and no matter what we do or achieve, it is never enough.

We live in a world of opposites, we have up and down, left and right, light and dark and so on and so forth and within life's lessons lies opposites as well – we live in a world of comparison and our free will allows us to create a life of our choosing.

So no matter where we stand in life, all that is not wanted is an opportunity for us to launch ourselves forward towards what we do want.

However, so many of us spend so much time simply resisting what is instead of reaching for that which is wanted, whilst fully acknowledging who we are and how we feel in the moment.

## Submission and Surrender

The word '*submit*' is a difficult word for most to digest. It conjures up images of submission, enslavement, acquiescence and being resigned to a given situation with no further freedom to change or do anything about it.

However, I use the term 'submit' in the meaning of accepting what is and what was. So why don't I just say 'accept' in its stead? Fate is a given and it comes to us from a power and a force that is much greater than ourselves, though I am not talking here about an individual God, the God of the Bible who has a personality, a will, wishes, laws and is almighty: I am talking here about the forces that govern human relationships and all life.

Within this force is not only the greater soul of humanity and the soul of all life on our planet, both seen and unseen by the naked eye, but also our individual soul. As I lay on the floor during the aforementioned armed robbery, a deep upwelling of desire emerged and part of that desire was a wish to complete what I had agreed to do.

The notion of soul contracts was not new to me, neither then or now, however, for the first time in my life it was crystal clear to me.

Whilst 'little John' was quite prepared to leave this life, the greater, deeper, inner part of me experienced a strong desire to stay and to complete a task. It is not as if I was given a map or clear instructions, or even that I now have a project plan with checkpoints, dates and an end time, but what I do have is a clearer connection to the longing of my soul and for the most part I allow that to be my guidance.

Also, this task is not 'grand' in the way that we may think of 'God given' tasks, it is quite simple really. It is simply to become a better version of myself, to evolve my personality to a level that is undefended, without masks and to be ever in tune with the longing of my soul. This in itself is a lifetime of work and it will find numerous ways to express itself.

Any task that is given to us is always about ourselves, it is about becoming the greater part of ourselves, living our essence and walking this planet in a more open and undefended manner.

So much religious imagery has led many to believe that a 'God given' task is some grand project, like 'save the world,' or 'heal the planet' and whilst our work may indeed contain elements of that – for example a project to preserve a forest or work that entails healing and education, the underlying principle is always 'healer heal thyself'.

It all revolves around us as individuals, so when we enter a life path of becoming a healer or teacher, then that is because *we have something to heal within* and *we have something to learn.*

We cannot possibly take anyone else on a journey that we ourselves have not already taken or are currently on. Our sacred mission is not to save anyone or anything else, but it is to save ourselves from the illusions we have built up to defend our wounds. We become Chiron, the archetype of the wounded healer.

The more we get in contact with our essence, our true nature and our connection to all life, it is who we love and how we love them, that becomes of paramount importance – it becomes our driving force.

However, to love and to be loved in the simplest of ways requires us to release our identification with our wounds and to surrender any investment we have made in resisting our fate and any investment we have in blame.

This is no small task, it is constant work, for along with our fate we have our stories and our images and very often we release them reluctantly as we have identified very strongly with them and they have become a defining part of who *we think we are* but not who *we truly are*.

Imagine for a moment that 'God' is the personality that some religions have described 'him' as. We die, we go to heaven, and 'he' will ask, 'I gave you your mother and father and your childhood circumstance, I also gave you your gender, your body, your ethnicity and your nationality, so, tell me, what did you do with them?'

Most of us, if honest, would reply 'Um....I spent most of my life resisting all of that, I didn't like the package deal at all'.

From the depths of our deepest wounds emerge our greatest gifts. Similarly, contained within the fate we were given, emerges a destiny when we choose to work with the fate. However, destiny cannot emerge until our fate is submitted to.

> *Who we are is our gift from God, who we become is our gift to God.*
> — **ELEANOR POWELL**

That means standing back and looking at everything that was given and has happened and asking ourselves where the opportunities for self-development and self-healing lie.

If we come from lack, then discovering the fullness of our being lies as an opportunity before us; if we come from conflict, then peace and reconciliation lies before us; if we come from abandonment and despair, then connection to all life lies before us.

Whatever the lack, its opposite awaits us. Therefore the difficult and challenging aspects of our fate give us the opportunity to springboard towards a destiny of our own choosing instead of bemoaning that which is less than desirable.

In submitting to fate, we receive this life and all of its circumstances as a gift and we get on with the task of digging for the gold that awaits us.

## Forgiveness

Forgiveness, like the words love and God, is another one of those supercharged, distorted and misunderstood words that is bandied about by religions, spiritual teachers, philosophers and society, along with off the cuff expressions like 'forgive and forget' or 'I shall forgive, but will never forget'.

Forgiveness very often doesn't work, even though it is at the core of many spiritual teachings. There is this idea of forgiving one's enemies, forgiving those who have hurt us. The reason why it seldom works is that most often it is the 'Good' struggling to forgive the 'Bad'.

Frequently contained within this attempt towards seeking resolution and forgiveness, is an inherent, and frequently veiled, sense of superiority. Forgiveness takes place when we meet what is and when we meet the other individual as an equal.

How do I meet the perpetrator as an equal? How could I possibly be equal to that which is odious, cruel or heinous? When we do our inner work, when we investigate our heart, when we have the courage to look at topics such as hatred, jealousy, bitterness, a sense of being hard-done by – our need for justice, or our need to punish – we will then have the courage to see how often our benevolence is not actually benevolent. It can reveal itself as piety, superiority and even manipulation.

The 'good' regularly triumph over the 'bad' with much more enthusiasm. With almost guaranteed predictability today's freedom fighter invariably becomes tomorrow's dictator. Our world is full of such examples and is still suffering under the heavy burden of the cycle of victims and perpetrators, with many groups of victims frequently claiming more 'rightness' than the previous group or other groups.

When we are able to face with absolute clarity, and through telling the absolute truth to ourselves, we can clearly see how 'goodness' can be the Devil himself dressed up as an Angel of Light. When we are able to face the inherent and hidden sense of superiority and look at our own shadow, we will then be able to meet the perpetrator as an equal. When we meet the other as an equal there is no need for forgiveness.

It doesn't have to be attempted, it doesn't have to be tried, it simply happens. And it happens as we bathe in the truth that resides in the silence.

What this requires is our ability to look at a perpetrator and feel, experience and know completely what it is that they have done to themselves. As we encounter the gravity of what the other has done to themselves and the consequences of what is in effect self-harm, we begin to see the truth of who they are – a human being who is lost and in pain.

When this is experienced forgiveness becomes meaningless for we have already witnessed the other through our awakening heart.

When someone murders, rapes or harms another; what have they done to themselves? What is the impact on their family? How many of their generations will feel the burden and for how long?

One of the problems we have as a culture is how the teachings of Christ have been distorted by religion. We have become a very punitive culture and within this philosophical framework the 'bad' have to be punished. What we are then left with is that 'the bad' need to be punished and the admonition that we must forgive.

How then can we expect to forgive a bad person who is to be punished and yet have it not look like some sort of pious benediction? We keep on trying to do that: the bad have to be punished, and we are supposed to forgive. Together with this is the message that as victims we are good, and that the perpetrator is bad.

Unintentionally we also believe that if we forgive, this confirms us as the 'good' person and although the forgiveness takes place, the 'bad' person remains 'bad'.

There is the huge contradiction in all of that. One is very 'old testament' in nature and one is part of a distorted teaching. Religion is almost always a distortion of the teachings of the master be that the Buddha, Krishna, or Christ.

One of the greatest crimes committed by Christianity on Western culture is to tell everybody that they were born in sin. This is one of the collective birthplaces of self-hatred. If that is the seed of our culture, if self-hatred is the foundation upon which we built our culture, how then are we able to forgive the unforgivable?

This can really only be done once we experience the depths of our own heart, for the heart is very broad and it leads us into a whole other universe that contains all at the higher and lower aspects of ourselves. Existing within those worlds is also our shadow and we often feel justified in wanting to be punitive towards the perpetrator, or even cruel.

We justify that by saying that 'they are the bad one' and we are the 'good one'. I'm not suggesting that we do away with our legal systems. Indeed sometimes society does need to be protected from an individual who can be very sick.

However, what kind of society created that person? What kind of society creates despots? What kind of society creates rapists? What kind of society creates people who steal and what kind of society simply imprisons individuals, treating them as if they are permanently bad and offering them little to no opportunity to redeem themselves through some form of rehabilitation programme?

Right wing politics have a big influence on how we view perpetrators and criminals. However, what is clear is that fear is the foundation of right wing politics and those who usually vote for right wing political parties and leaders.

We live in a culture where some of the greatest thefts are sanctioned or ignored. We tolerate corruption and lies in the world of big business, we allow our governments to take military action for invented reasons and yet we label those smaller groups defending themselves as terrorists – the 'bad' ones.

This is all based on fear. We seek to keep the 'bad' away and what is usually 'bad' is anything we don't understand. We live in a world in which someone from a disadvantaged background who steals a radio or car might find themselves in prison, and the elite who steal millions roam the streets and still run corporations – or governments!

We have a lot of inequality. We have lots of ideas about who is 'good' and who is 'bad', we have lots of ideas about whose crimes are not 'as bad' as other people's crimes. Within the seed of Western culture, and in all cultures on the planet, there is this notion that there are others who are 'badder' than us and there are others who are 'better' than us.

These belief systems are apparent in newspaper articles. If someone from a racial minority is shot the article will often state how this person had been in trouble before and what a bad area he came from – what it says in reality is this: it's probably his fault he got murdered.

Similarly if an individual from a privileged background walks into high school with a shotgun and murders a dozen people, the article may very well list all of his glorious achievements and say what a wonderful young person he was: in other words, he was a good kid, this was out of character.

As cultures across the globe we have fallen into the almost unquestioned habit of hating particular groups of people based on their perceived differences. What this allows us to do is to project our own self-hatred in order to create someone who is worse than us. What we fear may exist in us, we fear and hate in another.

As we have the courage to meet what is in our own heart we begin to experience that perhaps we are afraid to love, really afraid to love. What will it take for us to see those 'others' as ourselves?

Why are we perhaps afraid to love? Perhaps we were raised by a family in a neighbourhood or culture in which we experienced a lot of hatred; perhaps Beirut, Belfast or on the West Bank, or in an impoverished ghetto or in another part of the world where there is hatred towards or from other groups, or perhaps we were raised with religious abuse, or in a culture of blame that always seeks to blame others and especially outsiders for misfortune.

When we are exposed to such hatred as children we get to know that the core of hatred comes from a betrayed and wounded heart. Harsh upbringing, harsh rules, harsh religion and harsh opinions of others give little to no room for the heart to thrive and flourish and the only way to belong is to follow suit.

Such families or communities thrive on being against something and are invariably abusive amongst themselves. We can then become too afraid to love: because if we love, maybe that will happen to us, maybe we will turn to hatred too. In avoidance of this we close ourselves off behind a wall for we instinctively know that hatred and love are different sides of the same coin.

The only way we have of obeying the instruction to fear certain types of people and to reject them is to close our own heart which brings us into direct conflict with ourselves. It is our nature to love everyone, no matter their race, creed, ethnicity, gender or orientation.

It is simply, unequivocally, deliciously, exuberantly, gracefully and profoundly our nature to love. It is the very foundation of our existence and indeed of the entire universe.

So what happens when we obey the edict to hate 'those people over there', the ones who are 'bad' or 'different'? It brings us into direct conflict with our very nature and we begin to hate ourselves for it. I've yet to meet a misogynist, a racist, a homophobe, misandrist or bigot who is at peace with themselves and who can surrender to love. When innocence is lost, hatred defends wounded love.

Forgiving the unforgivable starts with an experience of one's own heart. This embraces an ability to really look at our own shadow, to really know what is present, to really know what is hiding there in the hurt. It behoves us to look through the heart with clarity at what the perpetrator did to herself, what he did to himself?

Can we cross the floor and meet the camp commandant of Auschwitz and stroke his cheek and say 'go home to your family, you are needed there'? It is very easy for us to say 'well, he deserves all of the suffering that is on its way to him' and indeed, the wheels of Karma turn and there are consequences for our actions.

However, what I'm proposing is that we bow with respect to the heavy consequences they have indeed brought upon themselves and have compassion for their family and descendants.

Do we really want to revel in the thought of another's suffering even if it is self-created? Can we be so far removed from the truth of the heart that our need for retribution is capable of overriding our true nature to the extent that what is truly prolonged is our own suffering?

When we look closely at the children, grandchildren and great grandchildren of such individuals we can know that the impact on them is grave.

What if you are a descendant of slaves, perhaps an African-American. Can you look through your heart at the grandchildren and great grandchildren of the slave owners? Or would that feel conflicting and disloyal? If you are the child of a Holocaust survivor, can your heart bear to see the suffering of Germans? If you are a Native American or Australian Aboriginal can you bear to look at the legacy of guilt inherited by the descendants of the colonisers?

When there has been ill gotten gain, shame and guilt have a very deep impact, not only on the perpetrator, but also on their descendants for several generations to come – what is apparent is that this negative impact is also felt and witnessed with the descendants of the victims.

The descendants of both victims and perpetrators mirror one another in many noteworthy ways. They struggle to be happy, they often struggle to have meaningful relationships, and they often work hard with little reward or lose all of the fruits of their hard labour.

The descendants of the victims often feel an unconscious loyalty to the suffering of their ancestors and the descendants of the perpetrators live out their lives as if it were a penance, often caught up in self-destructive and self-sabotaging behaviours.

With all of this is an invitation to look at the truth of that which says we are better, the truth of when we say that we are trying to forgive, or that we need to be more forgiving and inclusive of those 'bad' people. We really need to look at the truth of what that means.

One of my greatest awakenings was to realize that the thing being sought is not lost, it is the seeker who is lost. We do not awaken, it is awakening that calls us and it means letting go of everything we thought we knew, it is a death and re-birth into something new and yet to be re-discovered.

The heart's whisper is relentless. It calls us night and day, even when it is ignored it calls us, for our lives are but a pilgrimage of the heart to awaken to itself. We are relational beings and we are here to learn from the intricate and magnificent relationships of all kinds, and the mirror they provide for us.

Forgiving the unforgivable can only come from honestly meeting our heart with all of its contents; from our willingness to tell the absolute truth. When we let go of the story of who is the 'good' person and who is the bad person, the story of being hard done by and the need to punish or be punished, when we have the courage to do all of that, it really becomes the courage to choose peace and the courage to challenge our need to be right.

When we mourn the losses of the perpetrators, innocence and peace returns to us. Bow with deep respect to the consequences of their actions and peace will be upon you. When we await their punishment, only turmoil remains with us.

Our need to be right emerges from own need to punish the other in response to our deep pain. We need to ask ourselves this: When we need to punish the other, who are we imitating? We are imitating the perpetrator.

That which is unforgivable only becomes unforgivable within our own heart when we exclude someone from the human race. When we exclude someone as bad, it goes against the nature of our soul and the nature of our heart, which is to be inclusive. In reality it is ourselves that we cannot forgive.

When we came into this world brimming with innocence as young children we loved everyone and everything. Then we lost our innocence, and we are yet to forgive ourselves for the great betrayal of self, for being too afraid to stand in our light.

When we are unable to forgive another, and when we exclude them from the human race, the reality is we are unable to forgive ourselves for what we allowed to happen and for our participation in exclusion after that. *The soul can only include, the heart can only include.*

The heart encompasses everything, it excludes nothing. The awakened heart is the universe, it is God and everything and everyone belongs and as the heart awakens to itself, you will discover that everything is already forgiven.

WHAT THIS SECTION DID NOT SAY:
- Whenever I discuss this topic there can be reactions that lead either the listener or the reader to draw conclusions that stem from a wounded reaction – this is understandable when we have been deeply wounded.
- I am not suggesting that individuals such as rapists, murderers and those guilty of heinous crimes against humanity be 'let off the hook'. I am saying that we can bow to the fate that awaits them, the fate that either political forces or the force of law will deliver. The freedom of the heart allows us to love, pray for and include those who have been terribly lost.
- Not wishing vengeance, not wishing to see the other punished is not the same as saying that the law should not take its own course.
- Almost all victims blame themselves in some way for what was done to them. When we meet what is and see the perpetrator for what and who they are; a mother, a father, a son, a cousin, a child etc., then we begin to see ourselves for who we are.

WHAT THIS SECTION DID SAY: FREEDOM
- When we are able to see the other for who they are and lament their loss as well as our own, we are no longer bound to them, no longer bound to carry them throughout our life. This gives us freedom.

When we can bow with deep respect for the consequences to their soul
and on their fate we become truly free.

This is a deep and profound inner movement that can only take place in the
heart once we release our stories of right and wrong.

What about my memories?

Memories of events can seem to be etched upon us. However, as we do our
inner work, the emotional charge around what happened reduces.

What is important to realize is that we can only heal what did happen, not
what should not have happened.

Memories are bothersome, even tormenting, when we still have difficulty in
accepting what is. Acceptance of 'what is' is KEY to any path of healing. When we
are still crying out 'It should never have happened' then our memories of the event
will still plague us, perhaps for years. There is very little point in arguing with reality. We can only heal what actually happened, not what should not have happened.

The first step is to acknowledge that it actually happened and then accept that
it happened. Accepting that it happened is not the same as giving permission for
others to do the same, it is simply not arguing with reality.

## Love is Never Lost

One of the most common areas in which forgiveness has proven to be a great
challenge for many is in the realm of marriage, romantic and long term committed relationships.

In addition to the pain of separating form a partner, there are many who have
been the child that was afforded front row seats to what may have been a bitter
and painful battle between two people who have been charged with their care.

What is apparent is that in our woundedness we often fall into the clutches of
our own lower nature instead of surrendering to the pain of loss. What is noteworthy is that the person we once loved now suddenly becomes someone bad,
evil, disgusting and just plain wrong.

I have repeated over and over again through the pages of this book that we
have a strong tendency to choose long term suffering in favour of short-term
pain. Rather than face the deep pain that the loss of a relationship can bring, for
many, there is an unconscious choice to revert to backlash and attack in defence
of a breaking heart, and this is especially true when infidelity has taken place.

This wound of betrayal has a strong tendency to then tap into a lifelong pattern of experiences from early childhood onwards, thereby adding to the ferocity

of the experience and the emotional reactions. It takes courage to allow the love we still have for the other to remain unhindered in the heart. This acknowledgment of the love that remains is painful for most, however, when we seek to deny it or defend it with hatred, revenge and rejection, long term suffering is born.

# CHAPTER 6

# On the Edges of Infinity
## Journey to the Source and Back

In January 2013 I had a minor motorcycle accident that led me to contract a very serious case of cellulitis with multiple strains of infection. This caused me to be on an antibiotic drip for more than 16 days during which I underwent many procedures that involved removing dead skin.

I was in a lot of pain and suffered a fever that lasted for almost two of those weeks. I was very sick indeed. The daily change of wound dressing was becoming more than I could bear.

. The initial treatment I received was in a clinic in a very small town in the mountains of northern Thailand – this first procedure was done with no anaesthetic originally and then by injecting local anaesthetic directly into the wound. I screamed from a very deep place of terror and I was fortunate enough to be surrounded by friends who held my hands through this traumatic ordeal. The follow up treatments took place in a bright, modern and efficient hospital in Chiang Mai.

One day as I lay in wait for another wound change I was full of dread. It didn't seem to matter what drugs they gave me, my leg was so swollen that a mere gentle touch would solicit a reaction from the rest of my body. The nursing staff had been so gentle and so patient and tolerated my commands, my tears, my temper and my fear.

I'm sure they had seen it all before and I was witnessing first-hand what it is like when you have been in a lot of pain 24 hours a day for getting on for three weeks. Like sleep deprivation, it is enough to make one insane or simply want to give up.

This day, the day I journeyed to the edge of infinity, was in so many ways no different to any other of the days spent in the treatment room at the hospital, except it *was* different. I had had morphine on the previous day and was curious about how it caused me to dissociate from what was happening. I could feel everything they were doing with my leg, I could even feel the pain, but I was so dissociated I simply didn't care.

I did not know if that was how morphine was supposed to work or not, but that is how it had worked for me. It was a curious state of consciousness; to be in pain and yet not care about it. No emotional reaction, only dissociation. On this particular day the nurse administered the morphine and left the room immediately stating that she would be back in a few minutes. No sooner had she left the room I started to feel sensations that I had not previously experienced.

There was a strange electrical tingling throughout my body and a buzzing sound indicating some sort of voltage in my head that was interspersed with popping sounds. I tilted my head backwards and looked at the monitor – I knew that the numbers were not as they should be, pulse was low, blood pressure very low and in that moment, as I wondered if I would be ok, I found myself floating up above my body looking down at myself.

It was quite unlike the previous experience of being in pain but dissociated, for in that moment I was anything but dissociated; at first I was rather alarmed.

As I gazed downwards at myself, the first thing I noticed was the size and shape of my body and the thought, 'you really ought to go on a diet,' crossed my mind and then I spotted my dear friend sitting in his chair, clearly unaware of where I was. My heart filled with compassion for him and I became deeply concerned. I was worried that if this was the scene of my death than it may be too much for him.

How would he cope with informing family and friends and how would he organize all the practical aspects of someone dying? I wanted to shout at him, 'Don't bother to ship my body, just choose the easiest route for yourself,' and with that thought I found myself back in my body.

I was now back fully in my body and I noticed that I was gripping the sheets and that the buzzing feeling and sounds were back. In that moment I heard the very same voice, the same deep masculine tone that had asked me if I wanted to live during the armed robbery in South Africa some six years previously.

This time the voice greeted me with, 'just let go, it is more difficult if you grip, just let go'. As I knew this voice and had an inherent trust of it, for after all, a miracle had happened on that fateful night in Johannesburg, I followed the instructions and let go deeply.

A part of me was confused, as I just didn't expect this to be my time. I had assumed that I had survived a gun being put to my head in South Africa as there was still lots of work for me to do – so although I did not feel complete, I did however accept what was presenting itself and realized that on the level of my personality I could not possibly understand the big picture of what was going on.

I felt sad at the thought of death as I felt that there were still things I wanted to do and see, and yet I accepted it in that moment. I let out a breath, released my grip and once again found myself floating up close to the ceiling, looking down at the treatment room, my friend and my own body. This time however my vision had changed.

It was ultra-clear, ultra-sharp, no longer were my reading glasses going to be needed. In addition to being ultra-sharp, the colours looked different; there was a vibrancy I had not witnessed previously.

My vision also changed to encompass all 360 degrees, meaning, I could simultaneously see not only below me, but also above me and to the sides: my vision was spherical, for want of a better description.

In writing this, just as I have been aware of the same problem when telling this story live or on video, I am presented with issues of vocabulary and descriptions of linear and chronological time that are not strictly true. I will use words like 'up' and describe events in sequence when in fact there were no directions, no beginning and no end.

As I create the story of this experience I must use terms that make sense to both me the writer and you the reader, for in reality, there are very few words to actually describe where I was, what I experienced, what I saw and what I felt. What I mean by that is that time was fluid and many experiences seemed simultaneous and I even experienced colour for which I had no name, no equivalent.

This wasn't like encountering a shade of blue and not knowing whether it was cyan or turquoise, it was encountering something I had never experienced before. However, it was not in the moment of viewing the colour that I questioned it, for in the moment it seemed as if everything I saw was already known to me as it felt so natural. It was only afterwards on recounting the experience that I ran into word difficulties, 'What was that colour?'

My experience of floating up on the ceiling with 360 degree vision deepened as I noticed that above me was a vast black space encircled by what appeared to be an ultra-fine gold thread that was as thin as it was bright. Its brightness was astounding, along with its thinness. It appeared to be no thicker than the average hair and yet the energy and brightness it was emanating belied its insignificant size.

I gazed at the vast black space. I was curious as I had always heard that in these moments there should be a tunnel with light. However, I had no sense that I was disappearing into some dark underworld for the vast blackness I had become aware of was radiating a profound sense of benevolence.

I stared into it and could see what I can only describe as a black light. As odd and as contradictory as that sounds, it appeared to me to be a black light, maybe it was a deep cobalt blue, maybe it was a deep purple, but even today as I write this I know that if I say it was either deep purple or blue, it would not be true, it would only be for the convenience of avoiding describing something that I cannot even grasp in my day to day experience.

This black light was alive, more than that, it was conscious and it was aware of my presence. I felt as if its emanations were reaching across time and space to greet me, to welcome me, to simply say hello. I actually longed for it to touch me, I wanted it to wrap around me and coil up inside me, for the benevolence I felt coming from it was more than I had ever experienced in my entire life. It was more benevolence than I could measure or conceive of.

I became aware once more of the thin golden line which formed the boundary between this world and the one in which the benevolent black light resided. I noticed that I was being pulled upwards. It was a very gentle movement, a gentle tugging that felt as if my belly was being drawn by a magnet towards the vast space.

I knew instinctively that if I passed through the golden ring there would be no return and that I would then be in the world of the dead. As I started to pass more completely through the golden ring I looked down once more at my friend and at my body. I was at peace and knew that he would survive this experience and would eventually be more than ok. I released any thoughts of worry I had had about funerals and other inconveniences.

Finally I looked down and saw that I had passed through the ring of gold completely. At that moment I experienced only what I would describe as a gasp. I did not literally gasp for I was not in a physical body with which to draw the air for a gasp.

However, I use this word to convey a flood of awareness that was as astonishing as it was magnificent and full of wonderment. I can only liken it to a moment when, miraculously, each and every wish you've ever had comes true in the same instant.

This gasp, this astonishment was with the realization that I had merged with the black light, with that source of benevolence that was so complete, so very, very complete in every way that I could not imagine ever needing or wanting anything else.

To be merged for a second or for a few moments in perfection, bathed in perfection, embraced by perfection, felt like a thousand years of total contentment and resplendent bliss.

In my awareness I could experience myself being embraced by this deep dark velvet whilst at the same time being not only merged with it, but actually aware of being it. I was simultaneously aware of being 'me' in the experience of being embraced by the Benevolence, of being the benevolence itself, and of being the part of me that could observe both.

There was not a single moment when I questioned my ability to be focussed in multiple vantage points simultaneously, it all felt so very natural. For a while I did not know what to call this benevolence. It challenged some of my notions of God and it certainly felt as if I may be going out on a limb to say that I had met God.

However, for me this benevolence could not be anything other than that I have come to know as God. As part of this merging experience I knew that the Benevolence absolutely knew everything about me – we had no secrets, not at all. Absolutely nothing was hidden. I was as naked as the day I was born and each of my thoughts, my feelings, my pains, my sufferings, my joys, my hopes, my aspirations, my jealousies, my dishonesties, all of my history – everything was known.

To be that known and to be so deeply held in a way that transcended all sense of shame and unworthiness is a life changing experience. There was no hesitation from the Benevolence, and furthermore, we were now one.

ᕤᕤᕤᕤᕤ

As the realization of oneness totally and completely passed through me I suddenly saw myself looking down at the earth as if from space. How beautiful she was: A blue and white jewel floating in an ocean of blackness. The sight of her was breathtaking, I felt so much love for our home, and it was pure adoration.

Here again words fail me for as I choose terms like 'love' and 'adoration,' I know that they are each nothing but an empty carcass of a word in comparison to the true feeling that had passed through me. Just like the colours for which I have no name, the word love is only an estimation, a mere hint of what really transpired as I simply do not have words to describe something, that is adoration to the power of a number with too many zeros to count.

It was completeness in every sense of the word. Just as science describes 'absolute zero' on the temperature scale, this then is an absolute that breaks the rule by becoming infinite.

Just as I was gazing at the blue jewel my attention came to a covering of grass upon it. I suddenly found myself staring at a patch of beautiful green grass at very close quarters. It was very green grass and seemed so vibrant, so much greener than any other grass I had seen and it shone with an aura that seemed a little spiky, but very bright.

My entire consciousness seemed to fill with the presence of these blades of super green grass. As I became more completely conscious of them I became aware that each blade of grass was not only emanating a luminescent colour but also a tone, a sound. The tone itself seemed a very high pitch, and not something I had ever heard before, certainly not at that particular octave, or however that could be measured.

What happened next still astounds me today and in that moment it was the deepest and most profound experience I had ever had. I suddenly became aware that each blade of grass not only emitted a sound but that each blade of grass had a *unique* tone. In that moment I realized that a unique tone was no different to the sounds we make that are called names.

Just as that happened I became simultaneously aware of every single blade of grass on each and every continent and island of the earth in one moment – as I perceived the unique tone of each blade of grass I became aware that the name of each of them was known and remembered by the Benevolence – it astounded me and even now as I write this I am moved to tears once again.

Not only was each name known, each and every blade of grass was deeply valued. From this vantage point I experienced the merging of each individual tone into a grand orchestra of grass beings across the planet. This music was unlike anything I had ever heard. I could only describe it as the most adoring celebration of life through music into which I was folded.

Not only could I hear the music, I was folded up into it and it was playing inside me as if the grass had sung a song just for me. I had previously heard the choir of forests when meditating amongst the trees, but this experience far outstripped any of those extra sensory experiences I had had whilst in the body.

As if this was not enough I unexpectedly saw beautiful white sand on a beach that was bordering an azure blue sea. The grains of white sand glistened in the bright sunshine and once again I found myself looking close enough to take in individual grains of sand.

What I noticed is that not all of them were white and each not only had a unique shape but were also composed of different materials. Surprisingly these grains of sand were not still. Although from a distance they simply looked like stationary grains of sand, right up close I could see that they were moving – there was a general agitation, they were vibrating and then the experience expanded to understand the vibration I could see – it was sound, it was music!

Just as each blade of grass had a unique tone, so too did the sand. My awareness continued to sharpen and expand until I was holding within myself every grain of sand from every beach and desert across the entire planet and I became fully aware that the Benevolence knew each of their names and heard each of their songs, united into a vast, harmonious orchestral melody that was the epitome of perfection and pure magnificence: each grain unfettered in its essence, just happy to be a grain of sand.

I gasped and I gasped and I gasped but nothing prepared me for what came next. What came next was holding the grass and the sand in my awareness, being aware of each of their unique notes, their names, their history and origins and their locations, but what I was not prepared for, beyond this expanded and yet infinitely detailed awareness, was that the Benevolence held each and every one of them as exquisite and precious beyond any words I have to describe it, with any justice or true meaning.

Love is such an impotent word. I was in a total and profound gasp of realization of something that perhaps only a poet could grasp, a realization of the truth of love; it was beyond any kind of love I had ever experienced and even today words fail me.

I prefer exquisite and precious as they indicate the possibility of their being a Benevolence that exists above and beyond the very impoverished states of love we, for the most part, experience here on Earth. And there I was, all of it rushing through me as I gasped and gasped and gasped. It was like being on a wonderful winding road in the wilderness when every corner that is driven around opens up to a new vista that is even better than the one before – one wonders, just how beautiful can this get?

It was so profound to have the direct experience and knowing that even a blade of grass and a grain of sand was adored by the Benevolence, adored by what I am at peace to claim was God. Yes, I met God.

That's the truth of it for me, I met God and God was good and kind and more benevolent than anything I could imagine. God loved me more than I can comprehend even on this day, for it is not something to be understood, only experienced.

The greatest gift beyond being in the presence of God was the merging. The gift of experiencing myself as being a part of That which resides everywhere and in everything, to know *that* even for a second, even for just one breath, is a gift worth more than a galleon filled with gold.

The tone of the experience changed and now I was looking at humanity. At first I could hear music, Mozart, Brahms, Verdi, African Drums, Mongolian Overtone Singers, Indian Classical Music, Ballet, Jazz, Hip Hop, Reggae, Flutes, Violins, Mexican Trumpets.

I could see painters, sculptors, chefs of all persuasions, artists of all kinds, great and wondrous canvasses covered in paint, human expression creating a landscape of beauty and sheer magnificence, inventors, writers, poets, embodiments of compassion, farmers who loved the land, and those who tended the animals in their care with great respect and kindness; I was moved by the magnificence and enthralled by our collective beauty.

Then the tone changed once more and now I saw bombs exploding and the limbs of women, children at home and young men sent to war flying through the air in a macabre display of human creativity in total distortion.

I could hear and see the horror of every rape on the planet, I could see and feel all of the living beings affected by oil spills, deforestation, pollution, chemical waste and by the sheer lack of respect shown to them. I saw wars, tanks, bullets, crime, hate; I saw political factions, the extremists and all those who claimed to have God on their side.

I was witnessing the darkest nightmares that humanity had created: Auschwitz, Rwanda, the Middle East, Cambodia and much, much more. There was so much contrast to all of the beauty I had just seen and celebrated.

Then the view shifted again. I could see and FEEL every mother who abused and beat her children; every mother who neglected and abandoned her children; every mother who spoke harsh and cruel words to them and then I saw and FELT each mother who adored her children, who held them in safety and cared willingly for each and every one of their needs and encouraged them with love to become who they were meant to become.

Then I saw all of the fathers who were violent with their children, all of the fathers who had abandoned their children or who took no interest in them; every father who had abused his child in every way possible. I saw all of the cruelty, all of the damage and all of the insanity.

And then I saw and FELT every father who worshipped and adored his children, who loved them more than he loved himself, who would give anything in selfless service to them, who protected them, educated them and guided them with gentle and kind leadership.

My focus now returned to viewing the blue jewel from a distance and all I experienced was God's peace and love for all I had witnessed. My focus returned back to humanity and I was shown every hair on every head of every human who lived and had ever lived and will ever live.

Each hair was known and like the grass and the sand, it too was held as something exquisite and precious. God said to me, *'If I love the hair on your head to that degree, then how much more do I love thee?'*

In that moment I looked down at myself as I lay in the hospital bed and my heart was filled with compassion for the man I could see. I could see all of his attempts at being good, all of his trying hard to become something; I could see that he was still caught up in the idea that one had to become good in the eyes of God.

In that, I once again lost the distinction between myself the individual and the Benevolence that I call God. I began to see myself as God sees me and I was moved beyond words and a great sense of relief overcame me, knowing that no matter if I failed or succeeded, there was nothing I could do to either win more of God's love or lose it.

The only thing standing between me, and the awake and aware experience of the Benevolence, was my allowance of it, my ability to surrender fearlessly to what had always been within me and around me. With this I suddenly found myself back in my body and I laughed, and I laughed, and I laughed.

My laugh continued all day and into the next too, and here and there for several days more after that. What I was laughing at was what seemed to be some sort of cosmic joke – all of the effort to become 'good', all of the effort to be 'important', 'make a difference', to gain some sort of absolution for everything humanity had ever done.

I laughed because everything I thought I needed and was looking for was either not true or was simply as close as my own heart.

It was the mother of all 'aha' moments, the 'aha' moment to silence all of the others, so I laughed and laughed and laughed and laughed at the futility of all of my efforting.

My dear friend, my eternal friend, the Benevolence, had never left, had not turned its face from me, had never forgotten me and indeed loved every hair on my head. How could I possibly get more of what was already complete? How could I get more love out of a love that already encompassed everything I both was and was not? It seemed hilarious to me and I laughed for days.

Much of my time in the days that followed was spent in silence and drifting in and out of sleep. I would often awake with a laugh or simply start talking about what, to some, could have been experienced as gibberish.

However, the friend taking care of me had the foresight to record what I was saying on his phone. Almost every time I would re-enter this reality from the dream world I would laugh at the illusion of it all – it was a Divine Comedy on the grandest of scales and what was even funnier is that most of the actors had become so wrapped up in their soap opera roles that they thought that this particular episode of 'the truly bold and very beautiful' was absolutely real.

It is also true to say that most of my laughter was at myself for I had been experiencing many varied layers of coming to the realization that much of what

I believed was simply not true, or seeing that it was a futile attempt to get something that I was already in possession of.

Some of this process also involved deep sobbing for I also touched in to the hurt I had inflicted on myself and others over the years. It was as if in these days nothing was hidden, everything was revealed and I no longer had the capacity to keep secrets from myself.

Deep sobs would emerge from within me; deep feelings of regret, and also the movement of feelings I had kept frozen. I had come face to face with my own broken heartedness at how I had walked away from the God of my childhood convinced that 'He' did not want to know me, that I was in some way truly bad and truly not welcome.

I had forgotten that I really did know the truth. I had forgotten my childhood anger that the church was telling so many lies about my dear friend God. When I was a child there was an old man who stood by the tree in the front garden of our home in Singapore. He was not a man that anyone else could see, and I would see him standing in front of what looked like a doorway to light and behind him was the same presence that I now recognize as the Benevolent.

I am so relieved to be able to swap the word 'God' for the Benevolent, for that is such a fitting name and title that tells far more truth than all of the distortions and lies we have been feeding one another about the nature of God.

The 'old man by the tree' would tell me that difficult times were ahead but that one day I would not only remember him and his presence but that all of the suffering would also be understood.

๑๑๑๑๑

A few days after my life changing experience with the Benevolent, I begged to be taken to the shopping mall. I had reached my limit of simply staring up at the ceiling and being confined within the plain coloured four walls. I needed air, I needed to see people, I needed smells beyond iodine, disinfectant and mustiness, and I wanted those smells to be replaced with the fragrance of Thai food!

As I sat in the open restaurant I gazed at people as they walked by. I was captivated by the knowledge and the experience that the Benevolent was visible everywhere. As each person walked by I would smile to myself, even giggle, for I began to recognize that, which I had merged with, as residing inside everyone.

I could suddenly pierce all of the levels of what they presented as themselves to see a reflection of the Benevolent as the magnificence of their inner being.

I would smile broadly to myself with joy, knowing in my heart that all was ok. My eyes fixed upon one man who looked all gnarled, grumpy and lacking in any modicum of joy. His shoulders reflected great burden and he looked to be in a permanent bad temper.

As I looked at him I laughed to myself, not to mock him, but in the realization that no matter how hard I tried I could only see the Benevolent in everyone. In my giggle I said inwardly to God, 'You almost had me there, you are the last I expected to see when I looked, that's a really good disguise,' and I laughed some more.

Immediately after that a woman who I would usually be inclined to feel at least some judgement for, walked on by. Her apparel was overtly sexual and I spotted the lustful looks of men and the condemning glares of other women. As I wondered how she could possibly walk in the shoes she had on, for they looked to me to be at least 90 degrees, the laugh came back as suddenly as the first time – there 'he' was again, the Benevolence in disguise.

I was chatting to God as if she was a good friend, with absolutely no need for formalities. I found myself saying, 'wow, very good disguise. Who would have thought it? It's perfect, you're setting up everyone for judgement, and there you are, concealing yourself as this woman everyone loves to judge or treat as an object. You nearly had me there, I almost did not spot you'.

This dialogue in the shopping mall continued for a while as I began to recognize the truth of the Benevolence in each and every person, simply walking by, and going about their business. What I was perceiving was a reflection of what I had experienced during my total merging with the Benevolence and it was telling me that that merging is always present, in everyone and in everything even when the other, or indeed myself, is not aware of it.

It was reminding me of the truth that sat hidden under layers of what we perceive to be reality. In those days I was relieved to be able to see beyond what I usually perceived; I was no longer seeing other people's auras as I usually do, the astral and ancestral world had become temporarily invisible to me, I could only see distilled truth and essence beyond any other expression, dimension or aspect of any one person or soul.

Within all of that, all was well. There was no suffering, no pain, and no pointlessness. There was only experience, consciousness and the awareness of the all-pervasive Benevolence.

On the fourth morning after my experience I woke up and 'it' was gone. Somehow I was back to my 'normal' self before any of that had happened. I felt it the moment my eyes opened and I was back to seeing the world we live in through my usual limited perception.

Something was very different, but I cannot deny that I felt quite crushed by this. The experience of acceptance, being fully loved and being the presence of love held me in a place of deep peace. I was deeply disappointed that the experience had come to an end and I even wondered what could have gone wrong. Why was I back to 'normal' again? A great anger arose in me and as I went about my day I once again could see and feel the suffering of humanity.

Once my anger at God for allowing me to slip back into the 'old' me had subsided I noticed that I had far more acceptance about not only the suffering I saw around me, but also more acceptance of my own suffering. The deep knowing that all will be ok and the memory of seeing the Benevolence everywhere assured me that I would be ok.

My period of adjustment lasted for several months, and in some ways life was much easier with a deeper sense of inner peace, and in some other ways, life was more challenging. In the days after my experience I came to realize and to notice that my sensitivity had increased along with my extra sensory perception.

I could see more, hear and, especially, feel much more. On the one hand my greatest gift is my sensitivity, on the other hand it is my greatest burden. What had definitely changed for me was that I no longer felt the need to hide my extra sensory perception, I no longer felt the need to hide the fact that I speak to frogs and sheep and trees and butterflies and all manner of animate and inanimate beings. Consciousness and souls had always been everywhere for me.

## Being OK with it all being OK

I am very well aware that much, if not all, of what I have shared will be a challenge to some, of the belief systems that abound regarding the nature of life, the nature of God and our place in the Universe.

For some, the very fact that I've stated clearly that there was only love, being held in exquisiteness, being cherished and adored for ALL beings and all things can be very disturbing.

It is disturbing because there is the question of 'what happens to the bad people?' One religion will tell us that they are destined to go to hell and yet another will say that they will spend aeons in purgatory or in separation until fully repentant. Yet others will tell us that their future lifetimes will be harsh, perhaps being born into great misfortune or even not as human but as a stray dog.

These beliefs in divine retribution, punishment, or as Karma operating as a kind of punishment and reward system, have done nothing at all to increase compassion and love on the planet: quite the opposite. Many take comfort in knowing that those who hurt them will one day get their 'comeuppance'.

This difficulty exists only when we hold onto the identity that we are a victim. Releasing the identity of being a victim is not the same as saying it did not matter or did not happen – for both of those statements are indeed true – it happened and it was important.

When we hold onto the identity of being a victim we are waiting for someone to make it all good again or to acknowledge us and we can also be holding onto the distortion that through the punishment and therefore the suffering of the other we will perhaps be relieved of our own suffering.

It simply does not work that way, and it never has. More often than not those who have wounded us are not even aware of what they have done, for they are likewise lost in the quagmire of their own story of suffering,

What religion promises us is that another, something and someone else will take care of the suffering and putting things right. When we have been a victim of crime, violence, sexual violation, war, theft and humiliation at the hands of another there is a journey that must be undertaken.

When we sit back and wait for retribution to catch up with those 'others' we are then in absolute denial of being a child of God. We are in denial of our divine capacity to face it all, for our heart to grow beyond where it once was. As I recovered from having a gun to my head I was at first struck with hatred, I was incensed that anyone could possibly have the audacity to do that to me.

The first awakening around that was a question that emerged from within me that asked, 'What makes you so special for it not to happen to you?' The question was both startling and humbling. Once again I had found myself arguing with reality.

Armed robberies were a fact of life in South Africa; this does not mean that I welcome them, or see them as good, it means that I accept that I am no different to my neighbour, or someone in the next suburb, so why shouldn't it happen to me? Why should I be immune? That was the first freedom.

The second freedom came quite some time after, perhaps two years. I had experienced many flashbacks to that night in question and on one such occasion I could feel the three men from the inside out. I could feel their lot, their destiny, their hardships and everything that had brought them to the decision to live the life of crime and violence that they were living.

I felt keenly how burdened they were by the weight of their crimes. As I sat with this there was more than a glimmer of compassion and tears began to run down my face. I sobbed and said quietly to them, 'I am deeply sorry for everything you have experienced and for every blind eye that has ever been turned away from you'.

In that moment I could feel my bond to them dissolve and I only felt good wishes for them. Whatever God, Karma or the law of the land would do with them was absolutely none of my business. I had transformed hatred and a strong need to punish them badly and cruelly into a deep realization that the journey of their souls had simply crossed my path for a reason that was important to me, but that whatever was important to them on their journey had nothing to do with me.

Furthermore there was the deepest realization that life and consciousness is relentless. We long for love, peace and a deep sense of who we are and so life throws circumstances onto our paths that seek to get our attention.

We have made the call to awaken, not only as individuals, but collectively as a species. We only need to look at some of the effects of war and natural disasters to witness how they are forces of great change and when we challenge the reality of them and say, 'it should never have happened' then we deny all of the growth and evolution that has sprung forth from it.

It is apparent to anyone who cares to look that the position and liberties of women in western culture have been totally transformed by the two world wars. This is undeniable. Have all of the problems been solved? No. But there has been an enormous cultural shift that has broken the power of a corrupt clergy and church over the general population and there is more balance between the genders than perhaps ever before.

All of this emancipation of women has ushered in an era of examining our culture's relationship to racial and ethnic minorities and to the reality of the existence through the ages of lesbian, gay, bi-sexual and trans-gender populations.

Could we have achieved all of this without the great pain and suffering of the two great wars? Yes. However, would we? The stark reality is that most of us do not budge an inch until we are in pain. WWII in particular showed us the depth of our darkness and just how far from the light we had fallen.

It ushered in an era where unjust imperial rule started to crumble and the imbalances of power started to be re-dressed. All great leaps of consciousness usually need to be kick started, just like my own personal process and no doubt you have already identified some of your own as you read these words.

Had the feminine not seen the beginnings of liberation after centuries of subjugation, and had the power of the church not likewise been contested then the emergence of new spirituality that had been ushered in, in part by The Beatles in the 1960s, would probably not have taken place.

Today there are dozens of publishers dedicated to the work of publishing books like this one, read by people like you. We may bemoan 'big brother' and we complain of corporate and governmental corruption, however, in the west in particular, we have the freedom and the time to look at our lives and to listen to alternate views from many different sources instead of one singular teaching being handed down from the pulpit.

This is the truth of the evolution of consciousness. The invitation here is to discover it for yourself; discover if it is really true that all is already forgiven; discover that it is perhaps absolutely true that once you fall into the heart, that what is revealed is that love is the only certainty worth considering, for all else pales in comparison.

☙☙☙☙☙

When we give too much attention to what is 'supposed' to happen to the perpetrators or object on the grounds that it appears that they are getting away with it, with no accountability, then we are simply stuck in fear.

It is either the fear that 'they' are out there or it is the fear of facing what is inside of us. If you have been drawn to this book, its very title tells me that if you are reading this then somewhere inside of you is a light that flickers in your heart and that you want to know yourself more truly and fully.

When we only concern ourselves with our own business, the business of our own heart, of our own shadow, with the business of our own hatreds, jealousies, fears and our own belief in our lack and worthlessness, then we are fee to encounter and transform the very things that keep peace, love and happiness from our door.

If we continue to teach that hating others is wrong, through hating the haters, what is to become of us? Where do we stop? How do we determine who is to be hated and just how much or little they need to be cast out, rejected or deemed 'less than' the rest of us?

What we must be prepared to look at is our overall contribution to the planet. When we rage against those 'bad' people over there, when our whole focus is pointing out who and what is wrong, then our net contribution to life on earth is hatred, rage and anger.

What if you were to realize that all of your anger is but a diversionary tactic? What if you were to see, feel and know, without a shadow of doubt, that all of the hating, the fighting and the resisting of those who are bad is simply an avoidance of something much, much bigger? What if you were to know for certainty that in reality all of your anger is not real, really, it is not real. It feels real, it even sounds real, and its effects on others are surely real too.

However the stark reality is that our rage, our anger, our protest and our ranting have a function that we ourselves have assigned to them because we are deeply afraid to feel what is underneath all of that.

What is underneath all of that is a heart that yearns for peace, a heart that yearns to be free to love once more as we did when we were but young and innocent children. What we are truly afraid of is what I call the Profound Grief that hides in the shadow behind all of the anger, all of the hatred, all of the ranting and all of the righteous indignation.

The Profound Grief seeks to mourn the loss of innocence and for every ounce of essence that life and experiences robbed you of. The Profound Grief is the truth behind all of your need to punish others and when we meet it, truly meet it, truly surrender to it, we fall into the fires of Shiva who lovingly burns off all of our stories and then we fall upon the sword of Michael who cuts open our heart and flicks away the husk that we believed was protecting us but in fact was keeping us separate.

What I know is that none of us can be at peace with the world until we are at peace with ourselves. We so seek to punish ourselves, perhaps for simply daring to be happier than a parent or a sibling, or for having more than others or in the belief that there is something wrong with us.

The deeper we face our own versions of separation the more able we are to see the truth of what is. I do not know what happened with the souls and destiny of individuals such as Stalin, Hitler, Pol Pot and Idi Amin. What I do know is that just as my own armed robber's fate was created by the collective negligence of a culture, a government and of many people, I know for sure that these despots were created by us in the same way.

All such actions have at their core two things: deep separation from Self and the Self-hatred that keeps the split in place. Self-hatred emerges from repeatedly having our essence ignored, rejected or made to feel unwelcome. Which one us have never done this? Which of us has never turned away from the truth?

None of what I've offered is suggesting that we do away with our legal systems and protections against such individuals, for when an individual is marching down the road of destruction then we very often do need to protect ourselves. However, protecting ourselves and joining in a feeding frenzy of hatred are two different things.

The progress of humanity is slower than our personal progress, and the more of us who give up waiting for the world to change and fall back on ourselves, on our own responsibility to bring the light into the depths of our shadows, the quicker the world will transform in front of our very eyes.

# At Peace with God

Despite having extra sensory perception for the greater part of my life, none of what I could see, sense and feel had healed my deep wound with my relationship to God, that had been deeply affected at the hands of two established religions: the Catholicism of my childhood and a period of being a Jehovah's Witness in my teenage years.

Even though I had had the direct experience of the 'man by the tree', I still submitted as a child to the authority of the church. In fact it was one of my deepest longings, and perhaps it still is, to be a priest, although my concept of service through priesthood is very different today.

Like many young Catholics I was an Altar Boy. I loved it for I felt close to God and I loved being in the church building itself. I knew that in some way I was a burden to the priests for they would get impatient with my incessant questioning. I simply wanted to know everything.

One day as we were preparing for mass the other boys were late and it was just me and the priest alone with the preparations. I was rushing and forgot to genuflect before the altar as I scuttled past it. The priest turned to me and said 'Don't run so fast, you'll upset the Angels,' to which I replied 'But there are no angels, they don't come until you hold up the sacrament'.

In that moment of innocent truth telling I knew that I had erred. It was either after mass on that day, or later, that I was told that being an altar boy and a priest was not the path for me for all of my questions simply displayed a lack of faith.

I could not understand why these men appeared not to know God as I did or to love Him as I did. I left feeling cold and shut out. I never returned to that church and ceased going to mass from that day onwards.

My second foray into religion came, together, with great upheavals and difficulties in a home life that was marred with violence, neglect and sexual abuse. The promise of a paradise to come sounded very appealing when I was being bullied at school and even worse, dreaded coming home, more than anything.

Finally after three years of indoctrination and a six month period of voluntarily living with a Jehovah's Witness family as a means of escaping a very unsafe home, I was ousted from the religion on the grounds of being a 'homosexual'. I've placed the quotes around that word for that is how it was said: As if it was a mental or physical disease, some kind of pathology or an evil.

More than just being ousted there was a 'trial' during which I had to confess all of my 'sins'. As an adult looking back at this systematic and public form of humiliation, I have to question what type of men want to know the exact detail of my so called transgressions – all the way down to specific activities and details of the sexual encounter.

The excommunication, or disassociation form their organisation was very painful. As a teenager all of my friends were in that church and overnight, I had not one. I had escaped the violence and insanity of my family home and now found myself at the age of 19 friendless and rejected by God.

All of that, coupled with TV images of gay people being mocked and stereotyped through overly camp and effeminate roles and society's general homophobia, made me believe that I was a reject, in need of total redemption. I would pray and pray and pray to God to make me straight. I even married very briefly at the age of 19 in the hope that it would go away.

I also believed for a while that my natural feminine feelings would save me if I had gender-reassignment surgery. I believed that if I could achieve that, I could marry a man, be a straight woman and be good and clean in the eyes of God.

That is how far down the rabbit hole I went. Confusion around my gender identity had always been present and I very often felt like a girl in a boy's body, however, the Jehovah's Witness condemnation to certain death turned all of that into a desperate attempt to rid myself of something I saw as bad and evil.

ಬಲ

Many decades have passed since then and my relationship with the Divine has transformed from one based on fear and shame to one that now blossoms again through the inspiration of my guru Amma (Mother) and my love for Kirtan and nature.

My experience in the hospital in Thailand brought a chapter of my life to a close. During that experience I returned once more to my early childhood certainty that God is good and is not to be feared.

As I write this book I am reminded of the desire of a very young boy who said that he wanted to be a priest so that he could tell the truth about his friend God for so many were telling lies. Perhaps nothing at all has changed. Perhaps what has happened is that it has taken me more than four decades to return to the truth of my longing – which is to speak of the things of God.

Having read this book this far, then you will already realize that I too made a lie my story and took it on as part of my identity – the boy who was not wanted by God. Of course as children and teenagers we naturally acquiesce to the beliefs and edicts of our elders, for they are the authorities and we assume that they know all matters better than we do.

When contradicted by adults when we are children our automatic response is to make ourselves wrong. When not seen for what it is, a compromise designed to keep us safe, help us fit in or as insurance for our very survival this pattern can follow us into adulthood.

With each and every event that has forced me to either die or open my heart again, the abundant presence of that which knows no decay, that which is forever youthful, that which is beauty in all of its manifestations becomes more and more apparent to me. I sing to the trees and they sing back to me.

What I also absolutely know is that the only way to heal ourselves of all of the hurt, of all of the blame, of all of the hatred and self-hatred, is to be willing to tell the absolute truth.

That takes dedication, commitment and courage. Truth is not convenient, it rocks the boat and it means that we must relinquish the control we have on relationships. Truth is ruthless, not in the manner of its speaking, for when the truth is spoken it emanates from the heart. However, it is ruthless inasmuch as once it is spoken the ripples are irreversible.

I would not volunteer quickly to skid in mud on a motorcycle again and end up enduring the pain of having necrotised flesh removed. However, if I had the power to go back in time and prevent those events – I would not, I could not.

How can I measure the gift of knowing once and for all that we are all truly and deeply and completely held as exquisite and precious? How can I value the experience of not only seeing God but merging with the magnificence and completeness of that we have come to call God?

For me, today I use the term 'the Benevolence' for that seems to be a far better description of the truth of God that belies the 'god' of vengeance, jealousy and retribution that so many of us were raised with.

When we're raised with a God of wrath, violence, punishment and eternal damnation it reflects in the worshippers of that God and their treatment of one another, of minorities and of their children.

It is sad that the many churches built upon the words of Paul, who was not one of the original twelve, have steeped themselves in the tribal God of war and the anguish of Paul, instead of the Sacred Heart of our Lord Jesus, who sits equally with the other great Sons of God, the Buddha, Krishna and others.

Now perhaps it is time for the great Daughters of God to reveal themselves in an era when the masculine is becoming more balanced with the influence of the feminine.

It makes no real difference whether we pray to a deity or simply speak to our own heart. Devotion to the path of personal truth is the path of the heart, which leads to the discovery of self and to the discovery of God, for one cannot happen without the other, it is simply that way.

Under all of our layers of defence is a crucible of innocence that burns brightly with a love that is both greater than ourselves and defines who we truly are — without mask or pretence, authentically you, authentically me.

This is our deepest longing.

# CHAPTER 7

# Devotion

One of my favourite stories of devotion is that of Hanuman, the Hindu monkey God. To appreciate this story was quite a journey for me for the mere image of a monkey God challenged, and dare I say, offended my ingrained Christian sensibilities.

I had been invited by friends to attend a concert by Krishna Das in San Francisco. As I walked into the venue, a church building, I saw pictures of a curiously human looking monkey's face dotted all over the place. There were CDs and books for sale with the same image. I learned that this was the image of Hanuman, the revered Hindu monkey God.

In my mind there was a certain ridiculousness about it, how nonsensical was it to bow to what is clearly a mythical creature, half man, half monkey. However, as a lover of music I was not deterred and as my friends had raved about the man we were about to see, I was able to put my prejudice to one side and ignore the monkey.

I sat in the pews with my intimate gathering of friends and wondered how the evening would turn out. Krishna Das appeared on the stage and took his place seated, with what I was later to learn, was a traditional Indian instrument called a harmonium. He began to talk and the more he spoke with his deep voice and eloquence, more and more tears began to flow down my cheeks.

In part my mind was wondering why I had been so moved, I hadn't heard any profound insight that had given me an 'aha' moment, I hadn't heard some profound and deep spiritual mystery – none of that. As he spoke about his Guru, Neem Keroli Baba, what I witnessed was a man deeply in love with his Guru, with God and with the riches of his own heart.

His devotion was palpable, it filled the auditorium and similarly filled my own heart. As I left the concert later that evening I bought the monkey book and on returning home I sat up in bed and read it to completion in the wee hours. For more than a year I played the Hunuman Chalisa on my laptop, my iPod, listened to it on long flights and plugged it in to any and all rental cars when making trips – it had become my road trip song, I called it my 'happy song'.

Hanuman was a servant to Lord Ram and his consort Sita. Lord Ram is said to be an Avatar of Vishnu, in other words, a direct incarnation, or 'son of God', similar to Christ, Buddha and Krishna; the divine in human form. After fighting many battles and carrying out acts of courage on behalf of his lord and master, Sita offered hanuman a pearl necklace as a sign of her gratitude.

Hanuman on taking the pearl necklace bit into it, causing much alarm in the royal court. 'Why do you do such a thing?' the courtiers exclaimed. Hanuman replied, 'Unless my beloved Lord Ram and Sita are inside these pearls they are of no use to me'. The courtiers retorted with, 'They are right in front of you, how can they be inside the pearls?' With that, using his strong monkey like hands, Hanuman grasped his chest and ripped it open.

To everyone's astonishment the names of God were etched and written on each of his ribs and Rama and Sita were seated on their thrones inside his heart. Hanuman is seen, to this day, as a symbol of 'bhakti' – a Sanskrit word meaning 'devotion', and is regarded as the original bhaktau, the first to be identified as a devotee.

The Vedas themselves point to the importance of devotion in the Brahma Samhita with the words 'vedesu durlabam a durlabam atma bhaktau' – which means 'the understanding of the Vedas are sealed, except to the devoted one'.

It is not my purpose here to present the path of devotion as part of either a doctrine or as a religious edict, because then it would be truly misunderstood and lose its power and purity. Whenever we attempt to do or become something as a means of 'becoming good' – it loses both its life and its meaning, often leading to sculpted acts of devotion that have more to do with either piety or obedience than the way of the heart.

Throughout this book I've been asking the same question over and over again – are you willing to tell and to know the absolute truth? Once we begin to fully realize that the 'truth' is NOT the story we've been telling, but rather the deeper truth of the bonds of love that remain intact, perhaps damaged, under the story of our lives we can tell the story of having not been wanted and that story can be absolutely true and provable.

However, when this story is identified with and told repeatedly as something that defines us, it becomes a distorted way of avoiding a much deeper truth. When we feel unwanted what can lurk in the shadows is the belief that there surely must be something wrong with us to cause a parent or guardian not to want us. We were an innocent child of God, so how is it possible that we are not wanted?

രരരര

The path of Devotion is none other than a path of being devoted to the heart – to its discovery in all of its magnificent colours and the yet to be revealed caverns. As we reveal the layers that have kept us from our deepest longing for the heart to know itself as love, we can enjoy more peace and more meaningful connection to people, to nature and to all of life.

The heart is indeed the centre of our being, the centre of our personal Universe, it contains many aspects of who we are, the discovered and undiscovered landscapes of our human potential.

When we are centred in the heart we are at peace and we easily let go of opinions, stories and the drama of life. As we release the stories we begin to hear the language of the heart that is so intensely, deeply and profoundly silent that it becomes an ever-present whisper that beckons us with its call.

It feels good and deeply fulfilling to allow ourselves the freedom to love for it is part of our essential nature, it is indeed the truth of who we are. What is so very painful is a closed heart, one that is too afraid to love again, or too afraid to love too deeply or to love the wrong people for fear of ridicule or rejection.

As we make the absolute choice that peace is far more important than being right we are then supported by the heart to see what is really true through the eyes of authentic compassion – not the kind of learned compassion that seeks to see everything in a positive light, but in the depth of compassion that is able to pierce the veil wrapped around any story and embrace suffering in all of its moods, shades and colours.

Authentic compassion is deeply empathetic and recognizes the profound loss in both the self and in the other, no matter the actions of the other. When we are devoted to the path of the heart and to simple truths we have an increased capacity to lament the losses of those who have hurt us and to recognize just how often we ourselves have denied our deepest of longings out of fear of rejection or the fear that we will be solitary in our ability to love others as they are, making us vulnerable and defenceless.

The source of all human suffering originates with the limitations we have placed upon our own heart. We often wait in hope that someone else will love us enough to awaken us, or we wait impatiently for the world to wake up. Our fear of vulnerability is our Achilles heel. We long for connection, we long for peace, we long for the freedom that an open heart gives us and yet we sit in our prison cell often waiting for others to make the first move.

Our early formative experiences told us that it was not safe to be open hearted in a world that was harsh and demanded that we be a certain way in order to fit in with its expectations of us.

Eventually we capitulated so often and so completely that for a while, at least, we forgot about the depth of our being, the depth and capacity of our love and about the depth of our longing to know ourselves as we truly are and to know God, the great mystery of all life.

We came into this world knowing that the single goal of our lives was the great unfolding of the heart and that within it rests the Universe, the realm of all possibilities. All this, while we have known that the heart is the centre of our being and the crucible that nurtures everything we have ever longed for, wished for and truly desired.

When we rediscover our heart we encounter immeasurable dimensions of love which includes the fascination for all living things, not just human beings, but also wildlife, nature, trees, even stones. We begin to recognize that the foundation of all of existence is this love we have begun to taste. We begin to see it and meet it everywhere, including within that which had seemed so very unlovable.

๏๏๏๏๏

The deeper story of Hanuman is not that he was dedicated to a God that was outside of himself and the story was not necessarily telling us that a part of his God or Deity was inside of himself; the lesson is that through Devotion we can uncover the greatest mystery of realizing that the Divine is within us, inseparably, as it is revealed that we are one and the same.

When great teachers such as Christ proclaimed 'you can only get to the Father through me', it was their heart they were pointing to – for in the heart all is one, there is not separation, there is no distinction.

There are indeed colours and moods, flavours and nuances, as we can witness in the presence of the spirit of Christ, Buddha and Krishna, or lose ourselves entirely in the words of Rumi, St. Augustine, St. Teresa of Alvila, Hafiz and others who wrote so affectionately about the Beloved.

## The Path to Freedom - Truth

As we become willing to tell the absolute truth the path of awakening our heart becomes more about deconstructing what we have become and who we think we are so that we may return to not who we were meant to be, but return to who we truly are.

There is no *trying* to become who we truly are, there is only surrender. There is no forcing open of the metal manacles that gird our heart, there is only releasing our tight grip on it. The longest journey is indeed the shortest distance; all we have sought is as close as our very own heart.

It is a doorway to endless dimensions of unconditional love to which we have access when we are authentically grounded in the longing to know the truth of who we are beyond chasing images, wishful thinking, projections and expectations of who we think we should be or what we've heard will define us as good.

An open heart knows nothing else but the truth of our existence, it is whole and complete within itself. It requires no other to complete it, to sustain it, for it is a self-sustaining fulcrum of light and pure consciousness that has never been lost.

It is the abode of the eternal, of the Beloved, both the doorway to and the resting place of that which is eternal. Without the heart all is temporary and has very little meaning: with the heart, everything is eternal.

For if we once loved someone, where did the love go? Did it disappear? Was it consumed in a fire? Was it cast off like a spell into oblivion? Certainly not, for love is eternal.

Once we have loved someone, no matter for how long and who it is, the love does not go away. We may fool ourselves by turning a blind eye to the endless flickering of the flame of love, but it remains only shrouded in tales of betrayal, loss, bereavement and abandonment.

As we struggle with forgiveness we come to realize that our struggle is founded upon the lie that love does not live here any longer. We deny the love we once had for someone for that would appear to be easier for us than to face the pain of loss. As we face the pain of loss, the pain of betrayal and the pain of not having been met fully for who we are, we can once again uncover and allow the love we once had to reveal itself as a love that never actually went away.

As this most precious love reveals itself then we have no choice but to finally face the loss, face the forfeiture of the paradise that once existed between us, the paradise that is the heart in its open state. We never truly fall out of love with anyone, we simply shy away from the pain of loss, betrayal and disappointment.

Gradually as we awaken more and more to the vastness of our heart we begin to see that truth is the oxygen that feeds the heart and that without it we starve in the darkness of all of the stories we grip onto in the blind hope that somehow we'll end up being happy despite hiding in the shadows of self-deception.

What must be realized is that truth is not our 'take' on something, it is not a reasoned explanation, it is not our version of reality, it is not our opinion – the truth is in essence accepting what is.

The truth says, 'it is a great pity that things went the way that they did, for I loved you very much'; the truth says, ' despite everything my father did to me, there is a great love in my heart for him'; the truth says, ' no matter what other people expect of me, I simply cannot wish her ill fortune'; the truth says, 'my greatest heartbreak is not that my family neglected and abused me, it is that my love was not enough to save them from their darkness.'

When we become devoted to the truth, we start to uncover its immense capacity to be the crucible in which the power of love becomes boundless.

We cling to our stories and we limit telling and facing the truth, as we have bought into the illusion that we can control others. We withhold in the hope of keeping relationships alive whilst we wait for someone else or something else to change. We are afraid that if we truly express how we feel and allow our fear, shame or guilt to be seen then others will likewise abandon us.

Those we seek to control through not revealing who we are, in most likelihood are singing the same song and dancing to the same tune – they in turn are hoping to control you and their relationship with you, with more focus on feeling safe than on the love that exists, and both parties end up wondering why they feel so unhappy and unfulfilled.

Devotion to the heart, and therefore to the truth is not for the faint hearted. With the truth we risk everything. Every relationship, everything we've ever known, every belief we have ever held, every image we have ever chased, every dogma we have obeyed, every concept we've viewed the world through, our notion of God, our vision of who we are or ought to be and the images of who others are or ought to be...... all of it, every single last shred of it is at absolute risk of crumbling into the fires of eternal destruction as we commit and surrender to truth.

What most of us are hoping for is that we can keep a little contradiction in place: not much, just a little, a little lie here and there, a little Self-denial tucked away here or there, and yet still realize an awakened heart. The truth is fierce and ruthless, not in its delivery, but in the aftermath of the emergence of its bright light. Shadows and facades fade and crumble, and along with many things we thought we had under control.

When we invite truth in, we invite swords that slice us open and fires that turn once cherished belief systems into ashes, into the remnants of a life once lived.

In the Hindu pantheon of deities the once feared Goddess Kali can be revered as the conduit of this fiery energy that burns through illusion and delusion. She stands fiercely with severed heads, a rich symbol of what must happen if we are to truly enter the Kingdom of the Heart, the abode of the Beloved, the most sacred place in all of creation.

Indeed we must lose our head, we must surrender logic, reason and stories of woe.

◎◎◎◎◎

The truth is not convenient and can be unpalatable, and not because it is spoken harshly but because once it is heard, seen and felt, it becomes undeniable, making it increasingly difficult to clutch onto all of those things we were still seeking to control, out of the fear of having or being nothing once we relinquish all control.

The irony is that when we surrender to the truth of the heart we lose nothing but illusion. When our lives are pierced by the truth of the heart, rather than being nothing, we realize our own fullness, and nothing else can give us that.

What most of us are hoping for is that somehow, in some way, some condition, person, object or lover will give us finally what we did not get enough of when we were in our formative years.

We can hold out for years on end, keeping as much under control as possible, ducking every opportunity to face what we've been running from, in the vain hope that some strategy, new way of thinking, new partner or new belief will finally fill the gap between what is longed for and what was not given.

We have hoped in vain all of our lives that finally something or someone will provide us with the experience of love and fulfilment. However, we end up experiencing the impermanence of this so many times and the deep disappointment that accompanies this that we often simply become afraid to love and so we live our lives behind a closed heart, or one that yearns to fulfil its potential but is kept reigned in.

At long last we have to come to the conclusion that we have to give up, really give up. Inwardly we are guided towards saying the words, 'Mother, I give up,' or 'Father, I give up'. Inwardly we may have to say to our life partner or spouse, 'I'm sorry, I asked too much of you, you cannot give me what they couldn't'.

This is when we start to see the truth of our own strategies and our own self-deception. We begin to see the status quo we've set up in relationships, and how we have possibly put our entire lives on hold, just waiting for someone to give us what we didn't have, which is in stark contrast to the truth of who we are once we have the courage to face the Profound grief.

We must come to the full realization that our protection has become our prison and that fear is the jailer keeping guard outside our cold and lonely solitary confinement cell.

◎◎◎◎◎

The path of devotion is twofold. On the one hand it is the willingness to tell the absolute truth about ourselves and surrender to the purity of that, on the other hand, it is also the longing to realize the truth of others, of the world and to pierce each and every single veil that covers our view of the world.

This twofold journey is in fact the main purpose of the pilgrimage that we call our lives. The heart reveals it all. Once we start to view ourselves, and others, through the heart, we also begin to witness and experience the world as the heart does.

When that happens the many worlds that our heart has doorways to, begin to open. No longer is a tree just a tree, no longer is a mountain just a mountain, no longer is a rose just a rose.

As the heart truly begins to open with truth supporting its every move, new worlds are revealed to us and our perception of the nature of reality begins to shift. We begin to sense that we are not only islands of consciousness but that we are swimming in an ocean of awareness, consciousness and pure life force that is aware of itself.

One of my most profound experiences was when, after having received dar-shan (a blessing) from Amma, the hugging saint, my usual perception of the consciousness, spirit and aliveness in a tree shifted.

For the first time I felt the tree's curiosity about my existence and its relation-ship to me. This was profound beyond words. I was accustomed to seeing the en-ergy fields around trees and I had from time to time heard the beautiful orchestral sound they omit, but nothing prepared me for the 'hello,' I received, and what a hello it was – glorious!

What we witness is that everything is alive and that we can interact with all of it. We suddenly wake up realizing we had been a fish looking for water in the middle of the ocean. Devotion brings us into this ocean of consciousness because every non-truth we either told ourselves or lived out as 'not us,' simply brought us into deeper and deeper levels of separation from the multifaceted reality of who we are.

In reality, we are far more magnificent than anything the mind could conjure up and yet to realize this we must be willing to suspend almost everything we thought was true. If we look to the Gods' to bless us for having been good, pure or pious we are simply affirming that we are not 'that' which we are seeking – we are simply affirming that underneath all of the layers is the hidden belief that we are bad.

If we are to embody the teachings of all the great masters then we must at least be willing to believe that all that we seek is within. A grand and important key to this transition is the healing of our foundational wound. If we do not approach our early childhood wounding then we will forever project our relationship with our parents directly onto any Gods' we worship or pay respect to.

We will expect reward for obedience to a teaching, we will look to them to give us what we need as if we have no ability or must await permission. As we heal our foundational wound, not only do our relationships on the whole transform, especially the one with ourself, but our relationship with the Divine also transforms – it matures and becomes a joint journey of discovering the Gods' both within and around us.

# Bhakti

Bhakti, or rather Bhakti Yoga, is a path of devotion to God as defined in Hinduism through faith, song and ritualistic practice as a means of attaining the realisation of God.

Of course if you are a Christian reading these words the thought of devoting yourself to one of the many aspects of the Divine as manifest through Hinduism may not be appealing. In reality, it makes no difference, for in truth, devotion to God is indeed devotion to the heart and each great avatar or deity serves as a doorway into our own heart.

If we are fortunate enough to fall in love with a Guru, or a Deity, what becomes reflected is our heart's own truth. As we devote ourselves to the heart, we devote ourselves to the longing to be free to love and for our heart to know itself as love.

When we employ a doorway of devotion through the likeness of Christ, Buddha, Hanuman, Ganesh, Shiva, Devi or a Guru for example, we begin to uncover our deep spiritual longing for union with the Beloved, with the eternal flame that has burnt since before time began.

Bhakti, or devotion, is simply a means by which we can experience the depths and capacity of our heart to expand exponentially. Some come to the path of Bhakti seeking bliss, and still others redemption. However, when it is truly understood to be an expression of our devotion to the heart above all things and devotion to scrupulous truth, the rewards are immeasurable.

As we lose our outer selves in love for the Divine we have moments of profound silence in which we experience many flickers and moments of love for ourselves – this takes the form of truly appreciating the wealth that is our own heart. We become humbled by the realization that everything that we thought of as being God, or Christ, Buddha or Krishna is in fact inside us, is indeed *us*.

The sure indication that we have met something truly authentic within our heart, is that we are taken out beyond a blissful experience into the grand humility of knowing that there is the presence of something far greater than ourselves and yet this resides within us as the breath of God that breathes us as an extension of divine purpose and will.

Every spiritual path that is open to us can be used as a means for escape or as a way for meeting what is truly within us.

๏๏๏๏๏

Chanting and the recitation of prayers eventually lead to stillness of the mind and we can luxuriate in the silence once our mantra has been chanted and our prayer has been offered. It is in this silence that we can surrender to whatever is present.

If we enter devotional practice with the expectation that we will always feel good, or even blissful, then its purpose has not been understood: devotional practices, or the path of Bhakti, has the purpose of bringing us to the realization of God.

In order for us to realize the Divine we must experience ourselves, and the world, through our heart and the very opening of the heart is supported and initiated by our willingness to know the absolute truth. Truth destroys entire worlds, entire belief systems; it can destroy a way of life.

Therefore, as we surrender to devotion, all that has kept our hearts in chains and subjugation to images and dogma can reveal itself as it is – that which keeps the heart closed.

We clutch at dogma in order to feel safe. It may come from a need to belong, to be a part of a group in which everyone believes the same thing and it may come from a need to have some rules, some goalposts, to have some measurement of where we are and where we need to get to, in order to achieve something or to reach the next level of being 'good'.

The path of devotion is not about doing it correctly, it is not about achieving some imagined goal, level or status, although one could argue that the goal is the realization of God: that realization only comes through total surrender to what is here already.

For this deeper level of surrender to take place, we must be willing to be with what is, we must be willing to know the truth of who we are without masks, pretences and the deceptive promises made by our own piety which only seeks to keep us separate from that which we long for.

The false Self that we have constructed in defence of our wound of separation is willing to take us into the depths of devotional practice but ultimately seeks to negotiate its own survival. It wants to have the realization of God and keep itself in place. This is the grand deception. The false self will tell you exactly what you want to hear and when you want to hear it. It will tell you that you already know the truth, it will tell you that you are special, perhaps even a more favoured devotee, or even a chosen one.

It will convince you of the right way and the wrong way, the better way and will lead you perhaps into many blissful experiences that are more focused in the upper chakras than in the truth of the heart. We may have many profound spiritual experiences in which we see and come into contact with dimensions of life that exist beyond the limitations of physical reality.

Perhaps we see angelic beings, spiritual guides, and the manifestations of Deities and the many realms of light. With all of that we can be fooled into giving it some sort of meaning in terms of progress towards our goal.

These experiences can become addictive. So much so, there are many who are willing to throw themselves at the feet of so called 'shamans', 'gurus' and 'medicine men' for the promise of having just one more induced spiritual experience, with the hope they will get that one precious insight or answer that will solve all of their problems and eradicate suffering forever.

This is one of the worst deceptions of the false self, it bandies itself about like a spiritual whore who must simply get the next bliss fix. Far removed from bliss is the call to face everything we feared we might be and never wanted to be so that we can resolve once and for all the self-hatred and rejection that has kept us in the lonely place of separation.

When we step away from trying to please God and surrender to our longing to know the truth of who we are, our worship takes on a whole new dimension. Rather than paying obeisance to a God we imagine as an individual with needs and requirements, we begin to experience the Divine as an extension of our own heart and as the love that pervades all of existence – be that existence a sparrow, a sprig of grass, a cloud, mountain, child, man, woman or the stars in the night sky.

Until now we have clung to our own suffering and imprisonment out of confusion and fear. The path of Devotion affords us the opportunity to be nourished once more in the wellspring that is the wealth of our very own heart. As we begin to drink once more from the nectar of our heart, the fear that causes us to keep ourselves in prison begins to dissolve.

If we are saying that God is indeed one and the same as that which exists in our own heart, then why do we bow to a likeness of Krishna, Christ, Buddha, Durga or Kwan Yin and offer them our devotion?

As previously written our foundational wounding is seen and felt as an energy in the lower belly, much of it housed in and around our relational chakra – the second chakra or Swadisthana chakra.

This chakra houses and expresses our consciousness in the realms of relationships, emotional needs, pleasure and joy. This chakra formed at a very young age and most of its distortions and dysfunction find their roots in our formative years, the years in which we related to objects very easily and importantly; our best friends were perhaps soft toys.

If the path of Bhakti is to be a part of our path to healing and becoming whole, we must learn how to form healthy relationships with objects that are based on love. It is the younger part of us that that needs to see the figure of Jesus, that needs to be held in the arms of Mary, who needs to behold the beauty of Krishna and to experience the compassion of Buddha.

When our split is deep we can perhaps prefer to only conceive of God as a higher power or simply as an intelligence that pervades everything. However, whilst that is also true, on a path of healing this can become problematic as we may be attempting to heal one chakra with the consciousness of another.

That which is without form, omnipresent and yet unmanifest, cannot be felt consciously by our lower chakras for as the second chakra is our relational chakra, we need a form to relate to.

What is important to state here is that as we sit in devotion and our energy field opens up, we can start with a focus on the object of Buddha, Kwan Yin or Ganesh, but as our heart truly opens in devotion for the object of our love we can naturally follow this flow into the deep silence of formlessness, a realm that pulsates with life in which everything and nothing exists simultaneously.

In essence we have taken a journey up through the stacked layers of chakra consciousness. We start to relate from our lower chakras and as they open and become energized, their energy begins to move up the body to support the heart with its opening. An open heart is supported by the opening of our first two chakras, without this opening, it is difficult for us to sustain an open heart.

As a form of healing, the path of devotion can offer us a safe environment in which to open our heart again, from there we can start to feel safe enough to love ourselves once more, other people and eventually the world. Now that you understand how the path of Bhakti, or devotion, can be a part of your healing, it is important to look at the various avenues open to us as a part of practice.

## Prayer, Mantras, Kirtan, and Song

There is great power in repetition and by repetition I mean repeating the same words or actions for several minutes during our time of practice. Repetition has a hypnotic effect on the mind which allows our thoughts to finally become still.

If we sit and simply try to quieten our mind we are more often than not unsuccessful. The power of repetition is that we can create a stillness within ourselves that is deep enough for that which is beyond our normal sensory perception of ourselves, and the world, to reach us. We can be touched deeply by our own inner light, by spiritual guidance, by ancestors and indeed by deities.

During my own practice I have frequently been visited by many different types of energies ranging from deceased relatives and friends, to profound experiences of Christ and Krishna, by the love of my Guru, animal spirits and many beings from the shamanic realms.

## Prayer

The root tradition of your prayers makes no real difference. The prayers themselves can come from any tradition as long as the focus is on expressing love, honour or surrender. The repetition of the prayer will have the desirable effect of taking you out of thought and into greater silence. The effect of a prayer is to give the mind something to focus on instead of expending its energy on needless mental chit-chat and worry.

What is important is that there is repetition. The Divine can best reach us when the mind is quiet. The altered state achieved during the hypnotic repetition of prayer not only summons forth the presence of God but also prepares us to be in deep silence for the receiving of that presence and whatever awareness presents itself.

When our mind is occupied with distraction there is no doorway open for greater or deeper awareness.

## Mantras

The use of Mantras in Hindu Vedic tradition stretches back at least 3,000 years, and some scholars suggest many more millennia than that. What is often not apparent to many who first encounter mantras is that a mantra, rather than being simply a verse with literal meaning, is a collection of syllables.

Each syllable has a specific energy, planet, colour and vibration associated with it. What the chanting of a mantra aims to do is to change the energy field, or aura, of the chanter in order to imbue them with the consciousness of the mantra being chanted.

In addition, a mantra is associated with a Yantra. A Yantra is a geometric shape that is said to be the embodiment of the consciousness being summoned. When we chant a mantra from a deep place of surrender and devotion to the awakening of the heart, these Yantras can be seen in our auric field.

As a healer I have witnessed that there are many levels not only to the human energy field, but there are layers upon layers of consciousness that can be manifest as different dimension or worlds. On several occasions whilst working with the energetic template of the human body, I have witnessed a dimension that expresses itself with geometric shapes.

At times these shapes seem to be floating freely and are the size of a human hand, others larger still and on several occasions I have experienced myself as sitting inside a tetrahedron or similar form.

As we chant our mantra and surrender to the Prana they stimulate, allowing our mind to become still, a Yantra can begin to form in our energy field. There are those who will say that a mantra only has power if it is given by a Guru. Granted, a Guru-given mantra does indeed strengthen the bond between Guru and disciple, however, there are plenty of mantras in general use that do indeed have the power to uplift and take us within.

Very popular mantras such as the Gayatri mantra are not generally Guru given and are chanted by millions nonetheless.

If you do not have a Guru and would like to start chanting, simply try a few out to see how they feel for you or choose a mantra that is directed to a deity that you are particularly drawn to.

Once you've chosen a mantra, my suggestion is to build up a long-term relationship with your mantra and explore the many colours and moods it may have for you. Each mantra has within its syllables and sounds a manifestation of consciousness that we may wish to embody and realize within ourselves.

# Kirtan

Kirtan literally means 'praise' and is a form of singing mantras and prayers in call and response fashion. In recent years as yoga has gained in popularity, so has the art of Kirtan in the West.

Kirtan has become very popularized in spiritual, yogic and other alternative communities as it fills the gap of devotional practice, since so many have left Christianity. In recent years the west has produced many devotional artists who mostly play Hindu devotional music and song to an almost exclusively western audience.

It is very apparent that so many westerners long for spiritual devotion but no longer feel that they can find it in their traditional religions of either Christianity or Judaism. Across the globe you can attend a Kirtan evening in your local Yoga studio or join hundreds of other people when some of the big names in this growing movement come to town:  Krishna Das, Deva Premal, Karnamrita Dasi, Jai Uttal, Shimshai, Tina Malia, Edo & Jo, Snatam Kaur and Bhagavan Das to name just a few.

Although this could be viewed as a movement, it has no leader; most of the artists have studied under different Gurus and therefore there are many traditions, backgrounds and even beliefs. What unites them is the path of devotion through the medium of music.

Although Kirtan is traditionally sung in call and response style in a group, the power of music cannot be underestimated in terms of its ability not only to influence how we feel but it also has an impact on how we view the world.

Whether or not you are able to attend a group of singers and chanters, singing devotional songs at home on your own is still very valuable. Music is one of the most powerful forces in the Universe. It changes the direction of politics, it can take us into the past, define how we feel in a moment, and express that which is much more difficult to simply say.

Sound is the building block of the Universe and so what better way to explore consciousness than through the power of song. Song can move us to tears, help us clear out old pain, help us to meet our heart, it can cheer us when all seems dark and hopeless, and it can fill us with joy, enthusiasm, joie de vivre, vitality, deep stillness and even profound devotion to God. Music can do all of that!

One of my greatest pleasures is to present myself to an audience of birds, grass, trees, rocks and any other animal or plant that may be around and sing to them. I find a lot of my devotion is expressed through the magnificence I find in nature.

I sing to them in celebration of their beauty and out of gratitude for how they have adorned the earth with their presence and how they have adorned my life with their song and the richness of their various shades of green and other colours.

# CHAPTER 8

# Healing our World

## One Individual, One Family, One Nation at a Time

We are not islands. We are born into many histories that have formed and shaped our world, these histories are more than just the stories that have been told and are far more than the books that have been written to tell one person's or one nation's version of events.

History is a living entity for its energy and consciousness reaches across time and space to impact how we feel, what we believe and how we think today. The long reach of history informs us who is guilty, who is innocent: Who the bad people are and who the good people are; it tells us who is trustworthy and who is not, it tells us what is safe and what is not safe.

The long reach of history gives us a viewpoint of the world that has been passed down to us by our ancestors, it teaches us about God, the nature of the Universe and our place in it for we hold many beliefs concerning reality and 'God' that we simply assimilated without effort or question.

Ancestors are as close as your mother and father and seem as distant as your great-great-grandparents. However, your ancestors are as close as your own heart. Our DNA carries the memories and experiences of countless generations and part of our task here is to evolve from fear based living, that is founded on a false notion of who we think we are, into a more inclusive existence.

However, in order for us to do this we must first acknowledge that we are also our ancestors. When we grasp onto a transpersonal view of ourselves, we bypass one of the most fundamental lessons of human life – the lesson of compassion.

The only way for us to grow within and evolve our ancestral heritage is to fully claim our origins whilst at the same time not identifying with them as the ultimate truth of who we are. This requires balancing. Our transpersonal nature identifies with nothing, it simply merges with all that is. However, as we are in this physical body and must therefore go about our daily tasks, we relate very much through our identity as a human being. Those identities can be male, female, transgender, Asian, White, Black, Arab, Indian, Indigenous, straight, bi or gay. There are many different identities that we as humans express.

What needs to be recognized is that the earth and all of her peoples are an energy and that this energy contains information, experience and awareness; it is alive and it is conscious, above all, it is collective.

As we come into this world we are immersed in the energy field of humanity, we are immersed in the history of our family, our nation and our race and the land upon which we were born and live on.

We have indeed been plunged into humanity as if jumping into the ocean. We are wet, not only on the outside, but on the inside as well. As we swim in this ocean of consciousness we follow the eddies, currents and flows that were started not only by our ancestors but also the great forces of history and nations that shape this world for better or for worse.

When we fully own our humanity, our total belongingness to the human race, it is then and only then that we can really hope to have any influence for good. If we take the position that we are not part of the world then our contribution is one of further separation.

Indeed, what is required is for us to launch ourselves into the depths of humanity where we can fully meet all that has happened and that is happening. When we set ourselves apart or above we will never be able to experience the motives and see the truth behind human cruelty, human injustice, human greed and human frailty.

A big part of this process is the embracing of our ancestors, no matter who they are, where they are from and what they did.

So many who are spiritual seekers and healers in the world are, without full awareness, attempting to pay a penance for the acts, crimes and hurts committed by their ancestors. Some are attempting to pay a penance on behalf of their nation, their race or for someone in their family.

When we are not conscious of this we can end up bringing into the world a sense of guilt, which then sets us apart from the very people we may want to help.

Much of our personal development and education can be stimulated by the hidden motivation to fix what is bad about us. Guilt does not serve anyone and our guilt does not assist those who have suffered, for when we are attempting to fix something bad within us, then those who we are in theory helping are in fact giving us something in return through needing our help – the question remains, who needs redemption?

When we become fully aware that our own personal liberation is tied up with the liberation of those we help through teaching, sharing and healing, humility then becomes our constant companion for then we recognize the equality in both parties seeking liberation from suffering.

All of this hinges on the 'should' and 'should nots' we have told ourselves. If we look at the history of our nations and resist all that has happened with an attitude of 'that should never have happened,' then we cannot possibly embrace the human story with any equanimity.

What we end up doing is dividing the world yet again into who is 'bad', who is 'good', who should be helped and who does not deserve our forgiveness – what all of this adds up to is simply more of the same and a repetition of our history.

When we deny our own ancestors and set ourselves apart from the history of our people, we have little of value to offer any other group or the world.

A significant percentage of people in the more industrially developed world live on land that was forcibly taken from the indigenous population. In some countries those indigenous peoples have either disappeared entirely, through the effects of introduced illness and disease, or have disappeared owing to policies of extermination or genocide.

Many such peoples now live as impoverished and derided members of a minority within a nation to which they may not feel that they belong. Even as we move beyond the 'new world' countries such as Brazil, Argentina, Australia, the USA and Canada, these accounts exist, for conquests and fighting others for resources has been a thread throughout much of human history, along with greed and the lust for power.

Even in the 'old world' many have been displaced by invading armies, invading religions and landowners, leaving an energetic footprint that can be felt. If we are to heal as individuals and nations, then our past must be met fully. As we meet our past we can feel the energy it holds, for in many areas of the world and in many families, the legacy of history is like thick molasses that must be waded through.

Those nations who have enslaved and slaughtered millions in the name of progress, racial purity, or in the name of God, pay the heavy the price that no matter their material gain the spiritual poverty of the populace begins to be become a drain on resources.

More and more outward displays of wealth, status or religious piety is demanded in order to assuage the unspoken guilt of nations that can no longer feel the pulse of their spiritual and ancestral heartbeat.

Many of these nations gather together and point the finger at one another. They claim to have righteousness on their side, they claim to have the better, more pure, more reasoned sense of morality and differentiation between right and wrong.

However, their own histories belie all of this and the spiritual poverty of their populations has become akin to a growing cancer that with each passing generation separates their peoples from all of the other beings with which they share their land and their planet with.

Animals are not afforded the rights of considerate and compassionate treatment and populations are becoming increasingly estranged from the flow of life that blesses their tables each night. Under the yolk of guilt from generations past as to how we have treated women, other races, nations and those of a different faith, sexual identity or orientation, we have become numb to what is truly important.

If we were to face history then we would start to see clearly how the few, those who feed off the burden of guilt and self-hatred, prey upon our desire to have a blind eye turned to what we have done, to what we have ignored, to what we blame others for, so that they can rob our souls in the name of profit.

Those who claim to be conscious rail against these men of power in the name of doing what is right but for the most part what is simply being added to the world is more self-righteousness that is used to justify hatred and partition.

The men and women of corruption only get to blind us when we are willing to be blinded. Our focus is placed upon the one enemy, the one bad 'man', or bad nation, or bad religion, or bad ethnicity so that all of our fear, blame and hatred can be safely placed onto them giving us the illusion that we are free from the burden of guilt.

Humanity has committed heinous crimes, however, it is our choice as to whether we choose to single out the evil ones, choose to hate and blame ourselves, or choose individually and collectively to face the truth of separation from our true nature without the use of masks, projections, inflated ideals and defences.

It is within our power to recognize our fall from grace and, in saying that, I am not alluding to the teaching of 'original sin', but I am making reference to every moment each of us has denied the truth of who we are in order to feed the fear that somehow we need another to approve of us more than we need to love ourselves.

We live in a global culture of blame and one in which it is always someone else's responsibility. What we're being called to do as a species before we either destroy ourselves or most of life on our planet is to meet ourselves fully.

We must have the courage to meet our own prejudices and encounter every single place within us that would rather resort to blame than to face the collective human pain body.

This pain body that has been gathering momentum for generations is bringing us to a major crossroads in our evolutionary path: are we going to risk the heartbreak of truly facing all that we've done, embracing the truth of it all, or are we going to continue on a path of denial and turning a blind eye until it is too late?

Collectively we may very well need a few more knocks in order to bring to our attention what is right in front of us, but as individuals we must become the change we want to see.

Not through preaching, not through demanding that others adopt a certain lifestyle or demand that they 'wake up', but as we face our own personal histories and face our own personal burden of guilt, allowing it all to dissolve in the light of consciousness embedded in the heart, then we in turn give permission to others to follow suit.

Life will, more than likely, never be without pain, but it can be free of suffering. Pain is part of being in the physical body. We trip, we fall, we break a leg; that is pain. We meet, we fall in love, then decide to go our separate ways. That is pain. Suffering occurs when we make it personal, when we make ourselves, or the other, wrong.

When we have the courage to face the burden of personal and ancestral guilt we also have the courage and the wisdom to see through the politics of fear that simply seek to keep the status quo. In facing our own personal story we begin to see clearly that at the root of our own suffering has been stories we have told ourselves about how bad we are, about how worthless we are.

As we encounter that in ourselves and in our culture we begin to see the other more collective lies that have been told, and tell ourselves, continually. We need to challenge the notion that the perpetrators are less worthy of healing than the victims, we need to challenge the notion that either 'my people' or 'your people' are either more or less guilty than the other.

These are lies that must be challenged. They are lies because they deny the equality of loss. Somehow we have come to believe that the one who has caused the loss is not worthy of regaining whatever has been lost. The problem with that is what has been lost is a sense of divinity, our sense of connection to all of life, our sense of innocence.

So if we are to heal the planet, we must have the courage to recognize, to truly, freely, audaciously and boldly see and speak the truth of that. When we insist that only the victim has the right to heal, or has more right to heal then what we are agreeing to is that the perpetrators and all of their descendants live in separation from their true nature – this is how we end up with the world as it is today.

Those of us who have stood in righteous indignation demanding the downfall of the wicked, the cruel and the unjust have made just as big a contribution to this age of darkness as anyone else. We insist on separation, we insist that others live in darkness.

However, the inclusive nature of our soul and of the soul of humanity will not allow us to do that and therefore we carry the burden of guilt, for it is impossible to cut off one leg and for the other leg not to notice it.

Peace will come to us all when we have the courage to lament the losses of our enemies, when we have the courage to grieve their dead, when we have the courage to weep for the burden their children carry, when we have the courage to recognize that we ourselves will never be at peace individually or collectively until our sworn enemies are likewise at peace.

As we seek personal fulfilment and healing we must recognize that as individual as we may experience ourselves to be, we in fact live in a collective field of consciousness in which we are wanting to unfold the truth of our own inner light in order to make a fulfilling contribution to the whole.

Serving others through our gifts of music, art, carpentry, motherhood, leadership, compassionate care and myriad other ways, is the one and only path that truly feeds us. We are communal beings expressing ourselves as individuals and our deepest satisfaction comes from being of service to others.

This can be manifest in many different ways , it makes no difference if you are a stay at home mother serving the next generation of compassionate human beings or if you are a captain of industry leading the way towards more sustainable growth and development that seeks to respect all lives.

෧෧෧෧෧

Service is Divine Nature, it is at the core of the soul and it is through service that we get to experience the core and truth of who we are. When it is distorted by unresolved guilt and self-hatred it seeks constant affirmation or it needs to feed off fame.

However, when we surrender to service as the soul's pleasure we are content and fulfilled and allow others their nature and their path of service. We all came to serve and none of us came with a God given mission to save the planet, we only came to save ourselves and to realize that the pilgrimage that is manifest in the life we are living has as its intended destination our very own heart.

The heart is the jewel, it is the grand prize, it is what we came not only to uncover, or to discover, but we came to realize its own nature and that with a little attention we can recognize that it has always been here.

In its extreme 'good' Christians can invade the land of the heathen and subjugate them or a 'good' Samaritan can attempt to be better than the parent they despise through doing 'good' works. None of this is service, it is compensation for a much deeper problem. Shame.

What is apparent is that our deepest shameful secret is shame itself. We don't want anyone to know that we have shame and so we bury it deeply, as deeply as we possibly can. We are afraid that if another sees our shame they may go on to shame us further by agreeing with it – through telling us that we should be ashamed.

Shaming has sadly become endemic. It lives and breathes in our churches, our synagogues our temples and in our mosques. It lives in our homes and in our schools, it's alive and well on television, portrayed and played out in soap operas and in reality TV.

Shame shows its ugly head in our treatment of and commentary about women, the obese, assertive women, feminine or sensitive men or anyone who sits outside of what our culture deems morally or socially acceptable. Women shame other women, men shame one another – in fact as a culture we seem to thrive on shaming anyone we either don't understand or feel intimidated by, or shaming others through demanding that they comply with cultural standards.

Online forums and communities are awash with individuals who feed off shaming and negativity for negativity's sake.

Shaming others only seeks to hide our own sense of shame. It takes courage to face shame and this is what is needed at this time in human history that has coincided not only with the possibility that we may destroy ourselves, but it has coincided with an era in which our individual stories and messages of hope and healing can be broadcast easily to the world.

We need more teenagers to stand up and be counted, we need more of those who have been marginalized by society to speak to the masses through social media.

However, we are also being called at this time to invite the abusers to dialogue. We can no longer afford to allow our sense of being a victim to turn us into the next bully on the block, for this happens all too frequently.

Often, the very people who are championing causes and standing up for the rights of minorities, whether this be in the field of human rights, racial equality, environmental activism, LGBT rights, animal rights, and women's rights carry the very familiar energy of the perpetrator and can often be observed simply bullying, shaming and persecuting anyone who either disagrees with them or does not enthusiastically agree with their world view – this is not the solution.

We have witnessed generation after generation of the good triumphing over the bad and when this happens the 'good' tend to become paternalistic both in their viewpoint and in their actions.

Before we realize it another regime, another despot or another form of discrimination has been born and all of this is built upon the notion that the way to solve the world's problems is too weed out the bad.

Somehow, we need to fully admit that this approach has never worked and will never work. However, it would be far easier to point the finger at others than to face the truth of what is really underlying all of our issues of hatred and the need to separate, marginalize or control others – fear.

## Embracing Human Suffering

It is not possible to enter into a discussion on human suffering without including the spiritual, for without it, suffering and indeed all of life would appear to have little or no purpose other than the evolutionary mandate to ensure the survival of a species.

As a species of animal we are programmed to avoid pain and death at all costs. We equate pain with death and have become so identified with our physical bodies that death for us has become the threat of annihilation, the point at which we descend into an eternal nothingness in which we are not even aware of having ever existed.

Every achievement, every act of love, and every one we have ever known simply gone forever. No light, no consciousness, simply nothing and not even a speck of consciousness to observe the nothingness. We cannot even imagine this nothingness, the very idea of non-existence is not only terrifying for most, but also impossible.

The closest that we can come to imagining total annihilation and the descent into absolute non-existence is to imagine ourselves as a single dot of consciousness in a vast realm of nothingness. That would be enough to frighten anyone, in fact the death of total annihilation would, for many, be preferable than spending eternity as a single dot of consciousness observing a vast void in which nothing except our singular dot exists.

The reason why we cannot imagine non-existence is because even though our ego along with our body, are temporary containers for our consciousness, our consciousness is indeed eternal. Many of the great sages and avatars throughout time have spoken of eternal life. This has led many to assume that they speak of either a physical existence that is forever or that they only make reference to the soul.

Once we have cleared much of our defence mechanisms and strategies to avoid our deepest wounds, our ego becomes more refined as we feel less and less compelled to defend something that cannot be hurt or injured – our inner being.

The more our ego becomes refined and the more we are able to have the courage to lead an undefended life through an undefended heart the more aware we become of the silent witness that resides within us and remains constant no matter our external circumstances.

As we surrender to the grace anchored in the heart we become increasingly aware of the truth of our existence. We start to see more clearly and witness with peace in our hearts that we as human beings are but a temporary manifestation of the greater part of ourselves.

As we realize this more deeply we are able then to meet suffering in a more meaningful way. Whenever a discussion of suffering ensues one of the first questions that arises is the suffering of children and the 'innocent'.

This strong objection is frequently raised because it is often accepted that, for many, their suffering has been brought upon themselves and it is also inferred that all adults who exist outside the pure innocence of children are in some way guilty for something.

In this way we can have some peace with suffering if we can make it in part the sufferer's fault. However, even the most callous have difficulties in seeing young children as culpable in their own suffering – except those who are steeped in the notion of original sin that makes all humans guilty by default.

I do not pretend to have the answers as to why very young children suffer in wars or from terrible diseases. However, when I look at the journey of the soul to know itself in all of its dimensions it becomes clear to me that life itself is relentless in terms of delivering the experiences that will awaken us.

What I have learnt is that the reason why one person is born into immeasurable challenges and another into what is seemingly an easy life is none of my business, for we cannot truly measure another person's suffering through looking at their external circumstances.

When I attempt to make these things my business I run the very real risk of then avoiding the suffering of others through declaring that it is their 'karma' or their lot. The teachings of karma have likewise been distorted and used by many to either turn a blind eye or to condemn those who are suffering as simply being the reapers of their own past guilt or wrongdoing.

Similarly the teaching of original sin as transmitted down through at least fifty generations has led some to view 'sinners' as not worthy of our compassion, or that those who are suffering are merely sinners and likewise reaping the 'wages of sin'.

These religious distortions we now know to be simply a manifestation of the desire for control and power by the ruling classes who used the priesthood of all religions to support empires, dynasties and regimes.

However, it is too easy to make our lack of compassion and our inability to meet suffering as it is into a religious or political issue. The beliefs that those who suffer are wholly or partially responsible for their suffering serves the purpose of allowing us to distance ourselves from it.

If we can somehow turn suffering into a system of delivering personal and eternal justice we then have the illusory belief that we can in some way control how close it comes to us.

If suffering is linked to either karma and retribution or the 'wages of sin' we can tell ourselves that not only are we able to control it through being 'good' (or an image of what good is) but that we can distance ourselves from it for it is none of our business and perhaps not something that 'we' would earn or bring upon ourselves.

Secretly though, the suffering of others terrifies us. It terrifies us because our mind cannot reason it and therefore we cannot possibly view what is happening on the level of the soul. As we cannot reason it, we start feeling vulnerable.

On the level of the human ego, it is indeed all terribly unfair and unjust – there is truth in that, and one I do not dispute. However, we are multi-faceted beings and I have personally experienced aspects of myself that not only accept the suffering, but see it as beautiful and all in divine order.

In saying that I am not alluding to suffering being a noble path, but it is definitely an experience that can lead us to nobility if we allow it to take us on a journey into and through our hearts. When we argue with reality, eventually we lose.

On our quest for personal healing and spiritual development we frequently have as part of our agenda the hope of creating a pain free existence or a life in which something will be discovered leading to lifelong happiness.

Mostly what we're looking for is to fix ourselves sufficiently so that we may enter into a relationship that is designed to ensure our happiness for as long as possible.

When we seek to reject or ignore the suffering we see in the world, we are in fact ignoring our very own suffering. We are ignoring our own true self and ignoring our habitual denial of self.

The world is but a reflection of what is happening internally and what has already happened in our ancestral lines. We can only commit atrocities when we have disconnected from the truth of who we are.

The embracing of human suffering is not sanctioning suffering or encouraging it, but it is accepting it as a part of the human experience. When we turn from it we rob both ourselves, and others, of the opportunity, dignity and grace to surrender to a healthier, more authentic part of ourselves.

Suffering can be a gift. Not one that we pursue, but one we welcome when it arrives, for each and every episode of suffering is an opportunity to let something be burnt in the fires of Shiva and each time we are drawn into the suffering of another we are likewise being invited to discover the most precious parts of ourselves, our very own heart.

## Redemption

The heart's longing is to know itself as love and although its voice resides in the depth of silence along with the truth, we are often drawn to speak of love and its meaning. The greatest freedom we can give ourselves is the freedom to love.

Redemption is yet another one of those words like God, forgiveness and love. So much has been written, misunderstood and projected onto these words that they mean different things to different people. Redemption is no exception to that.

For me, redemption is about a personal journey of forgiving ourselves for each and every time we have ignored who we truly are and have denied what we are capable of. We have done this over and over again, often grasping at the image of what we believe we should be, or we have capitulated to fear and kept our more authentic Self hidden whilst presenting our small self, a mere cardboard cut-out, to the world.

Personal redemption is about finally submitting to the truth of our deepest longings and being authentic in meeting every place within us we have sought to deny.

Our constant denial of who we truly are, or ignoring the presence and longing of the heart, the God within, has caused us to amass a great deal of personal guilt for everything we have not expressed, for every moment of truth we have denied, for every opportunity to yield to love that we have walked away from, and for each time we have denied another in their magnificence, just as we have denied ourselves in our own magnificence.

Personal redemption emerges as an opening in the heart when we face everything we have ignored about our inner world and the truth of God that is all around us. We've perhaps had a lifetime of habitually seeing so many things as 'only'. For example, he's 'only' my mechanic, it's only a dog, it's only a tree, she's only an acquaintance, he's only my bank manager, and she's only my cleaner.

When we play the 'he's only,' game we are in denial of the importance of all relationships. The 'only' game seeks to keep us safe. When another is deemed 'only' we can turn a blind eye to their suffering and also turn a blind eye to our own heart's desire to simply love them.

Somehow we've told ourselves that love is limited and it is only appropriate to reserve it for a limited number of special people. However, is that true? Is that really true? We've been told that love has certain meanings and therefore it would be 'inappropriate' to love the 'only' people.

We make it difficult for ourselves because just as we have believed that love is only reserved for family, spouses, lovers, partners, children and close friends, we then limit love for the 'only' people because of the meaning we have attached to love.

Somehow we have convinced ourselves that if we love our gardener or baker then we have to give it a meaning beyond what is. We are quite capable of feeling deep affection for those with whom we don't have the bond of friendship.

What is truly beautiful about loving those with whom we are not in a deeper friendship with is that our love can flow free of any possible or probable karma. We have karmic bonds with our deeper relationships and they are often relationships of growth. We do ourselves a great disservice when we turn away from the 'only' people.

Redemption emerges as we face the truth of the pain of that ongoing and habitual denial regarding the nature of our heart and the nature of love. When we were just a toddler it was natural for us to love everyone and everything that came onto our path.

We have a deep, deep, deep yearning to return to the exquisite paradise that this fresh youthfulness gave us with our naturally unfettered heart. It is only as a result of our defences and being taught who to love and who not to love, that we have locked ourselves behind thick doors and told ourselves that it doesn't 'matter because it is 'only my gardener'.

Our heart longs to love our gardener, the grocery store assistant, our bank manager, our neighbour, our everything. When we ignore this inner call, and we do ignore it, just as we were ignored as children, we in turn ignore our inner impulse. It is not that it is not there and cannot be felt, it is that we ignore it and have developed very sophisticated strategies for convincing ourselves that there is no impulse to ignore.

However, when the impulse becomes impossible to ignore any longer, our guilt can gain the upper hand and we blame ourselves for living a constant lie that is slowly asphyxiating our heart.

Redemption comes when we have the courage to face the truth of our heart. When we acknowledge our heart and its deep longing, and when we face the fear we have of surrendering to our own magnificent and resplendent heart, redemption is ours for we are no longer turning a blind eye to the truth of another and the truth of who we are.

We are a child of god, we came forth to make manifest our magnificence and to realize the beauty of who we are through compassion and the heart's longing to know itself as love.

As we deny this we ignore the very existence of God in everyone and everything and this leads us to the fall from grace. The fall from grace is NOT having sinned against God or having sinned against another, the fall from grace is having 'sinned' against our true nature – habitually ignoring it.

Redemption is allowing ourselves to remember.

## The Constant Companion

The burdens and pain we overcome grow into our greatest storehouse of wisdom and compassion. They literally become the power that enables us to assist others in their healing. Our suffering has been our initiation of the heart for we can only assist the planet and humanity to heal and rise above our current deep crisis in evolution if we have been touched by suffering ourselves.

It is through meeting our deepest pain that we can offer the service and the knowledge of liberation to others. In this sense our awakening to who we are as we rise up out of our suffering likens us to Chiron, the wounded healer.

Chiron was reputed to be the wisest of the Greek centaurs. He was immortal and therefore could not die. One fateful day he was accidentally struck by an arrow that had been dipped in Hydra's blood. Had he been mortal then he would have surely died, however, in his immortality, instead of dying he suffered great pain as a result of his wound. Chiron traversed all of the known world in search of a cure for his affliction.

As time went by he amassed great knowledge and experience of what it was to heal and others began to seek him out. His very own wound created the destiny of becoming the wounded healer.

The wounded healer understands the pain of those he helps for he has suffered the same pain, the same anguish, the same loss of faith, the same grief, the same anger and the same fear. The wounded healer is most effective when the path that the other has walked is both felt and understood from the perspective of personal experiences instead of just theory.

When we embrace the path of the wounded we surrender our need to stop all pain, but rather we shift our focus towards uncovering the individual and collective human heart – the source of all grace, of all love and of all compassion. This pivotal shift in focus does more to alleviate and uplift than all of the energies we may have invested in either resisting suffering or trying to stop it at all costs.

When we stand alone against human suffering we are in effect arguing with reality and that is one argument we can never win. The forces of change and the forces that bring about the evolution of our species will bring us to the next stage that is beyond just being sentient, to a level of existence in which we will consciously co-exist with other worlds. Those other worlds are inclusive of all the beings that we share our planet with, the seen and the unseen.

We cannot rid the world of its ignorance and suffering through chasing the light for that has the effect of disconnecting us not only from the life we are living but also from what is standing right in front us.

When we become a 'light chaser' we often live life through the vision of our ideals and seek to remove or ignore whatever is painful of threatening. Chasing the light does not heal, it separates. Those who are lost in their suffering cannot see us or feel us when we are not fully present in our body and in earth life.

Our job therefore is to take the light of consciousness into every corner of our being that is separate, afraid, angry, hateful, enraged and feeling desperately lonely. Through this process of integration we create a template that many others can follow in their own good time.

We stand solidly with our feet on the ground, rested in the centre of our heart having run the gauntlet of our inner demons as a warrior of the light.

We've peered into the darkest corners and have sobbed the deepest of tears and have fallen, fallen, fallen time and again into the bottomless pit from which there was no return and no escape, only to discover that at the bottom of this pit, the dreaded abyss of separation, is a trap door that opens up into the resplendent and luxurious light of the heart – the sweet pure nectar of God, the essence of our true selves.

Each time we have the courage to come home to what is true, to what is really true, what is true beyond all the words that have been spoken about us, to us and by us that sought only to convince and imprison us over and over and over again with the grandest lie that we are inherently bad and that there is something wrong with us, we release more of the bondage we have imposed on our very own heart.

As we take courage and meet the abyss of separation not once, not twice, not thrice but a hundred times if necessary and fall into the deeper truth – no masks, no idealistic projections, we have an all pervasive experience that all is well with us and with our world.

This truth, as it is experienced by us each time we dare to cross the threshold of the abyss, paves the way for many more to follow in our footsteps. Neither the Buddha nor the Christ became the enlightened sons of God through chasing the light.

Each faced their demons and each faced them alone in the abyss of suffering and separation. This was their gift to us, not the dogmas that have spread in their name, but the gift of their inner journey.

## Spiritual Resource

As we become willing to see and tell the absolute truth of our existence, unlimited resource becomes available to us. Not only do the energies of the deities, saints, enlightened ones and gurus come in to support us, but the Shamanic world that contains all of the realms of our ancestors becomes available to us too.

The Ancients, the wise women and men of epochs gone by come forth to support us, for their evolution is intrinsically tied up with our own. Everything that happens on Earth and with humans is keenly felt in the many worlds that live intersected with our own.

For aeons there have been stories of unicorns, faeries, winged beings, dragons, gnomes, various tribes and talking trees. These stories exist across all continents and are common to all peoples.

Many of those  described are remarkably similar and some differ from place to place. It is not remarkable to me that some of these beings are as different in China as they may be in Ghana, Sweden or Peru, for just as there are different flora and fauna, as well as humans, in these, so it is with the shamanic kingdoms, also known as the astral world.

This world was very real to me as a child and is still very real to me today. All of my inner work has been supported by what for most people is the unseen world. When we simply want to dabble in predicting the future or are simply curious with no motivation to grow, we attract information and attention that matches our level of commitment to personal evolution.

As we progress in our personal journey of healing, our sincere longing to transform fear into the love we are in the process of remembering, is then met by beings of merit that take a keen interest in human evolution and healing.

We are supported and more than we can imagine. In the following chapter I will take you on a more detailed journey into this word.

# CHAPTER 9

# Other Worlds

## Seeing and Sensing
## Beyond the Veils

We are most certainly not alone. All of the aloneness that we experience is caused by inner separation. As we begin to meet and heal the splits within us, the places of deep separation, not only do we begin to feel our own heart again, we start to experience our heart centre as the doorway leading to the many mansions of God.

These worlds exist in the same space we do, but are simply separated by vibration. Once the veils begin to lift, our relationship to all beings similarly begin to transform, for our vision begins to clear. As these inner veils dissolve so too do the veils that keep us from seeing the truth of existence.

This seeing can become a literal seeing of the eyes, or it can become a seeing that is knowing or feeling the presence of the intersecting worlds. Trees become friends, they become repositories of information and we begin to see them as the benevolent guardians that they are.

Everything starts to take on more meaning and we realize more fully each day that we are living in an ocean of consciousness and realize that we had been the fish swimming eagerly and exhaustively looking for water.

Seeing, sensing, feeling and interacting with other worlds is very healing and is often a side effect of the healing process itself. The heart is the doorway and once we enter the kingdom of the heart we encounter many worlds before the witnessing of our very own Holy of Holies brings us to our knees.

Our relationship to this intersecting world has been tarnished by some major deceptions and attempts at controlling the masses. Firstly when knowledge of God and scriptures is placed in the exclusive hands of a priestly class it robs many of their inner experience. It does so because all authority becomes external and eventually we lose our ability to explore the truth of our inner world.

Generations of threats coming from the pulpits of all churches along with the Inquisitions, wide-spread Witch Hunts, and the heinous manner in which people were punished for both religious and political reasons, severed our ties to pre-Christian tradition, that had an open and acknowledged relationship to the intersecting realms of the ancestors and other beings.

This series of atrocities that cost the lives of millions, predominantly women, across the European continent, over a period of several hundred years, has left an indelible scar on the European soul, which translates into the 'western' psyche as the populations of the new world are largely descendants of Europeans or are of mixed race.

This deep wound of separation from our true nature has translated today into a deep distrust and indeed cynicism when it comes to any notion of the non-physical world being real. As we were severed from our inner connection we became logical and reasoned, for much church dogma was based on intellectual debate and the needs of political agendas, effectively removing the heart of spiritual experiences.

This remains with us down to this very day for the impact of Western culture has been far greater than perhaps any of us can imagine and we now live in a culture that honours and values good memory and intelligence above all else.

As I travel the world I witness many cultures that live with the intersecting realities and kingdoms on a daily basis. It is far too easy for those from industrialized nations to dismiss these cultural practices as simply being an aspect of the lives of uneducated peoples from undeveloped nations.

Miraculous healings take place, the ancestors are honoured and the spirits are consulted whenever major decisions are to be made. In truth many individuals in developed nations know this to be true, perhaps even the majority are aware of the intersecting realities.

However, the culture of elevating reason above intuition and the cynicism of scientific dogma places many in the dubious position of being seen to be strange, odd or not quite sane for acknowledging and interacting with this non-physical world from which our own world emanates.

What I've noticed is that for many westerners primal fears arise when the threshold of the spiritual makes itself apparent. The wound of the external God runs deep for it seems that whenever the possibility of a spiritual realm is entertained then the question of God arises. This is the point at which the deep wounding of our relationship with God becomes evident.

As 'God' comes into the picture our imagery of a singular being tends to come alive again and our fears around what is right and what is wrong also surfaces.

Additionally, within our family lines are indeed the ancestors who we burnt, hanged, drowned and otherwise dispensed with along with those of our ancestors who blew the whistle or were directly involved in the persecution of witches and the so called heretics.

# Lower Worlds

For generations we have had our hearts filled with dread with the stories that much in the spirit world is either dangerous or satanic in nature and therefore we have reluctantly given it no more credence than a passing glance.

It is however true to say the closest intersecting realm to this physical one is as varied in vibration, mood and manifestation as our own. Just as one can be walking down a green, leafy, boutique filled lane in one of our cities one moment and walking through a rough, shabby and dangerous feeling ghetto the next, so it is with the world that has come to be known as the Astral.

This world is roughly divided into three major zones: Lower, Middle and Upper. Anything in our world that creates, encourages and feeds off fear is interacting with the Lower Astral.

The Lower Astral is a non-physical manifestation of the personal and collective fear, hatred, anger and rage of humanity. Given the historical church's constant focus on evil, great doorways into this lower world were opened, and as they opened, the feeding frenzy of the lower astral began.

The lower worlds feed off fear and therefore all of the trauma from all of the wars and humanity's cruelty to one another over the ages has left doorways firmly open allowing these negative sludge like energies to migrate from one generation to the next.

However, all is not lost. As we focus on our inner work and on surrendering to the truth of who we are, we start to rise above the collective sludge of human fear and start being bathed in the light of the middle and upper worlds.

The world's population is for the most part entranced by what seems to be a very reasonable reality and state of affairs, unaware of that which lies just outside the average person's ability to perceive.

However, when we heed the inner call to awaken, the broader reality is no longer just outside our ability to perceive and starts to gradually come into focus. There are so many uncanny parallels with the movie, 'The Matrix,' however, my experience of these worlds are far more positive and the trance like state we find ourselves in has got everything to do with the evolution of consciousness and not much to do with the sinister agenda of the few.

The lower worlds must be respected but not feared. When we respect the existence of the lower world we honour our feeling when our gut tells us that a house, a location or a person 'does not feel good'.

# Middle World

The more aware we become of the intersecting realities the more our lives can become enriched by interaction with the Middle World. This world has been my playground for many years and this particular intersection includes many expressions, many kingdoms and worlds that have been expressed through the many fantasy novels that have been written.

It is my experience that so called fantasy worlds are a reality and that the tales are often the histories of real worlds that intersect with ours. These worlds can be very human and can be experienced to be as real as our own.

The soul's playground is not limited to 'heaven' and 'earth' and great epic stories that are manifestations of psychic metaphors for teaching purposes, run along beautifully in the Middle World as if they were on the Holodeck of Star Trek Voyager.

In fact aspects of our own soul play here regularly, especially during our dream cycle at night. In this world we can interact with our ancestors and interact with the grandfathers and grandmothers of all of humanity. This is the abode of the ancient ones and much can be gained from welcoming them into our lives.

Here in this world the grandfathers who suffered the horrors of WWI and WWII can be solicited to help us resolve the trauma and the fears that have been passed down to us. As much as many people would think of Family Constellation work as being purely a psychotherapeutic process, it is far more than that.

In reality it is the part that is 'more' than psychotherapeutic process that usually offers the healing solution. Through this modality we literally interact with, communicate with and listen to the abode of the ancestors. Each ancestor leaves their foot print on the family soul, or perhaps better said, its collective consciousness.

This collective consciousness creates a palpable footprint and manifestation in the Middle World and therefore we can solicit the assistance of the ances-tors to help us to heal ancestral patterns and traumas that are affecting living members of the family today.

As we interact with the Middle World we begin to see clearly that we simply didn't just arrive as a singular event. In reality what we arrived into and have become part of is a stream of consciousness that stretches down from the dawn time to where we stand today.

In our day-to-day waking self, yesterday is deader than a Dodo, however, like the Dodo it leaves footprints that inform us of its existence. In the Middle World time is not linear like our own perception of time. Therefore all of the Ancestors and all of the events that affected our family stretching back for generations are still very much alive and happening, as if in the here and now.

It is vital that this work is done for if you are a descendent of those who have suffered greatly, this suffering is part of your own personal footprint and one way to ensure that history does not repeat itself is to openly face our histories.

If we are to stop the madness that we continue to see in our world we must have the courage to face all of the genocide, all of the slavery, all of the wars, all of the injustice and look at the complete experience of both sides.

As we interact with our ancestors and their stories, the stories and their consequences we have inherited as our fate, we have the good fortune to ask them for their blessing. They, like us, are on a path of growth and it is often as important to them as it is to us that their story is told.

Do you have the courage to have a more blessed life than the great grandmother who was born as a slave? Do you have the courage to thrive even though many of your family members were lost in a war? Do you have the courage to be happy even though your people caused the suffering of thousands? Are you able to create a nurturing home even though five generations earlier indigenous peoples were cast off the land? Are you perpetuating the loyalties of your family? Do you dismiss members of certain groups because of your family's historical interaction with them? Are you loyal to the suffering?

As we interact with the Middle World a whole new sphere of opportunity for healing opens to us. The Middle World is but a hair's breadth away from us. Through ceremony, through Shamanic ritual, ancestral healing and through giving offerings we can interact with a world that carries the imprints of both our past, present and potential future.

The Middle World is delighted when we notice it and interact with it. This world I speak of is not 'elsewhere' for many around the globe. In many parts of the globe, interaction with this world is part of everyday life. It is not questioned, it simply is. The invitation here is to invite it in for healing opportunities and to seek out those who are sufficiently trained to be your guide.

# The Upper World

The Upper World can be seen as the upper levels of the worlds that directly intersect and interact with our physical world. The Middle World, in my experience, is far broader in terms of variety, expression and content, but the upper world is where form and aspects of formlessness start to meet and merge and where we begin to experience more specific and obvious expressions of the Divine in forms we as humans can relate to.

In the Middle World we meet Ancestors, Shamanic healers and Spirit guides, gnomes, unicorns, dragons, a phoenix, animal spirits, elves and the grandmothers and grandfathers of many peoples across the world.

The Upper World is intersected with what we could call the Celestial Realms and from the celestial on upwards: this is where we begin to enter realities that are less and less what we recognize and are more about the pure expression of consciousness.

These worlds can be an entire universe of geometric shapes, great lattice works of energy, vast void like expanses that are pulsing with energy and consciousness or realities of music, sound and light – the realm of the soul as pure consciousness.

Many who have travelled into the Upper World often confuse this world with the celestial realms for here in the Upper World we can come face to face and interact with Divine forms such as deities, saints, avatars and the angelic realms.

Many of the beings inhabiting this realm transmit energies and communicate with us telepathically – they are constantly pointing towards the truth of self and have the welfare of humanity as part of their highest concern. They communicate with those who reach them with pure intent form their heart and also with prayer.

It is my absolute knowing that all prayer is answered. It may not be in the way in which we want it, but our prayers are answered regardless. What I have come to learn is that many of the forms we can interact with in the Upper World are extensions of vast consciousness originating in dimensions high above the Astral.

I wrestled for a long time wondering if what I was seeing was real or imagined. Once I understood through personal experience that the person I could see in the mirror had been imagined by me, then I understood that everything and everyone was a thought form.

The conundrum was, 'Is that really Jesus,' and the answer is, 'If you believe it to be so'. This reality forms when millions of individuals across our globe believe in a deity: the Divine consciousness will take or 'incarnate' in that form in the Upper World.

It leaves us to ponder, what came first, our imagining of Ganesh or the form Ganesh? The answer is: yes. With a temporal paradox it is possible to see the effects before the cause. In this way the Gods are created in our image, however, as they are Gods, they are aspects of pure consciousness that have been made manifest in the Upper world for us to interact with, be blessed by and to learn from.

I no longer question their validity, or even the idea of paradox, and interact with them as if they are as real as I am – and the relationship is a rich one; I greet them, feel their kindness and their love and support. Each of the Deities are but an expression and embodiment of one or several divine qualities such as generosity, kindness, compassion, love, creativity, music, prayer, grace, wisdom and healing.

As it is difficult for our human minds to conceptualize the reality of God or even to process an encounter that makes any real sense to us, the Deities are manifestations of an aspect of the One. The One has many faces and many moods for it is All That Is. I was once told that 'God is a disco ball' – each tiny mirror being a facet, expression and manifestation of the one.

As humans, we relate to objects very well. It is how we describe our world and it is how we experience our relationships – everyone we love has a form. Likewise the deities are forms we can relate to and just as your loved ones are real, so are they.

I've had the good fortune during many sessions with my clients, during deep prayer, meditation and chanting to have encountered many Deities who have blessed me with their benevolence. Some of these experiences have been almost as intense as the hospital experience I described and have in their own way left their footprint on my soul.

What I have come to learn from these manifestations such as Buddha, Christ, Ganesh, Hanuman, Shiva and many others is that they are truly concerned with the evolution of our species and are benevolent. These worlds are vast, with many dimension of reality and many diverse expressions.

In writing this it feels somewhat as if I am offering you the history of the world and its meaning in a pamphlet – great volumes could be written on this topic.

## Encounters

Many episodes of my childhood had caused me to have encounters with several lower aspects of the unseen worlds, instilling within me a fear of many things non-physical.

However, as much as I tried to deny its very existence, my gift of sight and direct knowing, although suppressed, has never vanished. Following my journey into the ocean of peace that was Guangxi Province in China, after Johannesburg had left its indelible mark on my being, that which had almost been forgotten reawakened and indeed was re-acknowledged.

I had spent many years perfecting my craft through Family Constellation and Ancestral Healing work and although it was fairly obvious to anyone who had worked with me that I had an ability to perceive beyond the five senses, I was never very public about it, believing that I would never be taken seriously as a therapist, facilitator and a practitioner.

My inner journey of allowing my spiritual self to re-emerge was not only life transforming, but I could not do anything to resist it. Apparently it had taken a gun to my head to bring me back onto a path that had already been laid out for me from whence I was a child.

Today I gladly share with you my experience of the broader spectrum of the world in which we live, along with the message that it is our natural birthright and that the only thing standing in the way of this broader and deeper experience is fear and the mind.

We so often give the mind jobs that are not suited to it, and much to the mind's disappointment it is not the centre of consciousness, nor even our aware-ness. In reality, the mind is but a mere servant of consciousness.

The worlds I have experienced are as varied as countries can be and as dif-ferent and as odd as other planets. Not only has my perception of that which defines life changed, but also my perception of what constitutes intelligence and awareness.

It would seem that we live in a world within a world and that many, many worlds traverse our own, sharing the same space, simply separated by frequency, focus and vibration.

In many of these worlds the rules are pretty much the same, or can be quite different. There is a vast difference between the worlds inhabited by our Ances-tors and the Shamanic worlds of tribal spirits, healers and medicine women and those worlds where the astral embodiment and expression of various gods can be experienced.

There is indeed a stairway to heaven and each step has its own unique ex-pression of that. There are palaces replete with gold, overseen by Pan, Ganesh, Aphrodite, Kwan Yin, Hanuman, Unicorns, Sages and Gurus and also those worlds with vast temples holding the light and consciousness of Christ, Bud-dha, Krishna, and other great 'sons of God' and yet still other worlds that are civilizations going about their own business, unaware that we, for the most part, cannot perceive them and unaware that they are anything else other than ordinary beings.

The non-physical astral world ranges from dark and dense creatures with very little awareness all the way up to angelic beings and super-conscious light beings.

# The Gnome & Rose

Many years ago I had, to my great surprise, an encounter with a Gnome. I had once thought that they were fictional characters from children's storybooks, the stuff of Hansel and Gretel and The Hobbit, but no, I had an encounter that not only astounded me, but educated me to see a far bigger picture.

When I say Gnome, this is simply a word I've chosen to describe a being that was small like a toddler but adult in maturity, with roundish features and stocky in build. He was not wearing a red hat but was indeed clothed and was concerned with the land so in that sense he was a 'gardener', 'Gnome' then, seems to be the most appropriate word.

His complexion was ruddy and his face had the appearance of someone in their late 30s, a few lines here and there, and he had large dark eyes, his limbs being proportional to the rest of his body. I have since learnt that Gnomes and similar beings vary in appearance from region to region across the globe.

I recall being rather startled when seeing such beings in Thailand and on Bali, as they look so different! And why not? The people living there look different to me too!

I had ventured out on my bicycle to the nearby woods on a pleasant spring's day. Although the forest was a new forest, planted in rows upon land that was once a landfill site for garbage and waste, it was the nearest large green area near my home. I cycled along the pathways, which varied form paved to unpaved, found a secluded spot and sat to meditate in the dappled light piercing the fresh green canopy.

As I sat and took myself deeper with my breath I suddenly felt a presence, opened my eyes, and suddenly saw the likeness of a Gnome, not with my eyes, but as if a hologram had been superimposed onto the 'real' world. Once I had seen him, I could then still see him on my internal mindscreen if I closed my eyes.

I chose to keep them open as I was a little startled and it felt safer to do so. As his image was still very clear to me I decided to communicate with him and opened up telepathic communication with a simple 'Hello' in my mind. With my 'Hello' he looked directly at me and I went on to say, 'How are you?' The response that came was not at all what I expected and some of my images around spirit beings of this nature were about to be challenged.

*'Well, how would you feel if you were me? I work all day trying to tidy up the mess you lot have made here. Look at this place! Trees in a row! No bird is going to nest in here, no animal will play about...nowhere for them to hide, no place to nest. You think rows of trees are a solution? No, they just create work for the likes of me'.*

I was really taken aback! He was not only seriously grumpy but also seemingly telling me off for being a member of the human race. I said to him 'Sorry, so what more can you tell me?'

'Look over there' he said, pointing to a clearing. 'What do you notice about that young tree over there?'

I was unsure of what he was pointing out and after stating several of my observations he said the following, *'That young tree is surrounded by nettle. The nettle stops animals from eating the sapling. It's all in balance, to give the tree a chance. There's plenty for the rabbits to eat, they and the deer don't need saplings. Then you come along and plant rows of trees! Rows!'*

Our conversation continued and I learnt quite a few things about forests, harmony and the balance of nature. I then ventured more personal questions.

'So what is it you do? What is your job?' I asked

*'I direct, divert and plan energy flow into disaster areas like this. There are big rivers of energy on the land and I divert small channels of it here, it helps to feed the trees, soil and plants. Pollution degrades the energy flows, turning it thick until it almost stops, so I keep it going. It's a lot of hard work, all that plastic is poison.'*

I continued my conversation with him, learning more about the land and his function and then I asked him a question that solicited a response that touched me deeply. 'How long have you been doing this job? How old are you?'

*'I don't know how old I am'* he replied *'I've been doing this for a very long time, maybe a thousand years, long before this town was built, I don't know'.*

I then asked him what he aspired to. With that question his grumpiness left him and he began to shine with a twinkle in his eye. *'I long to be a Fairy. I'm tired of diverting energy and working in the muck and darker places. Fairies hold together the Song of a Flower in their bodies, they hold its tone in place, they sing to the flower and the flower sings back to them. Fairies do God's bidding, they hold in existence that which has been ordained. They are the most beautiful creatures in all of existence and I want to be one'.*

I was stunned into telepathic silence and had a tear in my eye as I listened to the Gnome's aspiration. He transformed from being somewhat grumpy to beaming with light, his longing to be something greater than he was, to grow into expressing and holding the essence of beauty was abundantly evident.

'I wish it for you' I said to him. At that he showed me for the first time a tiny being of light, it was immensely bright and from it emanated a single tone, which was more than a tone. It was as if all of time slowed down to just a trickle and within the single tone I could hear the many notes that made up what seemed like a choir of angels in perfect harmony, the notes themselves creating a choral manifestation that seemed to hold matter in harmonious form.

I could not differentiate between the tiny light being, or faerie, and the spring flower it was holding within its tone, the two seemed one and the same and I pondered if faeries were the external consciousness of the flower itself or if there was some sort of symbiotic relationship between them.

I did not get clear answers and neither did I need them for I was in wonderment with the song I was hearing – not something that could be heard by the ears, a pitch and range that was beyond anything I had hitherto heard, a choir of angels in an exquisite and devotional celebration of beauty and life.

Many years later I was hiking in the Sedona area of Arizona and whilst seated upon a rock with a friend we both began to spontaneously hear the song of the trees. It was mesmerizing, simply exquisite, and deeply transformative.

With this kind of deep listening, all of the sounds of nature can be heard differently and that which is generally experienced to be silent can be heard for the first time. I've often pondered our collective deep love of music and have concluded that the soul is a song and perhaps as the Hindu mystics will tell us, the primordial sound of creation is Om and that the 'Word of God' is indeed a single note.

So here we find ourselves in the 'One Song' – the Universe, which abounds with music when we have ears to listen and a heart to let it in. As we look out at today's world we can be deeply disturbed by all of the pollution and damage being done to our planet.

However, truly and clearly, the most important environment that needs to be taken care of is the one within us. When we surrender all of the lies, doubts and shame we have polluted ourselves with, we begin to see the Earth as she really is. It is our fear that clouds our senses, it is our fear that limits our perceptions of what is really here.

Some cling to the idea of extra sensory perception as something that either makes them special or that in some way provides an exit from the 'real world'. However, it is the opposite that is true. Seeing things as they truly are brings about the level of personal responsibility that is often a challenge to ignore.

When we lack sensitivity we have a far greater tolerance for that which is unhealthy, distorted and corrupt and as our senses broaden their range of perception, many of the unhealthy distortions can become intolerable.

Clairvoyance, clairaudience and all of the expanded senses not only bring us into a much broader perception of reality, it also introduces us to the experience of non- animated life being aware of our presence! This is in, and of itself, life changing.

The song of trees and rocks changes with our presence or their energy fields either expand outwards to greet us or withdraw from us. As I was to learn over many years, these expansions and contractions in their energy did not spring from an autonomic response but from awareness. We are not alone!

As my conversation with my new friend the Gnome developed over three separate visits I learnt that fairies and gnomes come in different sizes and that there was a hierarchy of beings, some of which could be called 'gods' of the land, sky, sea, river and mountains – far larger overseers.

I also learnt that my friend, Marko the gnome, had teachers and guides and that his desire to transform himself into a faerie was very real for him and taken seriously by his overseers.

Although he didn't say it directly, it seemed to me that maybe his transformation was wholly dependent on his development as an individual and not related to his skill as a gardener. What humbled me the most was learning that all of these beings were in service to humanity as well as being on their own separate and distinct evolutionary path to human beings.

They lived, they died, transformed, reincarnated and had aspirations. It was these very encounters that brought me to the realization that all of the folklore, and indeed the fantasy novels, were indeed very real; it was as if the authors themselves were having Elfic history dictated to them in the form of an epic 'fantasy' novel.

Entire kingdoms and worlds existed within the very same space in which we lived, just separated by a very thin veil, perceived consciously by few and unconsciously by the majority. The world in which we live, as well as other worlds are an expression of our consciousness for it is not matter that begets consciousness, it is consciousness that begets worlds.

Inasmuch as many of these tales of dragons and faeries are metaphors for inner journeys that require heroism and the ability to face our own darker natures, they are also, in a sense, very real and play out on the 'astral' in full technicolor, with fragments and aspects of our very own souls participating in a great epic reminiscent of the Mahabharata, Iliad, Gilgamesh or the Ramayana.

This encounter had brought me back to a childhood spent in nature or in the garden alone. I spoke to trees, even the grass and flowers and especially to the one I called 'the old man by the tree,' and yes, he did look somewhat like Gandalf!

Even today as I go about my business I tend to greet 'everyone' I encounter – I literally say good morning or good afternoon to the trees, to rocks, to plants and flowers, to frogs and even vehicles for I experience everything as having presence, as having spirit, as having awareness.

It may not possess the same sentience as I do, but this is irrelevant to me and to my personal joy of greeting and being greeted in return by everything that is around me. When we express our gratitude for everything simply for being present, it not only returns the compliment, but we are hugely blessed in return.

With the deep listening in the forest to the song of the trees, the trees themselves rejoice in our listening, they rejoice that we can hear them and know their essence and this is a great blessing, they naturally want to share with us. With this opening, life becomes a cornucopia of richly exquisite blessings that defy measurement in currency.

Life becomes enriched to a level of abundance that is far beyond the car we drive, the home we live in and how much money we earn. As we overcome the fear of seeing too much, a fear that was instilled in many of us during childhood when so many us saw and spoke the truth so clearly, the veils begin to lift.

With the veils lifted not only do we see the 'ugly truth' but also the vast riches of this vast Universe of ours. With light there is also a shadow and each great benefit has its responsibility and the seeing of that which is less comfortable.

One of my clearest memories was an encounter with a rock. I had been sitting on the doorstep of our home in Singapore so I would have been eight or nine years old at the time. As I was so accustomed to talking to everything I started a conversation with a rock. 'Hello Mr Rock, don't you get bored sitting there doing nothing all day?

At the moment of asking that question I found my awareness transported inside the rock and experienced the quickness of all of his molecules – he was undulating, vibrant, moving, expanding, contracting, as if breathing, and for moments I witnessed time from his perspective.

People came and went in a mere moment, trees grew and houses were built and crumbled in mere microseconds, the world evolved, continents moved and indeed he was moving across the land like a snail with direction and purpose, speeded up.

As I found myself fully aware and back on the doorstep the rock said to me, 'From where I am, you look rather busy.' Only years later was I able to fully understand how time itself is malleable: it has moods, ebbs and flows and that our own brain is wired to segment our own experience into time as we experience it – time is not fixed. As we step into other worlds with full awareness, our perception of time shifts.

I had wondered whether the gnome had in some way felt ugly or not worthy of the task of becoming a faerie, or greater than he was. This encounter challenged many of my beliefs around the nature of reality and life in other realms of existence.

I had assumed that all beings living in other realms were happy, wise and at peace with themselves. After all, if they were non-physical beings then surely they had absolute knowledge and experience of God and how could they possibly be anything else but happy? I had a lot to learn!

My encounters with Gnomes and similar beings have been transitory, somewhat like visiting a country on holiday instead of going to live there for a while. I have no doubt that there are others who venture into the realm or share our physical world with this magical realm more constantly, and therefore have a far richer and deeper experience of it than I am able to offer here.

What I can say is that the veil between our world and the many worlds that inhabit the same space as we do is thin. I do not have all of the answers regarding those worlds and their purpose, however, I do know that they exist with the same certainty that I know our world exists.

Just as I peered into China with 'western' eyes, I assume that I peer into these other worlds with very human perceptions and therefore my understanding can be limited, even distorted.

This entire encounter brought me to a place of contemplating ugliness and the place within me that held onto the notion that I was either too ugly, too bad, too unworthy or too 'something', to aspire to 'do God's bidding' or to excel and rise above who I was in that moment.

So many of us aspire to be 'good' or better and at times the very wanting to be 'good' can become a terrible trap of suffering as we avoid who we are. It is not that it is unhealthy to aspire to be greater, bigger, more magnificent with anything at all, it is only when we grasp at an image of what is good in avoidance of the *ugly truth* we've been telling ourselves – that we are worthless, ugly or stupid.

We cannot heal through chasing the light, but rather through bringing the light of consciousness into the places that are dark. I use the term 'ugly truth' not because it is a definitive truth that must be faced, but rather, it is an *ugly* truth for the very fact that we fear deeply that it may be true – that our unworthiness or ugliness is true.

Uncovering this can be a lifetime's work, or it can dissolve in moments, burnt off and evaporated in the realisation that we are that which we aspire to be. We are that which we are seeking.

Very often it is the weight of shame that keeps us from allowing our own magnificence to shine through and most often our 'shameful secret' is shame itself – much avoidance through using my mind, willpower and through clinging onto spiritual idealism has taught me that relief only comes when we face our shame.

It is having the courage to face the big bad wolf of shame that truly brings relief, nothing else. No amount of chasing the light will deter shame from running after us, pulling us back out of the light at each and every opportunity, like a heavy mill stone that defies any attempt to avoid its gravitational pull – even when we're in total denial of its existence.

Shame is the insidious constant companion of most of us, it lurks in the shadows and swims joyfully along with us down the river of denial towards false hope and wilful dreams that are a kaleidoscope of ideals, images and distorted beliefs about what it is to be truly good.

In chasing an image or an ideal of what it is to be good, we leave ourselves and the truth behind – for healing only takes place when we are willing to tell the absolute truth devoid of stories, analysis and blame.

Many of the images come from our childhood upbringing and education, the media and religion, while some of them are self-created. However, images are simply that – images. They are devoid of the essence of who we are and are distorted versions of a truth long forgotten.

෨෨෨෨෨

Some years earlier I had been attending a four day Zen intensive in a monastery. The days were rigorous with before dawn starts, minimal food, silence and long hours, sitting in front of another, whilst in direct self-enquiry as to the nature of my being.

As the third day unwound my senses had become hyper stimulated and I began to perceive much more around me. In one instant I found myself in a vast black space, which was both totally and utterly empty whilst being more full and complete than anything else I had previously experienced.

One of the teachers identified that I was deep into an experience and encouraged me to verbalize what I could about it. I was very grateful to him as it allowed the experience to be both real and validated.

What happened next was both astounding and life changing. Suddenly, the wall behind the person I was looking at dissolved and became a wispy transparent light and I could see directly into the courtyard behind what had been a very solid monastery wall.

I sat gazing in detail at the courtyard and in these moments of direct experience I did not question at all that I was indeed staring right through a solid object that no longer appeared to be the solid monastery walls that they had been just moments before.

Within and around me was a stillness and silence that was almost deafening. I was calmer than I had ever experienced myself to be and for once there was absolutely no mind chatter – no thoughts, no doubts, no analysis. Nothing at all, just silence.

Everything seemed so full and complete. The silence was fuller and more extensive than any concept I had ever grasped, more fulfilling than any energized thoughts, more satisfying than realizing that I now understood something I had struggled to understand.

The silence was full, total, all encompassing and yet unmistakably present – very loud.

As I was in the depths of this profound experience of silence we were instructed to take a meditative walk around the grounds of the monastery, remaining in silence and conscious of each of our steps. It was late spring and the first of the roses were just about to bloom. I approached a pink rose, still mostly in bud with the faint beginnings of opening apparent it its form.

In the depth of this silence I gazed at it and just as I had been contemplating my own self and the meaning of my own self and existence with our Self enquiry exercises I spontaneously asked the rose, 'Who are you and how do you experience yourself?' That which had just been solid was now see-through; the rose became alive, much more alive than just being a flower on a plant, it was alive with consciousness.

With my inner listening in the depths of the silence still present in that moment I heard, *'I am that which you are. Ever present, ever a witness to all that is. In this form I come to remind you of your own beauty. This is my function. In the east they celebrate the Lotus, in the west it is the Rose.*

*Why so? We are the fragrance of your Soul, we are the beauty of who you truly are and we are as aware of you as you are of us. Does your heart not sing to the tune of a rose? Do you not luxuriate in love with our sweet fragrance? There are so many and so much that is devoted to your well-being and yet you are blind to it, lost in the importance you have given to your own suffering.'*

It would take me many years to truly understand the meaning of this encounter. Contained within its brief communication the rose had shared timeless universal wisdom that would take the better part of two decades to realize, understand and embody.

Years later I developed a meditative relationship with a guru by the name of Baba Muktananda. In one of my vivid visions I saw him prostrate before me and he started to wash my feet. I was troubled by this and said to him, 'Why are you washing my feet and bowing to me, shouldn't it be the other way around?' to which he replied, 'The Guru is far more devoted to his devotees than they will ever be to him'.

I was humbled by the exchange and in the moments that followed I recalled the words of the rose and began to more completely grasp its meaning.

I was somewhat troubled by the sentence, 'lost in the importance you have given to your own suffering.' What did that mean? What was I supposed to do, make everything 'OK', forget it and move on? Think positive thoughts and hope for the best? After many more years of self-enquiry, healing and working with others in the capacity of healer, I began to truly experience what the rose had meant.

In referring to the importance we give our own suffering the rose was alluding to identifying with the suffering to such an extent that we begin to lose our sense of self and believe that we are that which suffers or that the suffering defines us.

The identification could be a perception of self that says; the unwanted child, the unlovable child, the ugly child, the bad child, the lonely child, guilty child, or the one who always does it alone. However, how could we not identify with the suffering if what we think we are is based on direct experience? What if all of our experience tells us that we are the unwanted one? What if we were literally given or sent away, what then?

To answer this question I need to return to the notion of the 'ugly truth'. When we are the unwanted child then there is usually something we've told ourselves about the cause of being unwanted. For example, that we were unwanted because we are ugly, stupid, bad etc.

What is important to understand about being 'lost in the importance given to your own suffering,' is how we separate from the essence of who we are and begin to identify with the persona we develop in defence of the original wounding.

For example, if we're asked to do too much too soon as a child, take on too many physical, emotional and financial responsibilities, such as becoming an emotional support for a parent, or having to go out and work at a very young age, then we are likely to have become a very capable individual.

However, very often in becoming that very capable individual we begin a life-long pattern of denying our needs and can separate from the part of us that is the child in order to fulfil the needs of the parent.

When this happens we have identified with our 'capable' personality in avoidance of the child with the deeper need. In trying to heal this we can get caught up in placing too much importance in the original wounding of betrayal or abandonment and avoid the underlying need all over again – the need to surrender to love.

Being 'lost' in the importance given to your own suffering' takes our focus to the symptoms which can simply become a hamster wheel of regurgitating the same issue over and over again. With this example it then behoves us to face what is really there – the fear of being nothing.

When we've built our whole life upon the split of denying our own deeper needs in favour of being capable, what we've done is to create the belief that capability is us and that without it we are nothing – of no value.

Even looking at this topic can be very frightening for the great fear comes in and says, 'But what happens if I heal this, am I to become incapable?' No. In healing this wound we replace perfectionism and will with magnificence and intention.

Capability built on a foundation of denied needs becomes a hard task master, dictating the needs of perfectionism and narcissism which eventually leads to increased amounts of energy being needed to keep the entire engine moving, and to failed relationships and businesses.

When the deeper needs of the child that has been separated from have been ignored then much of our life force energy is tied up in holding that deep pain of betrayal in place.

However, the deeper, weightier and more destructive aspect of all of this can be a profound and deep sense of worthlessness, even self-hatred. When a child is asked to do too much too soon and its needs aren't met, it simply learns not to have any needs or to view having needs as being somehow 'weak', 'irresponsible' or they are simply not felt or acknowledged.

Another way to look at how we make our own suffering too important is how we create an identity out of the wounding that has taken place and then fixate on the aspects of our personality that are 'dysfunctional' and try to change them.

This has its useful components, for it is useful to have social skills, manners, be assertive, confident and a clear communicator. However, if our underlying feeling is that of being 'unwanted', 'unwelcome', 'worthless' or 'ugly', then it will continually act as the gravity that will pull us into experiences and relationships that will reflect that.

However, what often happens is that we attempt to do in the mind what cannot be accomplished with thought alone.

## Three Queens

During and just after the period of Christmas and New Year 2011/12, I was having a whirlwind experience in India which culminated in meeting three queens:

The elegant and generous Rajmata of Jaipur, Oprah, the acclaimed queen of daytime television, and Amma, the Queen of Heaven.

Oprah struck me as being as warm and authentic as I expected her to be. It was rather surreal to be talking face to face with a woman I had admired for years. We chatted for around five minutes and I was grateful to have had the opportunity to thank her for her exemplary service to the world.

Earlier in 2011, just after my first encounter with Hanuman and Krishna Das, I planned a trip to India to spend three weeks following a yoga course in the Gujarat in northern India. In the days prior to finalizing travel plans and buying airline tickets I was asked by several people, at least six, if I was planning to meet Amma.

I had no idea who she was but I did vaguely remember being taken to see her in New York in 2006 or 2007 but did not stay as the crowds were too much for me at the time. I became intrigued, 'Googled,' her and found myself looking at her picture with deep curiosity.

So many people mentioning her in one week had already grabbed my attention so I was sufficiently drawn to change plans and go on a little detour. I contacted the ashram in the Gujarat and informed them that I would arrive four days later than originally planned. I figured that this would be sufficient time to visit her ashram and then continue with my plans.

I had not been in India since 2007 and suddenly I found myself in a rickety vehicle travelling for three hours on an insane road in sweltering heat towards the 'Mother'. I arrived mid-afternoon and stood at the ashram's entrance looking like a tourist with the pink Kali Temple towering above me. I rested my luggage either side of me, of course I had far too much, and proceeded to look around to see if I could spot any notices that said either 'Office' or 'Registrations'.

Before even deciding what to do and where to go, and wondering if I would fit in with all the 'alternatively dressed' westerners I saw milling around, a very excited and very short Indian man in his early sixties, clad in white from head to toe, excitedly rushed up to me and asked, 'Are you here to see Amma?'

I was hot and bothered and my smart leather shoes were rapidly turning into a pond of whiffy water and an object of shame and so I regrettably replied with a touch of impatience and a wee bit of sarcasm, 'This is her Ashram isn't it?' The darling man survived my Chihuahua bite, smiled and said, 'Then you must come with me!'

I fussed about my luggage and didn't want to go anywhere; I especially did not want to let my laptop and camera bag out of my sight. After a minute or so of further discussion I finally relented and asked a woman monitoring one of the lifts in an ashram tower block to take care of my bags. She nodded and smiled and although no word came to confirm a yes, I went on my way and followed the man.

'I thought darshan would be given tomorrow?' I enquired and he explained that Amma was seeing a smaller private group of students and it would be ok for me to go. He took me inside the temple and there were roughly forty or sixty people in a queue of plastic chairs, each person moving up one chair as their turn approached.

This small and continually smiling man spoke to a couple of people and before I knew it I had been queue jumped and placed just four seats away from Amma. I kept on looking around. Being British this was the rudest thing I could possibly ever do, which is ironic considering I was in India and queue jumping was a fact life of there.

However, my amazement at what was transpiring was taken to a new level the moment I was taken into Amma's arms. She whispered in my ears something so intimate and so personally important she would have had to have known the most intimate corners of my psyche.

In that instant I felt something like a heavy blanket had lifted up from me, it was so palpable it was almost shocking. As the embrace ended our eyes met and she smiled. I knew in that moment that something important has happened.

I wandered around the outside of the ashram for almost two hours afterwards. I was partly in an altered state and there were periods of deep sobbing and weeping that came and went. My mind certainly did not know or understand what had happened, but I had been touched very deeply.

As is usual with many ashrams, the hell began shortly afterwards. The combination of the relentless heat and humidity, shared accommodation and the sheer numbers of people started to create personal misery for me. Four days later I left as planned and headed to the Gujarat. The visit had been eventful and I had received one more hug from this so called 'hugging saint'.

The impact was nothing like my first meeting and although I was not disappointed by that, I was not sufficiently motivated to remain longer. I loaded my bags into a taxi and headed to the airport in Cochin and travelled by plane and car to the ashram in the Gujarat.

I arrived, I checked in, I went to my room, had dinner, went to bed and lay there thinking only of Amma. I could not sleep. She was in my every thought and in my every breath. I opened up my laptop and with a very unreliable internet connection I managed to book a flight back to Kerala.

The following morning I went to the swami to explain that I was leaving and offered to pay for the yoga course regardless. She was annoyed with my departure and I found myself taking a stand and speaking with absolute passion about my deep need to return to Amma immediately, a woman in whose arms I had rested for all of thirty seconds in total.

The swami saw my passion, accepted my apology and eventually wished me well. The following day I was back in Kerala and back in the ashram and it was worse than ever before. More people, more heat, more frustration and more annoyance than before – I was in hell but enchanted by the Queen of Heaven.

I could write so much about those days, a week in an ashram with a living saint is like a year out on 'Everyday Street', every defence you've ever had comes up for a breath of air. I found myself confronted with everything I disliked about people, about myself and about the world in general. I was hot and I was irritated to the extent that I simply wanted to slap most people.

I felt so very invaded, pushed, prodded, lectured, ignored, dismissed and distraught. Oh boy, what was I doing in this hell hole? On the second night after returning I went up onto the roof of one of the buildings. I was so miserable that I started to cry. I lit up a cigarette, which was totally against ashram rules, and sat smoking it as I looked up at the stars.

Had I listened to my misery I may have been tempted to simply jump and fall down the fifteen or so floors. However, I had a moment of clarity when I realized that somehow this ashram and this meeting with a woman I would come to call my Guru had engineered circumstances in which EVERYTHING I judged and disliked In myself and in others was more than just visible, it was in my face and it was relentless.

With that realization I looked up at the heavens as if staring God down before a gun fight and said, 'Game on, I'm not leaving!' With that I walked down the fifteen or so flights of steps towards the grand hall and checked the number on my darshan ticket to see when it might be my turn to be embraced.

I asked a man who looked to be an ashram volunteer where I should sit and he directed me towards a chair queue of people. The moment I sat in my chair a western woman stood up and glared at me and started shouting that this was the women's only queue and I should go over to the other side.

I was so astounded by her shouting and unkindness I could not muster a word of reply. I stood up and suddenly the man who had directed me there ran over and started to apologize. I shook my head and said, 'It's ok, I'm going home, it's time for me to leave'.

I shuffled my feet, feeling very heavy hearted and headed towards the ashram exit. I stood outside in the small lane, far away from the crowds and lit up a cigarette. As I puffed and puffed away I planned my departure. I actually decided that I would leave that very night and would pay any amount to do so.

I wanted a hotel, I wanted sheets, I wanted air conditioning, I wanted a steak and I wanted to be on my own. I knew exactly which hotel I was headed for and I wanted to leave right away, although it was almost ten o'clock at night.

Just as I had planned all of that and knew exactly what I would do next I felt a cool breeze at the back of my neck. At first I simply put my hand there to feel the chill. Then I felt it again and it felt curiously directed so I turned and looked behind me. As I did, there she stood, beckoning me to come.

In that moment I 'saw' Amma standing in her white sari beckoning me to come back into the ashram. As quickly as I had seen her, I could no longer see her. Her apparition disappeared as quickly as it had appeared. I returned to the great hall and just like the very first time I had met Amma, another small Indian man with a constant smile took me by the arm and led me towards the front of the darshan queue.

This time I felt too wrung out to muster up the energy to feel embarrassed by the queue jump. The embrace this time was gentle and I did not feel anything remarkable apart from her warmth. I went to bed that night wondering if I had blocked the darshan or the blessing for I had not felt much.

I awoke in the middle of the night with electricity coursing through my body. The current was so strong that my limbs were shaking and I could hear popping sounds which were more like bullets being fired in the centre of my head. I had to use my breath to accommodate this experience which frightened me a little, but also excited me.

It was the following day that my journey with Amma started in earnest. That evening she would not be giving darshan but bhajans (hymns) would be sung in the great hall. As a lover of both music and song I was strongly drawn to go and swim in the energies of several thousand people all singing at once along with her.

The evening's songs had already commenced when I arrived in the hall. I had lapped up a couple of precious alone-time hours in my dormitory room as all of my roommates were elsewhere.

As I entered I saw Amma on the podium and she was smiling and singing. I was transfixed by her and became sufficiently relaxed to enable myself to open not only to her, but to open my extra sensory perception which happened spontaneously.

I was not prepared for what I saw. Her energy field was huge, bigger than anything I had ever seen before. It stretched out in multiple layers for around 500 metres in each direction. The inner layers stretched out to 50 metres and a 100 metres and so on and so forth and I could see that everyone in the ashram was indeed sitting inside her energy field and as if that was not phenomenal enough, she then began to sing to the grandest mother goddess of them all, Devi.

As her song and chant continued in intensity there were moments when she would look up and stretch her arms upwards towards the skies and I witnessed something that literally caused me to fall to my knees.

As she stretched up to the heavens her energy grew in intensity and brightness. Her heart chakra expanded in all directions to become larger than her physical body and with one big gasp I saw eight beings emanate from her heart and levitate, four on each side.

I had never seen beings like this before. They were golden and were emitting a most intense humming sound or vibration. As waves of this vibration moved out into the grand hall I heard progressive waves of sobs amongst the people present.

As if that was not enough, with one more final call to 'Amma', as Amma lifted her arm up again, I saw the likeness of a great eye above her that was bathed in a purple cloud of silken energy. As I looked on mesmerized I noticed that with that stretching up to the heavens, that little Indian woman who had hugged me was no longer there. She seemed to have vacated all identity as an Indian woman and something else, much greater, was in her stead.

As I gazed I thought my heart would break, as I gazed I thought I would die from love. It was like gazing upon the very presence of God and I fell to my knees. I fell to my knees not only to the presence but also out of deep respect for a human who risked annihilation of her identity in order to make space for the Divine.

I was in love, I was in love with my Guru. I was in love with Amma. My entire being was enraptured with love for her and with profound humility for what I had witnessed. I felt so blessed to have been given the gift of sight but I also knew that just as I could see, many others had felt what I had felt in those moments, for truly, we had all been bathed in the heart of the Queen of Heaven, my Ammaji. Finally I understood what Krishna Das was talking about.

Less than ten days after this experience I found myself as a guest of the Rajmata of Jaipur in the City Palace. As I entered the general living and reception room I saw a large ornamental piece attached to the wall made up from several figures. I recognized the figures immediately, the unique shaped heads or headpieces which were new to me stood out. I was astonished; these figures looked exactly like the beings I had seen emanate from Amma's heart chakra.

I asked the Rajmata what the figures signified and she replied, 'In Hindu tradition we consider these to be Angels'. I smiled inwardly and also recognized once again that there is no uniformity in terms of the appearance of divine beings, they appear to be culturally specific.

# Who me?

During this period, which was a journey into a world I had never expressed interest in, I recalled a brief encounter I had had in Mt. Shasta in the late 1990s. I was in a book store browsing and the woman behind the counter made a suggestion regarding a book for me to read.

I have no recollection of what it was about, but I do recall that it was a book of teachings from an Indian guru. I declined her offer with the words, 'I'm not into gurus'. I smiled to myself with the memory of that encounter and was yet again amazed at how time and circumstance can change our position on just about any topic we care to think of.

My difficulty with the notion of having a guru was the thought of bowing to another human being. The memories of having to call catholic priests 'father' lingered long enough to influence my repulsion for giving any person that kind of reverence.

Time and experience changes us. As my healing work developed over the years, and especially through Family Constellation work, I increasingly became aware of something that was far greater than me or my own story.

As we enter consciously into the Ancestral field we become aware of forces, energies and influences that are far bigger than us and therefore I learnt over time to not only trust it, but to bow to its greater intelligence. This was a slow process over several years. Bowing to the greater intelligence requires us to have a healthy relationship with the unknown.

A healthy relationship with the unknown must either be built on absolute blind faith, or it is built up slowly based on experience. What becomes part of our experience is that the unknown can be trusted when we surrender to it fully and simply allow ourselves to be the empty vessel through which *That which is greater*, *That which breathes Us* along with the entire Universe can work.

If we are to participate in the healing of our world it behoves us to realize that we as individuals are simply not enough. The little me, with my day-to-day personality, my foibles and eccentricities is simply not capable of the work I do, it is far too much responsibility and simply 'trying' to do it all would exhaust anyone.

What is capable and what does work is when I submit to the unknown in the full realization that the unknown is greater, has more power, wisdom, love, grace than my ego would ever be able to match up to. Each act of service then becomes an act of submission to that which is, was and always will be.

As this had already been developing within in me for several years it was then very easy for me to bow to that which was greater – Amma. It is a recognition that no matter how experienced we are, no matter how popular we are, no matter our fame, fortune or intelligence, there is always someone or something that stands taller, grander and more important than us.

As we bow to that which is greater, in authentic humility, we realize that our greatest work comes when we do surrender. As we give up all of the trying and all of the self-importance, we submit to the message being more important than the messenger and step firmly onto the way of the heart.

For now I am very happy to visit Amma whenever I can and bathe in the luxuriousness of her magnificent heart.

As we step clearly on the path of awakening our heart, through being willing to tell the absolute truth, new doorways and windows open into worlds we could only previously imagine.

As we start perceiving the world we live in through the eyes of our heart our relationship to everything changes, including with the unseen. The process is one of remembering rather than being a process of learning or trying to get or grab something.

We cannot get or grab what we already are, we can only submit to it and remember. As we heal our very own heart the world opens up to reveal itself as the magical world we either lived in or had glimpses of when we were young.

This world awaits us, it calls us, it beckons us, it invites us – sometimes gently, sometimes with vigour. Either way, if you call it will answer, if you listen, you will hear its voice, if you stop looking you will see, if you stop searching it will appear, if you stop, you will be there.

Use of will is a poor substitute for surrendering to who we are: there is no trying to be who you truly are there is only surrender.

Our greatest fear is that we are nothing, even worthless. However, there is a different nothing from which all of these worlds not only emerge but through which are accessible. Not knowing is the doorway to experience. We must be willing to surrender the mind and to realize fully that our mind is but a servant of consciousness and is not consciousness itself.

Not knowing is the greatest gift that we have, for when we don't know we have two choices – walk away or surrender. It is in that moment of surrender, when we accept the condition of not knowing and not understanding that we can allow something greater to move through us.

In those moments we can also observe ourselves as a student enthralled with a teacher. We become the humbled vessel of magnificence, wisdom and beauty, we teach ourselves as we teach others, we heal ourselves as we heal others, we become ourselves as we assist others to do the same.

When we have the courage to challenge everything we have been taught about intellect, how to teach, how to gain knowledge and how to think, then we open up a doorway of possibilities for real miracles to take place: Miracles of compassion, miracles of forgiveness, miracles of love, miracles of healing a broken, worn out, embittered and crusty heart.

These miracles can only become manifest through the vessel of an awakened heart. For we as the little one, we cannot even comprehend what it is to have the capacity to look at atrocities and find a place in which forgiveness can take place. However, as we release the complicated stories of a self-important ego we give that which is great, that which has always been here an opportunity to make itself manifest.

What in effect happens in these sacred moments is that finally we let go of our tough grip on our very own heart and decide to let the greater truth of who we are emerge.

When that happens we are being held in the Grace of God as we enter God's domain through the heart. This cannot be tried, this cannot be whittled down to a technique or described as a system of processes, it can only be submitted to and that happens when we forget ourselves and bow to that which is greater.

# CHAPTER 10

# The Way of the Heart

B y now you have read the words, 'being willing to tell the absolute truth,' many times. But why? The deepest truth of human longing is that each of us yearns to be free to love and be loved.

Everything we keep hidden and everything we distort keeps us from the deeper truth of our longing, the hunger we have had since time immemorial. We have discovered that through allowing the simplest of truths to be apparent, we begin to release the story of who we think we are and start surrendering to the truth of who we are, for when we surrender our story, what dies is everything we are not.

This deep longing lives as a seed in the heart of every human being no matter their age, their background, their deeds, gender or belief systems. Love is the fundamental force that nurtures all life and our longing exists because we know that love is the oxygen we breathe, it is the breath of God that sustains all things, not least the human heart.

Love nurtures even a blade of grass to become its potential, it is the very underpinning of the Universe as we know it. We have grown afraid of love whilst at the same time we have romanticized its nature and have invested much of our hope in finding that one person who will fulfil all of our needs and the longing of our heart.

This invariably becomes dissatisfying over time for merging beyond bonding is not possible. The merging we truly long for is the dissolution of the separation we have experienced from our essential self which took place many aeons ago, long before incarnation in this particular body.

The separation that has taken place is the alienation from love, our own true nature. The existence of our world is for one purpose and one purpose only, to infuse physical matter with the same knowledge of self and the realization of love that has been possible in the many other worlds our soul has participated in.

Our longing exists not just as a seed in the heart, but also as a deep memory. We have always known that it could be different. *Do you remember? Do you remember knowing that? Do you recall knowing that things could be different? Do you recall that it was once different but it seems that you can no longer remember?*

It is as if the memory of it is a word on the tip of your tongue. We can feel it, we can sense it but we can't quite remember it fully. This process of remembering the existence of love and ourselves as being one and the same and inseparable from it, requires our willingness to tell the truth for it is everything we have constructed in defence of our vulnerability that creates and sustains the veils of illusion that both surround and suffocate us.

Love is an invitation. It does not push, neither does it pull. It invites. Gently. Therefore this process of telling the truth is simply a process of surrendering to what is in the moment. It is recognising the love that still exists between two people even though they may have gone their separate ways and even though betrayal, abuse or violence may have taken place.

The way of the heart is about recognizing that all love, once felt, never disappears, it simply becomes hidden from view. The way of the heart is having the courage to acknowledge to ourselves that what we truly seek is the remembrance of that which seemingly disappeared onto the other side of separation and appears to be no longer reachable.

The way of the heart is having the courage to risk everything in order to reclaim, regain and revive the exquisite innocence we have all known.

The way of the heart is about recognizing the human potential and capacity to overcome any amount of suffering and darkness in order to re-emerge as whole again and that no amount of facing the truth will result in us losing anything but the stories we have constructed and the inauthenticity that goes along with them.

When the heart speaks it does not cling to opinions for the undefended heart sees only what is in the moment. It does not judge, neither does it calculate, it simply invites the truth in all of its dignity to be silently present.

When we become devoted to the heart our focus is on our longing to know the truth of who we are in every moment, which in turn invites the truth of another to be present. As we become accustomed to bathing in simple truths, without grasping onto stories, opinions and demands, what becomes more important than being right about something is preserving the flow of love that exists between us and the other.

This can only be achieved and experienced once we start to willingly peel back the layers of defence, illusions and stories we've told ourselves about who we fear we might be.

The way of the heart leads us directly into ourselves, it cannot lead us anywhere else for truth starts with the Self and is expressed as the Self. Therefore, when we get caught up in the idea that living from the heart is all about being polite, kind and nice to people we have yet again floundered and have fallen upon an image of what it is to be good.

When we surrender our very own heart to itself and become willing to know the truth of our existence we become increasingly undefended. As this undefended state flourishes, acts of kindness, gentleness and generosity become a natural part of who we are rather than a set of behaviours we have deemed good to mimic.

The heart cannot help but love, it cannot help but want to embrace everything it sees with its affection so when we surrender the layers of lies we've both been told and have told ourselves, the true beauty and magnificence of the heart can be expressed. Wisdom is the voice of the heart, love is its expression and beauty is its manifestation.

As we surrender to all of our parts, the good, the bad and the very ugly we give our heart the opportunity to be exposed. Hatred, greed, jealousy, envy, avarice, judgement and resentment all have doorways into love from within their depths.

The way of the heart is dedicated to truth no matter what. It does not grab onto shiny objects as they float by, but rather it sits at the bottom of a pit until its own natural light illuminates all that must be destroyed in the fire of truth, the fire of Shiva.

A life led doing good can easily turn into a life of deceptively and subtly doing bad to others, especially to those we deem not to be good, when we do not allow the deepest cut of separation to be exposed. It is only through exposing the deepest cuts of separation that we can ever be free from childhood patterns and the idea that somehow we are either not good or are simply bad.

Until the deepest cut is exposed we may live life feeling as if we are a fraud. We may be gentle and kind, we may be reasonable, patient, even loving, and yet lurking underneath what appears to be so beautiful is a measure of self-hatred that is yet to be resolved.

As the years turn into decades the yet unresolved self-hatred turns our kindness and gentleness into persistent giving that eventually exhausts us, leaving us dissatisfied with life, with love and with relationships.

Our fear of facing the deepest cut has kept the self-hatred intact under all of the layers that look good from the outside. However, the heavy price that is being paid is our inability to let much or anything in.

Beneath the deepest cut is the truth of who we are, it is our light, it is our authentic self that does not and cannot ignore the existence of love and God in all things. This essential self is the breath of God and is also breathed by God.

As we surrender to this essential self our life becomes an expression of the universal breath – we have natural ebb and flow. We are able to give freely, as easy as it is to release our next breath, and we are also able to receive freely, just like taking our next breath.

Life's natural rhythm is one of activity and rest, sun up, sun down, giving and receiving. When we avoid the deep pit in our belly that screams of separation we can end up simply taking and taking and taking, for nothing, no matter how shiny, how glitzy, no matter the amount, will never and can never be enough until the cut of separation is resolved.

Taking is not receiving. Taking is an attempt to stuff into the void that is the cut, anything that will give us temporary relief from its nagging presence. We are so motivated to avoid the cut of separation at all costs that we will entertain almost anything, no matter how destructive, self-deceptive or temporary in order not to feel it.

We can line our pockets with money, with relationships, sex, perfectionism, status, titles, addictions, being busy, enslavement to a job or a career, religion, spiritual practice, meditation and all manner of things in the hope of feeling complete and at peace with ourselves.

However, taking the first step on the way of the heart is acknowledging the truth that everything we have tried, to date, has not delivered lasting happiness. It takes courage to see that although we may be mature in our personal process and we may have resolved many relationship issues and issues of self-worth, there is still this nagging, stalking and persistent presence that tells us we are not whole.

We may be very accustomed to expressing deeper feelings, and may even be courageous enough to look at our shadow, however, the simplest of truths are more threatening to our notion of existence than the story of our life we have taken into therapy, healing and to teachers.

The way of the heart places wanting to liberate ourselves, through experiencing the truth of our existence, above all other considerations. Until we are ready we will cling to that which makes us suffer. There is absolutely nothing wrong with that for everything has its day, its time and its season.

Most of us can only metabolize truth in measured doses. Some of us can digest bigger pieces at a time, and others need to spend time, perhaps years, nibbling around the edges of truth before taking a really good bite. The way of the heart is not going to force you.

However, truth is ruthless. Once it is revealed it takes a lot of energy to try and stuff it back down again. Truth eventually wins because the pain of keeping our heart shackled once it has been released for a moment, is simply too much.

The way of heart is not a new dogma, it is not a new technique or even a new spiritual insight that must be followed. It is a calling, in fact it is your very own heart calling you. Our heart longs to be free and this call to freedom is always there no matter when you choose to heed its call and respond to your dear friend, your very own heart.

There is no measurement, no assessment, there is only deep listening. The deeper we listen we can hear love's voice reach us from the depths of silence. As we listen we can hear love's voice call to us in the sound of birds, in the rustling leaves of majestic trees, in the smile and glinting eyes of a young child, in the wind that whips around a magnificent mountain.

Love's voice is everywhere and when we listen deeply within the stillness that is our heart, we can hear its beckoning and its invitation. The deeper we listen the more profound this silent voice becomes, so much so that we cannot resist but to speak of it.

One day, maybe tomorrow, maybe next week or next year we will allow ourselves to acknowledge that what we want more than anything is to love freely as we once did, to taste the sweet nectar of innocence, leaving all fear behind us so that we may luxuriate in the wealth of our very own heart.

As we allow this we come to realize that everything we've ever wanted is as close as our own heart.

*With love,*
*Shavasti, 2014*

# Teachings from an Awakened Heart –
## Embracing the Power of Truth by Shavasti

**IN THIS AUDIO PRESENTATION,** you will be taken on a journey to initially share in Shavasti's personal story of a tragedy and other events that transformed both his work and the core of his being. In addition to that brief account, Shavasti invites you to consider, experience, ponder and feel who you are on multiple levels of your being as he weaves almost two decades of a journey as a professional healer, author and seeker of truth together into a tapestry of profound teachings that will change the way you experiences yourself and see your place in the world.

In *Teachings from an Awakened Heart* you will journey with the stream of Shavasti's words that will bring you to new understandings and experiences of forgiveness, awakening, hidden loyalties and new opportunities for personal peace. With this audio journey, you will be invited to step inside the deeper questions of your being, your longing and the deeper truths of who you are and what you really want. *Teachings from an Awakened Heart* presents truth powerful, inclusive and pervasive ways that will invite to surrender to the core of your being – irrespective of what you discover about yourself along the way. You will discover that to love is totally natural and that there is, and never has been, anything wrong with you.

Available from all major audio stores including *iTunes*,
and also from *findhornpress.com*

# Acknowledgements

It has been more than seven years since I sat down to write a book. There have been several false starts as I entered a period of rapid inner change that also translated into very many changes in the way I worked with groups and with individuals.

As with any periods of growth and learning there are challenges and also those who come into our lives bless us with guidance, comfort and friendship.

In the past seven years since having had a gun held to my head in my home in South Africa, many people have touched me with their generosity, support, loyalty and understanding during a period of my life that has at times been the darkest.

My thanks go firstly to Lyn & Will Mitchell in Scotland. Fate would have it that they entered my life around a year before the real roller coaster began. I left South Africa feeling bewildered, lost and at times deeply unsure of my purpose and future. In so many ways this very ordinary and yet extraordinary couple provided much of the safety and a sense of home that I had not received as a child. I am also grateful to their sons Finn and Cai for their friendship and respect.

My deep gratitude also goes to one of the most fabulous human beings I have the privilege to know: Patricia White Buffalo. It is indeed a great blessing when we are seen fully for who we are.

In my darkest days she saw not only the deep wound and forgave the defences, she also saw the truth of who I am and encouraged me in ways that are a testimony to her magnificence as a respected teacher, Shaman and someone I am exceptionally proud to call a friend.

The blessings continued as I was introduced to a new teacher in my life, Amita. She has been a constant guiding light who through her wisdom has challenged me when needed, has been faultless in her support and who has in her own way changed my work forever – Amita is a true friend of my soul.

In the past two years much of how my work has developed has been supported by the loyal friendship, vision and unyielding truth of two special friends. Each in their own way helped me to see the value of my work and encouraged me over and over again to go out into the world. Special thanks go to Justin Bonnet and Letia Ayres.

There are many others across the globe I wish to thank for their friendship and for the constant presence of their support of who I am as a person and as an individual who longs to speak of the things of God through offering ever evolving teachings.

These include Reshma Murudkar Kalantri for jumping on a plane and spending two weeks at my bedside when I was in recovery from my motorcycle accident and for her friendship; Ayleen Chalidis for her guidance; Ursula Beller for her heart and healing abilities; Barbara Madani – Young for her friendship and support; Paulo Monica for being a constant source of love in my life for the past 16 years and of course Annebiene Pilon who has always seen the better parts of me, even when I could not.

So many have blessed my life with their presence and with their love: Liana Nenacheva, Susane Roziadi, Kate Targan, Annette Gates, Mina Marmol, Maria Jones, Yvonne Trafton, David More, Charles Lambrou, Paul & Grace Loube, Gary Stuart, Nancy Greenfield and many others.

In addition to friends, some very special teachers have crossed my path, each of them seeing a deeper truth of who I am beyond my human frailties: Kathy Bower and Tim Lowry for their support and teaching skills, and the wonderfully talented Karnamrita Dasi for helping me to find my singing voice once more. I must also mention the beautiful Edo & Jo for bringing the joy of song back into my life.

Finally I would like to thank the many countries around the world that held and supported me on my journey over the past seven years: China (Lu & Liang Families), Thailand, Argentina, Mexico (Pedro & Gina), the USA, Scotland, Bali and of course, India. Travel has always been in my bones and whether I journey inwards or to another destination on the globe, it is a constant uncovering of what is really true.

My gratitude also goes out the many clients and students I have across the globe. You continue to assist me in discovering my greater potential. Thank you. As this is my sixth publication through Findhorn Press, there is much gratitude for my publisher, Thierry Bolioglo, and for my editor, Michael Hawkins.

And finally I bow deeply to Amma for embracing the world and for embracing me in the truth of her heart. Jai Mata Di!

*Love, Shavasti*
*2014*

# Contact the Author

Shavasti's deep exploration into the truth of who we are is available to you as a healing journey in gatherings, workshops, privately in your location or one on one over Skype or Phone.

*shavasti@shavasti.com*

Or leave voicemail:
*Los Angeles (323) 315-0058\**
*London 020 8123 9608\**
\*voicemail services for callback. Shavasti is not based in either city.

*www.shavasti.com*

## Gatherings

As part of the exploration in an awakening heart, gatherings are offered to groups anywhere in the world on invitation. Whether you are part of a large group or seek a gathering for your smaller group of seekers, contact Shavasti for a quote and scheduling possibilities

## Private Sessions Skype/Phone

When you work with Shavasti you will be guided to discover the more authentic truth of who you are, beyond relationship entanglements and a distorted self-perception that has been keeping you from the more complete awakening of your own heart.

Shavasti brings to his sessions years of deep experience working with hidden loyalties, relationship entanglements and burdens that may exist in ancestral lineage. Beyond his finely tuned high sense perception that allows him to pierce many veils of illusion to see, sense and feel the subtle bodies of the auric filed, chakras and ancestors, Shavasti works from a foundation of simple and yet profound truths that will assist you in re-awakening your heart to its natural state of flow.

## Family Services

Shavasti brings together his more than 15 years of deep experience with Family Constellation work to assist you in uncovering the hidden dynamics that may be causing disruptions to the flow of love and harmony in your family.

## Exclusive Services

This service is for people whose status prevents them from attending public workshops and individual sessions due to your position in society, whether it is political, financial or celebrity status. This work is extremely important for those in influential positions not only because without having deep roots within, peace of mind is impossible, but it also engenders a strength and stability that is required to make important life decisions that impact so many people

FINDHORN PRESS

*Life-Changing Books*

Consult our catalogue online
(with secure order facility) on
*www.findhornpress.com*


For information on the Findhorn Foundation:
*www.findhorn.org*